1/12/88
Budd,
Thanks for
everything.
Betsy

A FIRESIDE BOOK ○ PUBLISHED BY SIMON & SCHUSTER, INC.
NEW YORK   LONDON   TORONTO   SYDNEY   TOKYO

COMIC LIVES

INSIDE THE WORLD OF
◇ AMERICAN ◇
STAND-UP COMEDY

BETSY BORNS

A FIRESIDE BOOK

Published by Simon & Schuster, Inc.
Simon & Schuster Building
Rockefeller Center
1230 Avenue of the Americas
New York, NY 10020

FIRESIDE and colophon are registered trademarks
of Simon & Schuster, Inc.

Designed by Bonni Leon

Manufactured in the United States of America

1 3 5 7 9 10 8 6 4 2

Library of Congress Cataloging in Publication Data
Borns, Betsy.
Comic lives.

1. Comedians—United States—Biography.   I. Title.
PN2285.B65   1987   792.2'3'0280922   [B]   87-11893

ISBN 0-671-62620-5

To My Family/Friends and Friends/Family:

Sandra, Bob, Sylvia,
Lillian, Sam, Irving,
Stephanie, Emily,
Jim, Glenn, Ann and Lisa

ACKNOWLEDGMENTS

Portions of the following interviews appeared in
Interview magazine :

Paul Provenza
Alan Havey
Carol Leifer
Judy Tenuta
Emo Philips
Alan King
Bob Goldthwait
David Brenner
Phyllis Diller
George Carlin

SPECIAL THANKS TO:

Glenn Albin and Gael Love, *Interview* magazine
Caroline Hirsch and Peggy Reed, Caroline's Comedy Club
Herb Schaffner, Fireside Books
Roberta Myers, for getting this book started
Jim Ackerman, everything

C O N T E N T S

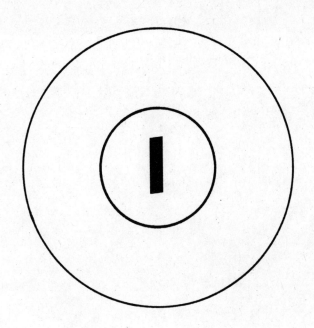

AUDIENCES MAKE LAUGH NOT WAR

The comedy club, as it exists today, is a stormy sea of conflicting purposes that manages to stay calm long enough each night to let the show go on. It is an establishment dedicated to the making of money, the creation of art, the furthering of alcohol consumption and the performing of both humorous insights and filthy smut—often by the same person. But perhaps the most bizarre aspect of the comedy club is what its patrons go there to do: laugh out loud among strangers, unashamedly, for an entire evening. One has to wonder, simply: why do they do it?

For starters, it's the only place whose raison d'etre is sending patrons into paroxysms of uncontrollable laughter. If you want to hear jokes, you don't go to a bank . . . or a supermarket, or a doctor's office; you go to a comedy club. In movies you find humor, with friends you find mirth, but in the club, you find comedy in its alternately lowest and most elevated forms—stand-up. Bill Grundfest, owner of New York's Comedy Cellar, sums it up this way: "Visiting a comedy club is like going to a hooker. You don't want the flowers, romance and candy; you want to *get it* and go." Catharsis, you see, comes in many different packages. And while comedy clubs may be short on romance, they make up for its absence with pure seduction, thus providing an irresistible promise of satisfaction for potential paying customers—the promise of catharsis through laughter.

Comics make their living by lampooning what we quietly accept as "the way things are" and by demystifying those things which we have spent lifetimes endowing with mystery. Surprisingly, however, comics are not knee-jerk iconoclasts; they are simply habitual questioners who, in seeking the truth, reject those sacred cows that stand in their way by rendering them absurd. Comics are cerebral strippers, seducing us, ever so slowly, as they peel off layer upon layer of our collective repression until finally, when the laughter dies down, we find ourselves naked, brains exposed to the cross-ventilation of comic insight and age-old inhibition.

Alan Havey, in a recent club date, was in the midst of discussing "morning erections, when I was a teenager, so intense I used to levitate off the bed . . . I'd have fantasies about being one of the floats in the Macy's parade: 'Hi kids—it's me, Alan . . .'" when suddenly a mother and daughter group came in. Havey said, "Make yourselves comfortable ladies, we were just going to talk about masturbation . . . when I was a kid, I called it my mini-vacation." He then proceeded to do a verbal celebration of the word "taboo" by discussing every subject from cannibalism ("Aw, come on, you know you've thought of it . . . maybe when you're on a train late at night, with just one other person in the car—you think, 'why not, who's gonna know?'") to sexual technique, always managing to tap dance around vulgarity, while never actually falling in.

As opposed to telling "dick jokes," (scatological jokes which rely primarily on shock value to get cheap laughs) Alan spins yarns like a village storyteller—using slightly kinky thread; onstage he's Blue Bard, come to save the masses from their freshly laundered opinions. About sex he says, "I think it's genuinely interesting—it's a part of people's lives." As for the story-like quality of his bits, he explains that "I don't do real one-liner type of humor and I don't want to do dick jokes, so I try to set it up gradually . . . it's an important topic. I like to draw people in, like how I talk about going into the lingerie store and the women show them to you by sticking their hands into the panties. One comic I worked with in Connecticut said, 'Man, I got a hard-on when you told that,' which was kind of a compliment. I don't want to change the world but I do want to involve people in my act. I don't do it for shock value."

On the topic of sex, comics adhere to a very definite distinction between sexual material, like Alan's mini-monologues, and the standard "dick jokes" frequently told by less experienced or less dedicated comics. In general, sex is used by comics for the same reason it is used by advertising agencies; it arouses and stimulates people, and having gotten them to drop their guard, convinces them to buy whatever is being sold—in this case, humor. The distinction between a dick joke and sexual joke lies in what makes the joke funny: if people laugh because the word "fuck" is used, that's a dick joke (and an easy laugh); if people laugh in reacting to an insightful observation about sex, that's a sexual joke. The sole intention of sexual material is not to get cheap laughs; it is viewed by comics as a valid subject with which everyone in the audience can identify. If the material sometimes embarrasses or shocks audiences, that's the price they must pay to watch non-censored material in its raw form: like eating steak tartare, one must relinquish age-old prejudices and just dig in. Once a taste has been acquired, the thrill of experiencing humor's "raw meat" is intoxicating—for both comic and audience.

While comics themselves know the difference between dick jokes and sexual humor, audiences often don't care to make the distinction. Existing alongside the audience's desire for witty, urbane, adult entertainment is, very often, their desire for lowbrow, adolescent "no-no" humor. The preponderance and popularity of scatological jokes in clubs makes one wonder if, following Freudian psychology, anyone in America has received proper potty training. As for dick jokes, forget about it! From New York to New Brunswick, nothing gets as many laughs. Comic Paul Provenza says that even in Las Vegas, where comics are told to "'keep it clean,' in reality, if you work dirty, they'll love you even more, because dirt always kills." The tremendous response to dick jokes is in most cases simply a mixture of R & R (release and recognition) and the more repressed the audience, the better. R & R works as follows: Sex is something we think a lot about, but can't seem to talk much about; so consequently, when the comic brings it up, we feel tremendous release. Soon, we find ourselves laughing in recognition, then we notice others laughing, and we feel a sense of group recognition. So it seems the dick-joke lover isn't nearly so depraved as one might think—just, perhaps, in need of a good . . . laugh. It is important to remember, in the face of even the most base body function reference, that the resulting laughter one hears is the sound of freedom—a kind of psychic spring cleaning that knows no season.

Laughter, as catharsis, is serious business. As a physical response, it stands alone in its respectability amidst its uncouth siblings. While we are prohibited from screaming, crying, snoring and burping, among other things, in public places, we are almost always allowed to laugh. In a comedy club, this behavior is not only permitted, it's written into the establishment's charter. Of course the same is true of theater and film, in many cases, but both lack an ingredient as crucial as laughter in comedy clubs—the interaction between performer and audience. This does not simply mean *live*, but *living*—an organic, growing, developing monologue that is as reactive as it is active.

As stand-up Jerry Seinfeld explains: "Comedy is a dialogue, not a monologue—that's what makes an act click. The laughter becomes the audience's part, and the comedian responds; it's give and take. When the comic ad-libs or deals with a heckler, it gets explosive response because it's like, 'Hey, this is happening now! This isn't just some pre-planned act.' So whatever lends itself to that feeling is what makes comedy work—that live feeling. That's why comics ask, 'Where are you from?' It brings a present moment to the show."

As with any audience, there is an element of voyeurism, a willing passivity and a desire to be "shown and told." Many comedians see themselves as adventure surrogates for those in the audience. Onstage, they are free to act out our boldest fantasies and should they cross the line of acceptability there's always the safety net: "Just kidding." Comedian Bob "The Bobcat" Goldthwait says about his unconventional, aggressive brand of humor: "I think part of my appeal is that a lot of people would like to scream, tell everybody to get fucked—so they pay money to watch me say it instead."

Alan Havey feels that, while some audiences view comics as daredevils through whom they can live vicariously for the evening, this isn't always the case. Instead of adventure, people are often just looking for a little release and relief: "People work all day and when they come in to see a comedian, they want to be grabbed. They want someone taking over for a couple of hours, or twenty minutes, or whatever—it's like going to prostitutes, therapists or the movies."

We go to the comedy club for a couple of hours to relinquish our frustrated ids to the stand-up comic, so that he or she can strike them against the rocks of blind fury and hand them back to us, clean as a whistle. It is this cleansing effect that attracts us to comedians after a long day spent slaving over the hot stove of reality. We want to be taken back to our innocence and youth, when existential inquiry meant nothing more than a rousing game of peek-a-boo. In the comedy club, we replace peek-a-boo with "here's the punch line!" and the trust we placed in the hands of grown-ups is transferred to the hands of stand-ups. Like a group of children playing "house," we become a single entity playing "life," responding together to exaggerated problems that are close enough to the real thing to make the game interesting, yet abstract enough to keep it fun. We draw strength from the sense of community and comfort from the group feeling of "me, too."

But we do not let go of ourselves completely. We retain the right to mutiny at any moment, to regain control of the ship if we don't like its course. It is actually in these terms, of a voyage, that stand-up comics often view their acts, saying, "I'm taking the audience on a trip," or "They've got to hang on and trust me while we go on a ride." Usually, with a skilled performer, the audience lets themselves be taken, willingly, but on other, rare occasions, they just won't budge. Paul Provenza says that the most frustrating thing in the world, for a comic, "is an audience that won't open its mind—that won't give you any creative freedom. This usually happens because they will not hear you. It's a sheep mentality. I know it's happening as soon as I hear an 'Oh-h-h' over something slightly over the edge of good taste. I know immediately I'm dealing with sheep. It only takes one person to screw up the audience, to say, 'Hey, guys, we're getting out of hand here, we can't let him take us that far over the line.' Then, suddenly, everyone agrees with them."

The reluctance of an audience to laugh at certain subjects is not simply out of prudishness but because, according to George Carlin, "People vote when they laugh... if the comic's saying something about 'the mechanical dildo...' and you laugh, it's like, 'Hey, the big dildo—like the one I have!' This happens when you get to any subject where people don't want to reveal their comfort with it—even if it's not something they're intimately involved with. They don't want to show they're comfortable talking about baby rape—instead of saying, 'Geez, he's talking about being in a nursery knocking off a couple of female kids,' he doesn't want to reveal that—so he goes, 'Hmm, I don't understand this at all,' and he certainly isn't going to laugh at it."

Soviet born comic Yakov Smirnoff says that this type of reaction is most common in groups that have rigid standards of behavior or propriety; he noticed it when he began performing in Russia: "Audiences there were more careful about laughing; if things went too far, they wouldn't budge. But since you usually said things that were already approved, that didn't happen much. If you want to see it here, go watch a performance before a religious group—you'll see that they're afraid of laughing at certain subjects because their pals are there, their bosses are there... it's like being back in the Soviet Union."

An audience's attitude toward a comic's material depends on its members' general range of acceptance. George Carlin feels that while the counterculture may be gone, today, its legacy lives on: "What remained with people, out of that era, was a more relaxed approach to personal morality. Now movie stars can have babies out of wedlock—three kids with different guys—and it doesn't affect their careers at all, because everyone at home is doing that too, or knows someone who is. So the audience's line of shock has been expanded—things that were once sensational and outrageous no longer are—the territory is much broader." This makes the dick-joke comic's job harder in that it's more difficult to get easy shock laughs, and the good comic's job easier in that there are fewer untouchable topics: "Certain areas can be opened up now without fighting that initial revulsion. At least you can say, 'You know, I was raping my sister the other day,' and they'll say, 'My, he's a little nuts, but let's listen.'"

In an audience, the power of our fears is defused; gathering strength from group recognition, we become larger than life and therefore in vulnerable. We can laugh at our primal fears—even death loses its bite when given the proper set-up. When we surrender our fears and insecurities, whether consciously or subconsciously, to the comic, it is with the understanding that he or she is in complete control and will handle them carefully. If the performer suddenly loses control, the audience senses it instantly and pulls inward, gradually at first, then sharply if the comic's footing isn't regained. To the performer, this response can seem callous and unfeeling—the audience becomes like a shark, gliding through the water easily, secretly sniffing for blood and finding it, turning on its prey with no trace of compassion. For the audience, however, their response is one of self-preservation. To leave their unguarded anxieties in the hands of a comic who lacks complete control is annoying at best, frightening at worst.

Comic Richard Belzer believes that there is rarely such a thing as a bad audience and that the mistake many comics make is to "mistake their own ineptness for indifference or stupidity on the part of the audience." Stand-up Carol Siskind agrees: "I always claim full responsibility. I never blame the audience...my job is to do what I do. Sometimes it's harder, sometimes it's easier, and I have to evaluate that." She says that, instead of blaming a crowd for not laughing, a comic's job is to evaluate the audience immediately after getting onstage, find what they like, where the source of their energy lies, and give them what they want. She believes this can be done "because the audience takes on one personality. You can see it in three minutes. I could tell the audience last night didn't really want to reach for my jokes; I sort of got away with the bit, 'I know I've had other lives—that I've been here before. I have clues. First of all I'm exhausted...' I knew, from their energy, that was a borderline joke for them—but I decided to risk it and I got away with it."

In addition to people who are too tired to laugh or who refuse to laugh at subjects that lie outside of their dogma-scape, some people prefer not to laugh at anything at all. Jerry Seinfeld describes a situation known to all comedians: "You always get the couple who comes over to you after the show and the wife will say, 'My husband thought you were very funny and he doesn't laugh.' Imagine living with this guy! You just have to smile and say, 'thank you,' while the guy's sitting there saying, 'I enjoyed the show—I don't laugh.' It's like, I don't eat prunes or I hate anchovies... I don't laugh." Some people would just like to be heard, to exert a little influence on the course of the show. David Brenner remembers getting to the punch line of a joke, when suddenly someone shouted out, "That's not true!" and ruined the whole joke. He said, "Wait a minute, you're right it's not true, but these people didn't pay money to hear truth; they came here to laugh! I was going to tell you a wonderful joke attached to that lie, and you ruined it. And *that's* the truth!"

The relinquishing of control by a comic, even if the crowd seems to want that on any given night, is the absolute stand-up taboo. An audience may imply (through heckling, interrupting, etc.) a desire for the comic to break down the fourth wall and "join the crowd," but experienced comedians know that this would only make the room more uncomfortable. Jerry Seinfeld, acknowledged by many comics to be the ultimate in professionalism, explains that contrary to signals being sent out, the audience does not want the comic to lose control, because if he does, they realize, "we're all in trouble—we're in it too." He describes this subtle balancing of power, between audience and comedian, in terms of a judo match, in which "two guys are standing there holding on to each other's costumes for three or four minutes, until one perceives the slightest little error in the balance of the other one, and then flips him and he loses." Killing, in comics' terms, is synonymous with an exceptional performance, as in, "It was the best show of my life, I killed them."

Seinfeld, along with a majority of comedians, believes that his craft is by definition a battle, stating simply, "To laugh is to be dominated," and, conversely, to make someone laugh is to dominate. Domination and control have an impact that can not be emphasized enough by stand-up comics.

To maintain control, comics must transcend the need to get laughs for every joke, says stand-up Paul Reiser. "I do this every night, so I'm used to anything. My goal isn't to get the most laughs, especially in the work-out clubs, where it's like an exercise gym, but to work on new lines, new segue ways. And also, you have to realize that when people laugh, it could be for the wrong reasons—maybe it was a good spot, or maybe the audience was drinking... I was watching comics last week at the Improv, and aside from really enjoying it, I realized how insecure we get up there. It's a matter of knowing what to hear and how to handle it. The audience gets shaky if they see you panic for no reason, or if you turn on someone unjustly, or if you ignore people. To me, that's when a comic bombs—if someone's up there not getting laughs, or getting laughs for the wrong reasons, and the guy presumes they're on his side. That, to me, is pathetic; it makes me cringe."

Part of his need to control is purely selfish: "The stage is the only place in the world that I control. That's why I feel my best up there, my most assertive." He adds that he will vehemently protect this territory, with the microphone as his only weapon. In stand-up, the microphone as a means to gaining and holding power is viewed by comics in literal terms and, by male comics, in psychological terms revolving around virility and impotence. Paul describes a situation early in his career when his microphone was taken by someone in the audience: "It's like having your balls grabbed... you have no control." His feelings are corroborated by other male comedians, several of whom use the metaphor of "microphone as dick" to explain why there are many more men than women in stand-up comedy.

Bob Goldthwait says, "Did you ever notice a lot of comics hold their dick onstage? The reason is, for me, I get the feeling everyone's taking from me, and I'm so naked up there... I'm hiding my last fucking thing, I think. I hate the cliché that you feel naked onstage, but it's true, you are naked up there. That's why you hold your dick—and I find the more honest I get up there, the more I'm grabbing for it. It's not really honest, it's more when I'm feeling vulnerable, when I feel like everybody's bugging me—I'll be playing with my penis the whole night up there." But for comic Robin Tyler, this concept is ridiculous: "When male comics are talking about stand-up being phallic, what they're talking about is aggressively controlling an audience, and women aren't supposed to be allowed this. My answer to that is, 'Tough shit!' They think, somehow, the prick is the most aggressive thing and that's not true; the mind is much more powerful than the prick—and the mind doesn't go down in two minutes."

Control is a necessary tool for the stand-up comic; it is also a highly seductive drug that drew many into the profession, and keeps many working at it. Its allure is described most vividly by Yakov Smirnoff who, ironically, came to America to escape the yoke of governmental control: "Part of the addiction of comedy is the control—you control the audience. They're there because you're there, otherwise they wouldn't be around. Most comics say, 'I'm just here to hear laughter,' —that's bullshit. I'm secure enough to admit that it's a feeling of definite power. You're in control of whether they laugh or cry...that's great. It's not just about laughs. It's like being the conductor of a huge orchestra—you point your finger and they do it. It's the same thing."

Steve Mittleman, who describes himself in pre-comedy days as having been "unheard," found in stand-up the perfect solution—the comedian is not only allowed to talk and be listened to, but he is paid to do it: "It's addictive—the most addictive thing I've come across in my whole life. A lot of it is the power over the audience—the manipulation of people—being in charge, the center of attention. Getting approval, hopefully. John Hinckley would have made a great stand-up; he needed to be heard."

Beneath the push and pull of verbal dominance, another, more subtle battle takes place between comic and audience—emotional seduction. Just how this love-in ends depends on just how charming a stand-up can be. Bob Morton, segment producer of "Latenight with David Letterman," sees hundreds of comics throughout the year, and says that while being funny is important, "being likeable is the key. You won't laugh at someone you don't like, especially when they're hitting so close to home. They're doing jokes about your wife, or your habits or the way you conduct your life and you aren't going to laugh if you don't like the person."

Jerry Seinfeld says that, because taking control is an aggressive, dominating action, it must be done with subtlety, or the crowd will fight you all the way—particularly the men. "So the main thing you have to do is make them like you first. Once they like you, they'll say, 'Okay, I'll look at things your way for the next twenty minutes—you seem like a nice guy, I'll go with you.' That's what you're doing when you laugh at a comedian, you're going along with his point of view. It's easier with women; they're more open. I've always felt an audience dominated by women is great for me, because they don't have any withholds on getting silly and doing things for fun. A woman's sense of humor is much more free, more fun loving—it doesn't even have to make sense. If it's fun, great."

An audience does not go to a club to hate comedians, but neither do they go to fall in love; the comedian must, as the saying goes, pitch woo. Richard Belzer is often perceived as treating audiences in a manner bordering on ruthless (comic Lois Bromfield says, "I've seen him say things to people that I'd get up and punch him in the face for, though he has gotten better"). But he says, ironically, that in order to do stand-up well, one must "make love" to the audience: "First you warm them up, say hello and greet them . . . and by the time dessert comes around, they're ready to go wherever you want them to go." While this sounds a bit forced, like the kind of lovemaking that takes place over a stick shift in a '57 Chevy, Belzer insists this isn't the case. He rejects the word "force" and says it's the term "win an audience" that is apt: "I don't think you can mug an audience into liking you or your material. They have to trust and like you."

In cynical terms, the whole procedure could be viewed as an encapsulated version of every love relationship: initial contact is made, enticement begins, trust is built, infatuation and finally love set in . . . then the comic leaves. Seen in less cynical terms, it is a love based more upon coaxing than seducing. Comic Larry Miller sees it more in terms of Mother Goose than Casanova, explaining, "It's like looking at a child when he's coming up behind you, and you're going, 'C'mon, c'mon . . . that's it . . . ' then you take his hand. It's never, 'Get over here!' You have to make the child trust you. It may go a little slower but it will get there." Reiser says, "I used to do this when I came on late, or opened: 'Do you want to skip this and go for coffee?' If you don't force it on them, if you relax, they're more likely to go with you."

Often, the audience itself is responsible for the type of wooing it receives. A crowd resembling Genghis Khan and the Golden Horde is not likely to respond well to perfume and bon bons. The experienced stand-up feels the mood of a room instantly upon hitting the stage and he or she will entice accordingly. The important point, however, is that no matter how rough or easy the crowd, it must still be made to love the comedian.

The procedure of courting is made infinitely easier for the comics because they do not think in terms of a room full of people; they view the audience as a single entity. This entity has a personality, which is established immediately. Often it also contains several outstanding members: the spokesperson, the asshole, the drunk (see asshole), the scapegoat (see drunk) and the out-of-towner (preferably very naive and very stupid). Carol Siskind remembers that one night the audience, as a cohesive entity, struck her as being so warm and cooperative she stopped toward the end of her act and said: "You are just adorable." She adds, "It wasn't like talking to a group, it was like talking to 'someone.'" Comic Paul Rodriguez believes that audiences are a cohesive unit in the sense that people are basically alike: "It's like Maslow's hierarchy of needs; people have the same basic wants and desires— shelter, relationships, food—and I have in my act these basics." But the sweet, wonderful entity can, conversely, turn into a "thing," as in "The Thing that Wouldn't Die"; it's at these times that, for the comic, stand-up can fall several steps below that magical place called fun.

Lois Bromfield takes a stoic, pragmatic approach to the problem: "Sometimes you think, 'I don't want to do this,' because they're mean strangers and you don't give a fuck about them, but then you realize this is what you do for a living—so put up with it or leave." But most comics have a harder time separating themselves from the emotions of the mob. Carol Siskind says that the same strategy she uses to "read" the audience is what also makes her particularly vulnerable to them: "Someone once said to me that I remind him of Jackie Vernon because of the way I really look at the audience. Some comics work with a kind of glazed expression, but I really do look at the people . . . and sometimes it gets me in trouble because I'll be looking at them and realize, 'I'm looking at them and they hate me!' That's not a good thing."

Comics' descriptions of this fear—of being turned on by the mob— can best be approximated by a famous scene in every gothic horror movie: an angry mob of villagers, brandishing hoes and pitchforks, gathered outside the castle walls screaming, "Kill the beast! Kill the beast!" Jerry Seinfeld describes a joke by Larry Miller about the comic's protective bubble bursting: "He says one night you're going to be performing and suddenly, in the middle of your act, someone is going to stand up, point at you and say, 'Wait a minute, he's no good.' And everyone in the audience will say, 'You know, you're right! He just had us fooled with that rhythm he talks in and the jokes . . . he's not good at all!' And they rush the stage and try to get you. The next scene is this big crowd and there's this body being thrown up—and it's a dummy body, you know, with the arms flailing the wrong way." Though individual hecklers often seem to have the strength of millions, it is rare that a comic is actually turned upon by the group. This is a result of the tight-fisted control a comic maintains on the audience, and, of course, it's a result of the audience having a good time.

Still, there are those audiences who believe that when a comic says, "Where are you from?" they are supposed to not only give an answer, but elaborate as well. They're wrong. Apart from elaborations that make the comedian funnier, the general feeling of the group is, "I paid good money to laugh, and I don't give a damn where the jerk at the next table is from." Comics, however, continue to initiate this type of interaction for one reason: it's the most profound way of saying, "Look at this! You're not watching a videotape! This show is happening right now, and anything can happen!" The excitement and beauty of this concept usually overwhelms even the most boring, overextended story about someone's trip in from Des Moines.

This ability to talk back to the performer is particularly interesting in light of stand-up's current popularity. Obviously audiences today desire "contact entertainment"—but why? The logical explanation is that, in the face of growing isolation and powerlessness on the part of the individual in the real world, there is an increased need for direct contact in entertainment. If you're not satisfied with the proceedings of a movie or play, you can either keep quiet and smile—or leave. If you're not happy with a stand-up comic's act, you can always yell, "Hey, what the hell are you talking about?" and, most likely, you'll get an answer.

For Alan Havey, this is one of stand-up's greatest attractions: "I really want to know about people's personal lives. If I wasn't doing this, I think I'd want to be a therapist." And he assumes the audience enjoys it also, based on the very personal things people tell him: "They feel comfortable with me. There's something very intoxicating about the lights, the attention, the microphone—look at Phil Donahue, women on national television talking about losing their virginity. I think part of it is that people love to confess."

People's desire to be "part of the act" takes many forms, and often extends beyond the confines of the stage, with audience members approaching the comic after the show in order to discuss his material, his persona or the world in general. While a feeling of camaraderie between comic and audience is usually desirable, there are cases when it extends too far, if only in people's minds, and trespasses into the "peculiar zone." Judy Tenuta, who refers to herself as "Judy the Petite Flower, Giver/Goddess, Fashion Plate, Earth Mother Hostess, Geisha Girl, Buffer of Foreheads, Blesser of Bunions, Healer of Hermaphrodites, Queen of Candy Pants, Monarch of Malcontents and Tower of Babble," says (not surprisingly), "Some people really think I'm a bondage princess, that I have people tied up in my house—that's real sweet, but I did that when I was a teenager and baby sat."

She also says that many people, apparently feeling they have spiritually bonded with her during her act, approach her after the show and through the mail, presumably to form friendships. "I got a letter recently that began, 'Dear Judy, I am an incarcerated man.' So right away, I'm ready to get a blood test—how appealing. It goes on, '...could you please send me a lock of your hair...' and it ends, 'I will be out of prison in two months.' I'm thinking, 'Yeah, babe, pick up the pink courtesy phone!' I got another guy who brought me sea monkeys, which was fine, but then he thought I should pollinate with him. He worked at a nuclear waste dump or something—like I can't wait to have cauliflower for kids, right? Some of these people, you want to say, 'Did you ever think of maybe growing a career somewhere?'"

Jerry Seinfeld tells a touching story of being approached by a man, in a car wash, who had seen his act recently. He remembers, "The guy came up to me and said, 'Could we be friends?' I said, 'Well, that's really the nicest thing you can ever ask someone, but I'm a little busy.' I mean how do you invite someone to be a friend of yours—there's got to be some kind of mutuality I think. Want to be friends?! If someone wants to be your friend, you shouldn't have to ask. Who wants to be your friend because they're asked? It would be like, 'How did you become friends with him?' Oh, I was invited."

Generally, this feeling of kinship—of shared energy between comic and audience—can be used to the stand-up's advantage, but it must be genuine or they will know. Larry Miller says that "energy from the audience makes you relax; you realize you can do almost anything to mold it, delicately. You can be more of a bullfighter with it, let the bull come and use its energy as it goes by . . . you pull them this way a little bit, then draw them in and then try to get a little coy. You hope, as a performer, that you can really touch people, and connect with them, so when you say, 'Watch me, you'll like it,' they will. The better you get, the more sincerely you work on your talent, the energy starts to come out of your body and you can touch people from two feet away, then eight feet . . . And they know right when you walk out, that energy can touch them. Lenny Bruce has a great phrase. He says, 'Audiences individually may be idiots, but together they're a genius.' They know and sense everything—for good or for bad. They know if you're not honest with them, they know if you're just yanking them around, they know if you're being sincere."

According to A. Whitney Brown, a former street juggler/comic and, of late, writer/featured performer on "Saturday Night Live," audiences fulfill an important function in communicating with comics: "Hemingway says being a good writer is having a good shit detector, and that's what the audience is for us, a shit detector. I knew that, through this process, I could learn what was funny and what wasn't . . . and I figured it would probably take me at least ten years to learn the language of humor, and when I learned, I'd be a writer who could make people laugh."

Stand-up comedy serves as a fun-house mirror through which audiences can look at their lives and laugh; it presents the truth in a deadly serious light, but distorts it just enough to be easily digested, so it won't clash with beer and pretzels. Richard Belzer describes this phenomenon, saying, "I think there's a tremendous amount of guilt among the young, upwardly mobile generation, that they will not directly address.

When they go to these comedy clubs, they get to laugh and forget that they're stepping on the backs of the poor people, and that they love Reagan's tax breaks. . . ." Stand-up comedy is the once and future politically correct palliative for a generation clamoring to "make laugh not war!"

On the other hand, there are those who maintain stand-up's importance as a catalyst to social change, as opposed to a Band-aid for spiritually decomposing bond traders. For George Carlin, stand-up's primary attraction is that it allows him to dig into the skeletal closets of his audience, bring to the surface all the volatile truths and detonate them onstage: "If I can say something that will shoot down a popular notion, especially if it's something people are mindlessly flocking to because they're supposed to, I'll do it. Or if there's something that's ugly and unpopular, I enjoy advancing that—and appearing to be blithe about it. I love just tossing it off. I like dropping in little turds . . . like, I'd love to be at a wedding and there's a nice big punch bowl —and I sneak over and take a turd out of a bag and drop it in the punch bowl. Then I go, 'Hey, look at the turd in the punch bowl!' I have a thing I say about the fitness craze: 'America has lost its soul, so now we're going to save our body. We won't be good people, but we'll be able to run around the block eight times.'

"I have an angry spot that enjoys saying, 'Fuck you and your favorite thing, you asshole! You haven't thought it through!' Stand-up is a socially acceptable form of aggression. You get to name the targets, you get to fire the bullets, and what you're doing is putting people in an impossible situation where they're forced to like it. There's a great deal of hostility and aggression involved—and the wonderful part is, after you've finished, you then say, 'Hey, can't you take a joke? This is humor, sir! What's a matter with you?' You shame them into agreeing; nobody wants to be accused of not taking a joke, so it's a double bind for them."

The fact is, stand-up is satire and, regardless of how comforting or confrontational it is for angst-avoiding audiences, it is also planting some serious seeds. Logic dictates that if you want to get a message across and the frontal lobe is locked, you go in through the back door. Regardless of how non-provoking it may seem at times, stand-up is by nature an asocial endeavor; the status quo and punch lines mix like Petra Kelly and atom bombs. The premise for every joke is that something is wrong—with you, with the country, with your mother, with something! If nothing is wrong it's not a joke, it's making conversation. Ultimately, the audience chooses whether to view what they see onstage as thought provoking or thought preventing. But the important point is that it is thought.

or... "Hey, Waiter, There's a Fly in My Primordial Soup!"

Jokes, in varying degrees of crudeness, have existed since the beginning of human life. Before man learned to walk erect, there was comedy; after he learned, there was stand-up. It's possible that the sense of humor in human beings is an evolutionary survival trait—if you can't laugh at your problems (which were probably quite numerous in the Mesozoic Era), you're going to have a hard time reproducing. Comedian Kip Adotta believes that stand-up comedy is the world's second oldest profession—which, if true, proves that man cannot live on making whoopie alone; he needs a whoopie cushion.

History seems to back up this theory; from the dawn of time to the present time, stand-up comedy, in its various incarnations, has remained firmly entrenched in the consciousness of humankind. We have survived the Fall of Rome, the Birth of Christ, the Bubonic Plague, two World Wars... and still maintained our sense of humor. Stand-up has changed dramatically through the years, of course, but whether you're talking about Royal Fools or Catskill Mountain tumlers, the formula remains the same: funny person telling jokes + laughing audience = stand-up comedy. The major difference today is that stand-up comedians are enjoying the critical and popular acclaim that has, for the most part, been denied them throughout history. As comic Jay Leno explains, "We're just lucky to live in a time when it [stand-up] is marketable. Had I tried to be a comedian at the time of Attila the Hun, it would be like, 'Who's that guy the troops are giggling at? Kill that annoying person! Behead him!'"

In 1963 there was one showcase club in the country—the New York Improv. It had just been opened by Budd Friedman, a former ad man, and his singer wife, Silver Friedman, as a coffeehouse where singers could congregate and perform. For the first two years there was no cover charge; after that, it cost fifty cents to get in. Friedman says, "It wasn't until we got our liquor license that comics started hanging around"; but he got it—and they did. Between the club's opening and his departure for Los Angeles in 1975, he estimates that he introduced more than 10,000 new acts, including comics and singers. (In October of 1975, after he and Silver were divorced, he opened the L.A. Improv. In 1979 a court ruled that he could not open another Improv within a 100-mile radius of New York City. No other restrictions were placed on him, however, and today, on the West Coast, there are seven other Improvs.)

The list of stand-ups who worked at the New York Improv includes virtually every stand-up comic who attained prominence in the 60s and 70s—Freddie Prinze, Jimmy Walker, Robert Klein, David Brenner, Rodney Dangerfield, Gabe Kaplan, Bill Cosby, Dick Cavett, Steve Landesberg—and several prominent singers, including Bette Midler, whom Friedman managed for a time. For aspiring stand-up comics in America, the New York Improv was the mecca, and the reason was far from mysterious—it was the only showcase club in the country. There were some paying gigs around for comics, but since the demise of nightclubs in the late 50s, they were few in number and were immediately seized upon by more established acts (in elegant rooms like the Copacabana in New York, Mr. Kelly's in Chicago and the big rooms in Vegas) or by more traditional acts (in the Catskills).

Virtually the only paying gig where up-and-comers could work out new material was a place called Pip's in Brooklyn, and this kept many a young comic afloat between the Improv and the streets. Among the comics who worked Pip's for the all-important $30 a weekend were David Brenner, Robert Klein, Andy Kaufman and countless other struggling stand-ups who needed the money and work-out time. But that was it. There were other rooms in New York, like the Café Wha?, the Champagne Gallery and other Village clubs, but these were oriented toward singers and musicians; for stand-ups who wanted to work out new material, there was the Improv—and it paid nothing.

In 1972 Mitzi Shore, her husband comic Sammy Shore and comic writer Rudy DeLuca opened the Comedy Store in Los Angeles. Like the Improv, this was a work-out club for stand-ups and because it provided this "service" for comics, its owners said, the talent would be working for free. From the beginning, Mitzi says, her concept of the Store was more along the lines of an "art colony" than a club. Her aversion to "saloons" (the term she uses to describe the Improv and other comedy clubs) began in the early years of her marriage to Shore. As a comic, he traveled around the country working the variety club circuit and in those days, she says, "there were no clubs with only comics; comedy was something you did to warm a crowd up for a stripper or singer. . . ." In 1973, however, the Comedy Store partnership broke up when she divorced Sammy, then bought him and Rudy out of the club, and began to build up her "art colony." Among other comics who worked out at the Store during its early days were Richard Pryor, Robin Williams and David Letterman.

The success of these two showcase clubs was both artistic, for the performers, and financial, for the owners. Because of the "discovery" of several new stars on these stages (Freddie Prinze, Gabe Kaplan, Jimmy Walker, David Brenner. . .) more and more young actor/comics were attracted to the clubs. Paul Reiser remembers, in the mid 70s, "when Freddie, Gabe and Jimmy made it, that gave all the clubs a big boost. It was different than the environment at the Improv eight years before when Klein came in every night with a tape recorder, and Bette Midler was practicing her act. Back then it was a more beat crowd, but after these guys were discovered, suddenly it was TV! I remember thinking, 'I want to be Freddie Prinze and go on Carson.' I had no act, nothing, but I wanted that."

These discoveries made the same impact on the West Coast. In the mid 70s, Tony DePaul was booking a tiny, paying club in San Francisco called the Holy City Zoo. He remembers the effect of Robin

Williams's "discovery" and sudden rise to fame on the increase of the number of comics who came to him for work: "Right after 'Mork and Mindy' hit, *Playboy* did an article on Robin [at the time, he and DePaul were both members of an improvisational troupe called Papaya Juice] and it mentioned the Zoo. Within a couple months, comedians from all over the country started coming here. People looking to get into comedy didn't know where the hell to go before this, because there was almost nowhere. Because of this, the Zoo started expanding and I began putting on shows in neighboring towns—Santa Cruz, Sacramento, Sebastopol, Monterey. . ."

DePaul also attracted comics because he was paying them: "I would take the door and divide it up. Comics could get more exposure in Los Angeles, but they could come to San Francisco and get fifty to seventy-five bucks a show—that's nothing now, but then it meant a lot to a lot of people. A. Whitney Brown started coming in off the streets, and Michael Davis, who keeps getting called to the White House—he just did his fourth show for Reagan. I used to make fun of him, that thing he does with spitting the ping pong balls. One time I squashed his balls, and he couldn't do any goddamn tricks." Quickly, demand threatened to overwhelm the supply of comics and material, but DePaul says they came up with new programming innovations: "Nobody had developed enough material to do a whole set, so instead of using just three comics, we needed to use five or six of them doing fifteen minutes a piece to fill the bill."

In addition to attracting stand-ups, the much-publicized discoveries of several new stars in the comedy clubs drew increasing numbers of audience members who wanted to see the new TV stars-to-be. This, comic George Calfa feels, encouraged the growth of the industry, but downgraded the level of audience sophistication. He blames the owners who were more interested in keeping a club full than in maintaining order: "What's happened is, about six, seven years ago, because of Freddie Prinze and comics like that, people started to go to comedy clubs that never went before—people from the outer boroughs. So there would be this one table of 'Vinnie, Tony, Joey and Frankie,' but the rest would be the old, more discriminating crowd. You could still work out and develop new material and you wouldn't have to kill-kill-

kill. Then, more of these people started coming. They'd scream and nobody stopped them. They'd disrupt the show and have a good time, but nobody else would. So, little by little, it became more 'Joey and Tony' and the other group got smaller and smaller. Now, the second show Friday in these clubs is crazy. That's why there's a whole new breed of comedian—they kill at these clubs. If I go up before them, I have a shot, but if I go on after, it's very hard. Most of their stuff is all generic: 'I just signed a cable deal—now I get fucking HBO! Thank you! Boy George, there's a real man! He says, "Do you really want to hurt me?" Hurt you?! I want to fuckin' kill you! Thank you!' Do that kind of act in clubs today, and it will work . . . it will kill."

In response to the growing supply of and demand for comics, other showcase clubs sprang up in the mid 70s. In 1975 Rick Newman's Catch A Rising Star opened in New York, along with the Improv in Los Angeles, and in 1976 Richie Tienkin and Bob Wach's Comic Strip opened in New York. As the major outlets in the country, these clubs drew hopeful comics from across the nation who hung out until 2 A.M. waiting to work out onstage—for no compensation.

Many business people in the industry look back on this time as the last hurrah for the true American comedian; because there was no money involved, live stand-up was still a pure art form, pursued only by those willing to do without material gain, instead of those who were in it to get rich. But this fond reminiscence takes on a sort of *Gone With the Wind* tone—sure it was a romantic, dramatic time, but that doesn't erase the fact that there was slavery involved!

So it's not surprising that the late 70s brought a civil war to the tiny comedy club community. At the heart of the argument lay the question of whether or not to pay comedians for their onstage performances. The comedians argued the point that if they were good enough to merit a cover charge from the audience (standard practice in the showcase clubs), then they were good enough to be paid, and Mitzi Shore was the first target. In March 1979, twenty-two comedians, after estimating Shore's yearly gross at roughly $2.5 million, formed a group, called "Comedians for Compensation," and began their strike. Shortly after the Comedy Store strike began, the Improv was severely damaged in a fire that left only a small portion of the club open for business. If the comics struck him then, Friedman would have gone bankrupt—so he gave in to their demands immediately. Shore hung tough, however, refusing to negotiate with the growing number of striking comics.

By late April, when the group had grown to almost one hundred fifty members and the Comedy Store was severely crippled, Mitzi decided to negotiate. On April 25, 1979, *Variety* reported that, after rejecting Ms. Shore's latest offer, the comics submitted the following counter-proposal: $25 a set on Tuesday–Thursday and Sunday nights in the two-hundred-seat capacity "Original Room" (at the Sunset Strip club and at her Westwood club, which was then temporarily closed), with a guaranteed schedule of eighteen paid comics plus two nonpaid new-comers on each of those nights, and on Friday and Saturday nights, a guarantee of eleven sets per night at $25 each, with no unpaid new-comers. In the seventy-seat "Belly Room" at the Sunset Strip club, they demanded eight sets per night at $25 each, Tuesday–Sundays, and in the club's five-hundred-seat "Main Room" (where she featured "The Best of the Comedy Store Regulars"), a guaranteed fifty percent of the gross nightly covers, which could be up to $150. All comics would restrict themselves to one set per night in the various rooms. After several squabbles, the terms were agreed upon. Budd Friedman, after fully reopening his two-hundred-twenty-five-seat club, settled on $15–$20 per each twenty-minute set.

But the strike produced a serious rift in the California stand-up com-munity that has only recently eased up as more and more post-strike comics have diluted the former small group. Tom Dreesen was the leader and one of the founders of "Comedians for Compensation" and he walked the picket line in front of the Comedy Store for eight weeks. While other, lesser (at the time) L.A. comics, including David Letter-man, Jay Leno and George Miller, gave their time and support to the cause, Dreesen was particularly important to the group because of his level of success at the time. Earning more than $300,000 a year at that point, he commanded more respect and had more leverage with owners, and his presence also served to reassure struggling comics that the "big boys" were involved too.

According to Dreesen, the strike began with several informal meet-

ings in which comics discussed their frustrations over the issue of performing gratis. "These comics were college graduates," he recalls.
"They were people who had been politically involved in anti-war pro-
tests and things like that. I got them organized and went to Mitzi a
dozen times before the strike and said, 'You've got to realize these kids
know what they're doing and they're serious. . . .' To make a long story
short, she said, 'No, I will not pay the comics.' So we, the comics,
decided to go on strike. But eighteen other stand-ups crossed our picket
line. Had they not done that, the strike would have been over in
twenty-four hours and all the comics would have gotten paid. But,
because they crossed, it took eight weeks, and in that time so much
went down that it's hard to imagine."

Meanwhile, at the Improv, a mysterious fire (caused by a more mysterious case of arson) had destroyed the back room. The front room,
however, remained intact and could seat roughly one hundred people.
Dreesen remembers: "Budd came to us and said, 'Please don't strike
me. If you do, I'm dead.' We asked him to sign a memo that said once
the place was built back up he'd pay the comics. He said yes, and so
when we walked the picket line at the Store, we'd send customers over
to the Improv, and then we'd all go over there and work." Friedman
does not try to appear as the martyr, however; he admits, "If I were in
her [Mitzi's] position—if they came to me first—I might have done
the same thing. Because I truly believe that the showcase clubs were
like schools, and I didn't want to pay them to go to school."

Regardless of his reasons, Friedman gave in. Meanwhile, some very
ugly things began to happen because of Mitzi's refusal to negotiate with
the comics. Dreesen says: "Several nights, some of the women on our
picket line were attacked. They [nonstriking comics] were going to beat
up one of our comics, Jimmy Aleck, who had polio as a kid. The
people who crossed the picket line thought that, with all the 'stars' out,
they'd have a chance to get better time spots. One night, one of their
guys drove a car through our picket line and almost hit Jay Leno. In
fact they scraped him and he hit the ground."

A comic named Steve Lubetkin became a real tragedy of the strike.
"He had walked the picket line with us, and when the strike was over,
he couldn't get on. Finally, he jumped off the top of the Hyatt House

and left a note that said, 'My name is Steve Lubetkin . . . I used to work at the Comedy Store.' Before he died, I gave a speech to the comics and said, 'I'm going back to work now in Vegas. I have a family, but you young comics should form an organization that will keep things in check.' When I was leaving (to meet George Schlatter, who wanted me to host 'Real People'), Steve came up to me and said, 'Tom, I need to talk to you!' I said, 'Steve it's late, I'm in a hurry.' But he said, 'Tom, please don't leave the group, because if you and the bigger guys go, she'll retaliate—she won't let us come back.' I told him, 'There's a no retaliation clause, and I won't go back until you go back. That's a promise.' I left and he tried for three weeks to get on, but she wouldn't let him. Finally, on a Monday night he called in for time slots and was told once again there were no openings—and he went and killed himself. Jay Leno called me in Tahoe, fifteen minutes before I went on-stage, and told me. That was the hardest performance of my life. I'm not blaming anybody directly for what happened, but I just made my mind up that I never wanted to return to the Comedy Store.

"A year after Steve's death, on the very spot that he landed, there was a dummy lying there with a sign around its neck that said, 'My name is Steve Lubetkin, I used to work at the Comedy Store.' The next year, the same thing happened. Some people think it was his old girl-friend, but they don't know. Also, when it happened, someone had taken his picture off the wall in Mitzi's office and put it on her chair." This incident served to fuel the already burning antagonism between strikers and "scabs." "To this day," Dreesen says, "I still do not talk to those comics who crossed that picket line."

Lois Bromfield is a comic who did cross the picket line. Having arrived in Los Angeles at the time of the strike, she explains that she was unaware of the situation's gravity. She only wanted to work as a stand-up, and in retrospect feels that "I made a big error and I've never lived it down. I've had to go to people at the Improv and rekindle my friendships with them—people I knew from New York. I've had to say, 'Look I fucked up and I didn't realize it.' I was new and I didn't know what was going on. I just walked by the picket line and went in, and there I was. It's like walking into a hotel past a picket line and not seeing what's really going on. When I realized . . . it was too late. I got out of my car that day and walked into the Comedy Store. I'd just come from New York; Mitzi was giving me spots. I was a kid... I didn't realize what had been going on for all the years before that."

Aside from having no idea why there was a strike, she felt some loyalty to Mitzi, who was the first person that helped her in L.A. After realizing what was going on, however, she took a stand; but it was too late: "I was angry—but it was like being attacked and wishing you had done something. I didn't perform during the whole strike but it didn't matter; they saw me cross the picket line. There were other people who knew all about it and went in to work anyway; they really got reprimanded, and cut off. The only repercussions now are that there are still some people who remember me as crossing the picket line. There are people I've had to work with, who don't like me because of the strike. I say, 'Hi, how are you?' and they don't talk to me. There's no reason to be an asshole—I made a mistake—so what. Also, I don't work in the L.A. Improv at all; I'm not welcome there because of the strike. I've had to work with most of the people who were strikers, though—we're on the same level, and a lot of them have gotten over it."

Lois's habit of working only one club is not unique; generally, in Los Angeles, there are "Store" comics and "Improv" comics. While some may cross over between the two establishments, this is not the general rule, and those comics who do are known to be more loyal to one club or to have a "home club." Paul Rodriguez, who works both clubs, believes it is only possible for him because he came onto the scene in 1980—after the strike. While he doesn't actively subscribe to the two clubs' rivalry, he feels that in one sense it is beneficial in that it keeps the clubs competitive, and therefore more concerned with quality. "I think rivalry is part of the American way; there wouldn't be a GM if there wasn't a Chrysler. Rivalry is good for all consumers—including the ones who buy comedy." But, on the other hand, he acknowledges its darker side, which has trickled into the industry as a whole: "It's unfortunate that a lot of comics were harmed or stifled by this kind of competitiveness. There are some industry people who won't go to the Store, others who won't go to the Improv, and some comics, too. So let's say if you're a struggling comic/actor who works at the Improv and you're right for a part where the agent only goes to the Store . . . you blow getting a show."

In New York, at the end of the Los Angeles upheavals, the comics began to plan a strike of their own. Chris Albrecht, then manager of the New York Improv, remembers that he, Rick Newman (owner of Catch A Rising Star) and Bob Wachs (owner of the Comic Strip) got together to talk to the comics and it ended up with a big meeting at the Strip: "I was willing to come up with some money but the other owners weren't. I didn't want a strike because I'd worked hard to build a relationship with these people and besides, I could afford to pay them ten to fifteen dollars a set. Sure it was money, paying like ten acts a night, but it was tax deductible—it was an investment in our business!" But the other owners did not agree with him; they worried that it would set a dangerous precedent—"Where will it end?"—and they used the same argument as the Los Angeles owners: "If you want money, we want perfected acts . . . otherwise, remember—this is just a work-out club."

But before a strike broke out, a compromise was arranged. Dreesen credits Albrecht and Silver Friedman with having the foresight to bargain with the comics, which prevented a New York version of what had happened in Los Angeles. The L.A. strike also had repercussions across the ocean: "In London they started paying comics after reading about our success," and around the country, "Because we were getting paid in L.A., it was more difficult for other rooms around the country to keep prices artificially low." His response to the showcase's argument of, "You guys need a place to develop your craft—you should consider yourself lucky we provide it," is: "There's a thing called 'cover charge,' which supposedly is to cover the charge of the entertainment. I said to Mitzi, 'You pay the waitresses, the bartenders, the parking lot attendants, the guy who mops the floor . . . this place is called the "Comedy Store," and you don't pay the *comics* anything!' " He argues that not paying comics for their work places them in a degrading, childlike position that he finds intolerable. "Once you pay a person for their work, you give them dignity and respect; you no longer control them."

Many credit the strike with being one of the most important elements in creating the current comedy "boom" because, although the payments were modest, they produced a significant result: comics could now, with a full week's worth of sets, afford to support themselves *by doing comedy.* This infusion of money brought about an increase in the supply of comics and, because they made a lot of noise, a growing audience for comedy. Soon a small group of entrepreneurs began to recognize the phenomenal growth potential of stand-up comedy—and thus began the phenomenon of "the road."

In the late 70s, these people started booking comedians into the rapidly declining dance halls and watering holes of the previous decade. Mirror balls and mechanical bulls made way for rabbit ears and "These two guys on a bus . . ." The response they got was strong and it was immediate. Clubs that had been battling declining attendance with "Ladies Night," "Happy Hour" and "Wet T-shirt contests" were suddenly filled to capacity on "Comedy Night." This was the beginning of the comedy club industry and the resulting comedy boom. Today, there are an estimated 250 to 300 paying (non-showcase) comedy clubs in the country; in 1980, there were approximately ten.

These nightclubs differ from the showcases in that they do not encourage experimentation or the working out of new material (though some critics say that, after the strike, comics have been less inclined to work out in the showcases as well). For professional operations that require polished acts, the evening schedule consists of an opening act, a middle act and a headliner, with the weekly salaries for each ranging from approximately $150–$300 for an opener, $400–$800 for a middle and $1,000–$15,000 a week for a headliner. "Five years ago," says Chris Dipetta, a former partner in The Punch Line (an Atlanta-based comedy club franchise), "the top headliners were making eight hundred dollars maximum . . . Today, even a bad headliner who works every week will make at least sixty thousand dollars a year."

The reality of stand-up's dramatic growth in recent years is as indisputable as that of VCRs and Tofutti boutiques; less apparent, however, is the reason for it. The most sensible of the various opinions holds that once stand-ups were able to make a living by performing (or at least earn enough to feed themselves), it became a viable career option for many more young funny people. There are those who feel this growth has hurt the art of stand-up; mediocre talents, they believe, lured into the business by the promise of possible stardom and guaranteed income, would not have been pursuing stand-up before 1979.

Mitzi Shore is notable in this group: "Paying comics had a big effect. It's diminished the artistic growth of stand-up comedy because now their money comes first, and their art comes second—and it's not supposed to be that way. Now, all these clubs have opened up [the road clubs] that are nurturing untalented people for money and that goes against my code of honor: it is a sin to encourage mediocre talent." She says also that "I didn't have to give in, but I did... I just didn't believe in paying for a workshop. Instead of creating on the stage, they wanted to do a sharp act for money; that's why it diminished stand-up comedy. That's why these clubs are terrible around the country—they encourage bad talent."

Budd Friedman believes that while money is not necessarily the reason for all young comedians entering the business today, it is the main draw for club owners: "The explosion of comedy clubs has to come as a direct result of my opening the Improv originally. Over the years, the Store, Catch, the Strip—everyone and his brother said, 'Jesus, what a gold mine,' but I struggled for fifteen goddamn years. It's been very successful, financially, for a lot of people."

Like Shore, Friedman abhors owners who perpetuate mediocre comedians, citing as an example his refusal to franchise hundreds of Improvs across the country: "It was years ago—and Chris Albrecht, who was then my partner in the New York club, never forgave me for this decision. I said, 'You can't do that' [he laughs]... and of course there are now hundreds of clubs anyway.... But I was right in that it would really prostitute and cheapen what we're doing, because a lot of the guys in these clubs aren't comics; they're imitating their lessers, not even their peers. I would not be happy doing that. We've been open for a year in San Diego, and I take a lot of pride in the quality of shows I produce there week after week. When I say 'headliner,' it's usually a real headliner."

Chris Albrecht, now Senior Vice President, Original Programming, West Coast at HBO, feels the same way. "Now, since they started paying, it's great for the comics, monetarily, but it keeps a lot of mediocre guys in the clubs. If you do five sets at the Store and four sets at the

Improv in a week, you can make a living, which you couldn't have done before. But that doesn't advance the art; it just keeps a lot of guys in these clubs. Character guys [comics whose entire act is built around a single character] or good-looking men and women can go into a club with five minutes of very mediocre to bad stuff and play at being a comedian. There's a certain rhythm comics use (da-dum-da-dum . . . boom!), and because they've heard it so often, audiences know they're supposed to laugh at that rhythm—so they do."

During the week, payment for showcase club sets ranges from $10–$20 a piece, but the money is greater on weekends: the Comic Strip pays $30, Catch pays $50, the Comedy Cellar $50, and the Improv is $30, $35 and $40 depending on what time a comic goes on-stage. But still, says Alan Havey, "When you look at how hard we work—I think comics are still underpaid." Havey is one of many comics who, instead of regularly working the road, opts to live and work in New York where he can be seen in the showcase clubs by film and television casting agents and producers. In addition to the payment he receives for his weeknight spots, he supports himself by doing occasional road work and by performing up to five showcase sets a night on weekends.

Comics who lived outside of New York and Los Angeles once found ways of making money through comedy that had nothing to do with the clubs. Judy Tenuta recalls that in 1982, before the road circuit hit full steam, she performed her show at a Chicago nightclub called Byfield's in the Ambassador East Hotel, at which time she also made contact with people who hired her for their "private functions." She says: "They would come to me with requests like, 'Would you come to our home and abuse my husband for his birthday?' So I'd go there. I'd show up and say, 'Hi, it's your birthday, pig. Come, let me play my accordion in your face.' It was a lot like strip-o-grams. They actually asked for abuse. I thought, 'It's too bad you weren't around during World War II—Germany had a lot of that going on for free.' No one else I know was paid to abuse people from home to home." In addition to the money, it was great for free food: "Right when I got there I'd say, 'Bring me some food,' so I could eat while I abused them."

She also did a feminist twist on the old male-comic-as-emcee-for-strippers routine: "In 1980 there was a club called the Rose. Women came in, men stripped and I'd do warm-up. I'd say, 'Okay, Mr. Troll is coming out next—get out your scissors so you can snip some unwanted body hair from him.' Talk about crustaceans and neanderthal men . . . the owner paid me to talk about them, sort of like Lenny Bruce with the strippers, but they only went down to boxer shorts. It was unusual work, but at that time the clubs hadn't begun opening yet. Other comics were at home practicing in mirrors—and they still should be."

Even if the money in the showcase clubs can not be held completely responsible for the tremendous growth in the stand-up industry, it can be held responsible for some increase in the number of comics— which created a greater supply of "product" and led to the appearance of the road circuit—without which that growth would have been impossible. Since about 1979–80, the business has changed from a series of cottage industries into a major show business genre. According to Tom Dreesen, "What's happened is that the big time has gotten smaller and the small time has gotten bigger. Vegas has shrunk and they're using more production acts, but there's a new comedy vaudeville that didn't exist when I started. There's a whole club circuit: Crackers, Titters, Giggles, Jitters. There are outlets for these kids to develop in. Years ago, comics came out of the ghetto, à la Tom Dreesen, but today they are college-educated middle class kids."

Paul Provenza, a comic who began performing shortly before the "circuit" came about, concurs: "I think it's the first time since vaudeville that there's a middle class in comedy; what used to be the vaudeville circuit is now the comedy circuit. There are musical comics, jugglers, acrobats. A guy can make twenty-five to seventy-five thousand dollars being a total unknown. A guy with no TV exposure can make forty thousand dollars a year!" He says that, in the "old days," it used to be that a comic either made it big, or he just got by. But today, a stand-up can lie firmly in the middle, which has its positive and negative aspects. "It's good because now people can make a living doing what they love, but the bad side is that you can fool yourself into thinking you're a good comedian because there's a lot of work. It's easy to fall back and get comfortable. That's why real professionals like

Leno and Seinfeld are constantly moving and growing—they don't just sit back and relax."

And in many cases the choice between the comfort of mediocrity and the risk of innovation is not made easier by the fact that there is little artistic encouragement from the club owners. In the pre-growth days, there were so few outlets for stand-ups that, unless they consistently wrote new material and their act was constantly evolving, they simply would not get stage time. Today, on the other hand, there are plenty of stages, so it's more of a sellers' market and there is a strong temptation for comics to just float from one town to the next, never changing their act, and stopping only to pick up the not insubstantial checks along the way. As Alan Havey says, "Today, if you get down twenty to thirty minutes of good material you can work for the next ten years. There are so many clubs and the way they're set up, it's not conducive to being creative—it has to come from within. Owners are rarely going to come up and say, 'Write new material.' As long as they get people in to laugh, it doesn't matter. You can live in a dream world."

Comic Adrianne Tolsch says that with the industry's growth has come not only a greater tendency toward mediocrity, but an increased number of strongly derivative acts. In smaller towns, where shows are emceed by local comics, she says that this is more of a problem because these stand-ups aren't really part of a community of growing, developing artists—they simply copy what they know works.

Another incentive lures comics toward derivative material; very often, it's a guaranteed crowd pleaser—it "kills." That's because it has already been perfected but, unbeknownst to the audience, by its originator—not the comic delivering it. Jonathan Solomon, who works out of the New York Improv, echoes many other comics in saying that because of these types of acts—and because of dick-joke comics (stand-ups who rely primarily on scatological jokes and shock value for laughs)—it is harder for more cerebral, original acts to work: "I don't do as well on the road because of them; they get audiences used to a certain kind of inferior comedy and it's hard to win them back."

But before the road circuit—or the strike—came something that, with the possible exception of the joy buzzer and the exploding cigar, has had the single greatest impact upon stand-up comedy: television. To understand this phenomenon, it must be examined in two parts— B.C. (Before Cable) and A.D. (Anno Davido) [Latin for "Year of David Letterman"]. Before cable, a comedian's longest stretch of stand-up time on television was about five minutes. Even during the "Golden Age," when comedy was king, the king's subjects were *comedy characters*, not stand-up comedians: from 1948–53, there was the "Texaco Star Theater" with Uncle Miltie, and from 1950–54, Sid Caesar in "Your Show of Shows," to name only a few. During these years, television threw open its golden portals to the stand-up comic who knew how to bleach his burlesque roots to a pure kinescopic white. But there were rules: long stand-up routines were out; television comedians performed in sketches, situation comedies, musical numbers and as masters of ceremony with bite-sized monologues. The stand-up routine, with its stink of Borscht Belt bungalows and cheap vaudeville houses, was first-generation entertainment; television was a medium for "real" Americans, a perfect back beat for the "assimilation dance."

And so it went. The best comedians of each successive decade were discovered, nurtured and channeled into an appropriate television format. If the networks could afford to provide lavish sets, lots of extras, big-name talent and high production value, why give air time to some hyperkinetic guy who wore a plaid jacket and made libelous statements about his mother-in-law? So years passed, the distinction between "a legend in your own time" and "a legend in your own time slot" was blurred, the system worked, and everyone was happy.

Then, in the mid 70s, came cable, and with it, the need for low-cost, easy-to-produce entertainment. Stand-up comedy filled the bill; it came fully assembled, with writer, star and supporting cast included. Beginning in 1975, with Home Box Office, comedians began to appear on cable television specials, doing what their title implies: standing up, talking into a microphone, facing an audience and telling jokes that make people laugh. Not only did this provide comedians with a new opportunity—the chance to be seen in concert—as Chris Albrecht says, it also solved the age-old problem of television as the great equalizer of stand-up comedians: "Network TV buys comedy in five minute hunks, which isn't nearly as difficult to achieve as the hour-length set which you need for a cable special."

Once freed of their network restraints, the anarchistic vibrations of stand-up began to pulse in earnest, and the new beat was heard immediately. The ones who heard were the children of video, who, after years of scanning the airwaves for the voice of dramatic truth, had found it, speaking in the dialect of humor. Little Janie and Jimmy, raised on Campbell's Soup and Wonder Bread in lemon-freshened suburbs, schooled in politics by the Vietnam War and President Nixon, were taking control of the telly now. Unlike their parents, the new generation did not want their comedy pasteurized; they wanted it hot and heavy, and, since the price was right, they got it.

When it became clear that audiences were accepting comedians in full-length formats, the blitz was on. A comedian could now be seen in the context of his own act—not just as the funny character on a situation comedy. The advantage was that, although there was less money to be made initially, a comic could get the all-important television exposure and not run the risk of becoming over-identified with a character. Unfortunately, this new possibility came too late for people like Freddie Prinze. After gaining national recognition as the character "Chico," on the situation comedy "Chico and the Man," he found that audiences would come to see Chico do stand-up, but they had much less interest in seeing Freddie Prinze perform. Comedian Jimmy Walker had a similar experience. As the character "J.J." on the series "Good Times," he became an instant comic superstar. When he began performing stand-up again, people turned out in droves but many of his jokes were drowned out by the audience's pleas for him to say J.J.'s famous tag line, "Dy-no-mite!"

Comedians of the post–situation comedy era began appearing on television in both the long (cable) and short (talk show) formats. A successful appearance on one of the ever-expanding number of cable comedy shows, such as HBO's "Young Comedians Special," Cinemax's "Comedy Experiment" or Showtime's "Big Laugh-Off," often led to the next step—an appearance on "The Tonight Show" or, after 1982, "Latenight with David Letterman." This increased exposure only seemed to further whet the audience's comic appetite. Stand-up comedy, which had been resurrected as a cost-efficient broadcasting ploy, was turning out to be that most elusive of commodities—something that left audiences begging for more.

Michael Fuchs, chief operating officer of HBO, feels that there is a definite correlation between the introduction of cable and the growth of stand-up: "I think we rekindled the interest in comedy. It was almost a dying craft when we started." But he gives credit to an "institution" more specific than cable. "In the club realm, I think HBO had a seminal influence, and as an institution, I don't know of any other company that's been more directly involved with that world than we have."

There are others who claim that they planted the seed for the current growth of comedy even before HBO or cable. One of these people is Lorne Michaels, creator and producer of "Saturday Night Live": Although stand-up, per se, was never emphasized on "SNL", "I think the more important effect we had was in changing the general climate. In show business, things go in cycles and in the mid seventies, when we began, we helped focus attention on comedy again, and that created, in economic terms, more of a market, which led to the formation of lots of comedy clubs, which you see today." But generally, those who credit television for creating the current boom, single out cable.

Tom Parks, a comic who has worked the road over ten years (playing colleges before the clubs began opening) says that, with regard to the current boom, "I think it's all because of cable TV—that's what exposed America to stand-up. In 1974 and 1975, it was the Improv and Catch in New York and the Comedy Store in L.A. and that was it; there were no comedy clubs. If you were in Birmingham, Alabama, and said, 'stand-up comedy,' people would think, 'Bob Hope'. . . that was all they knew. It took cable to expose America to comedy as an art form—and they sure went for it."

Cable television created a new comic format that brought comics a step closer to rock stars—a link that hadn't existed before: "Cable," says Chris Albrecht, "created something new to strive for—to have an hour-long show on pay television—like a concert." But at the same time it created a new division among comics, which hadn't previously existed in television, between those who could sustain an hour-long special and those who couldn't: "In this sense, HBO separates the men from the boys."

In separating the men from the boys for their hour-long specials, HBO made good use of many "men," but left a lot of "boys" hanging around. Other cable channels like Cinemax and Showtime, incorporated after HBO, noticed this growing supply of not-yet-established talent and quickly made use of it. Today, in addition to HBO's comedy specials, which use well-established acts like Robin Williams, George Carlin, Robert Klein, and Buddy Hackett, there are many other pay-cable outlets for lesser known acts. Stu Smiley, today vice-president, comedy programming, at HBO, formerly vice-president, variety programming, at Showtime—at the time of this interview—explains how smaller pay-cable stations have taken up the comic slack: "We're trying to innovate, because we have to. HBO is the biggest, so we need to be hungrier. I think, in the last three years, they've followed our lead as far as going after young people . . . because we're doing it, they have to. In the mid seventies, when they had to be more aggressive, they did some terrific stuff. They did the original format with Robert Klein, Steve Martin, but when you get fatter you change . . . obviously, I have to feel this way. If I thought they were greater, I'd have trouble waking up every day."

Because Showtime can't afford to hire top comics for their specials, they try to discover soon-to-bes, and nurture them into stardom: "We have several tiers to our comedy program. We try to give up-and-coming comics a chance to show the best of what they do in the clubs. Then, if they get a career going, we can give them a special. So there's a farm system, really. We give them the opportunity to work and not hamper them too much—that's the most we can do . . . and out of that will come a natural growth of the art." And a growth in the business as well, he adds: "We're investing in these comics—and we hope to share in the profits down the road."

According to Chris Albrecht, in the case of HBO, comics' specials tend to be "produced," which means that once the deal is set with an established comedian, the show goes right into production. In the case of Cinemax, specials tend to be "developed," which means that, because the comedian is not as well established, the show will have to be sculpted in a way that will best highlight his specific performing style: "In terms of stand-up there are two major focuses here—HBO specials and Cinemax Comedy Experiments, which aren't for stand-up per se, but for comedy artists to use their abilities to put something together that wouldn't get a forum somewhere else. The only effort I put into stand-up at HBO is making a deal with Billy or Robin, trying to talk Eddie into doing another one, Joan Rivers into doing one . . . making a deal with Rodney. With the Cinemax experiments there's a lot more effort because there's a lot more creativity involved—they're concept based, not just performer based."

Because Cinemax and Showtime make use of up-and-coming talent, as opposed to HBO, which is able to afford those who have up-and-come, cable audiences are exposed to a greater number of stand-ups (whom they will then be more likely to see in the local comedy club), and young comics are given a broader range of possibilities with regard to television exposure—both of which add previously nonexistent dimensions to stand-up and contribute to its general growth. They also give exposure to comics who, because of the uniqueness of their acts, would never have gotten television exposure before cable. As Albrecht says about two of today's hottest comics, "Sam Kinison and Bob Goldthwait are two people who would have had a big problem fifteen years ago."

But cable has not only opened up the small screen for lesser known acts, it has also expanded the previously finite limits of television for well-known acts by freeing them from the shackles of network censoring, and allowing them to perform in a manner previously unheard of on TV. Michael Fuchs explains that, while HBO could not compete with the networks financially, they had a greater advantage in attracting top comic talent—the ability to offer artistic freedom: "The networks have never been able to do live comedy concerts because they can't handle the content, and the comics don't want to do censored acts. When we did 'Comic Relief,' all the comics wanted to do it on HBO so they could do their thing uncensored."

Instead of targeting their product to the maximum number of people in order to satisfy advertisers, as network TV did, cable programmers targeted their product to a particular audience they felt was most likely to pay for television; in other words they stressed demographics, not just numbers . . . a concept that has recently caught on at the networks as well.

Producing full length, uncensored stand-up specials enabled cable to be something that network TV couldn't be, and it was also economically efficient programming. Compared to original series and movies, its production costs were next to nothing. Stand-up, filmed live in a nightclub setting, also worked ideally to convey a strong sense of what Michael Fuchs calls "perceived value." "We believed, back then, that pay TV meant 'pay TV,' literally, and people had to feel that they were getting what they paid for. We often showed openings of our shows and you could see people pay for tickets. We wanted viewers to see that these shows were from nightclubs—and if you went there to see them, you'd have to pay."

Since Fuchs's early days at HBO in 1976, the industry has grown tremendously, and comics' perception of TV exposure has changed dramatically: "In the beginning it was difficult to sell certain comedians on the idea of doing their full act on television. There are some who have an act they've been doing for twenty years—they've got fifty-two minutes and they were afraid if we put it on tape it would give away their act, and that's how they made their living. But people learned, in time, that audiences *would* go see the same act that they'd seen on TV—it was like hearing a hit song. Finally, they realized how valuable the exposure was. Buddy Hackett will tell you today he's bigger in nightclubs as a result of his HBO shows."

The numbers have also changed since the beginning, says comedy agent/producer Rick Messina: "Today, someone who does an HBO Young Comedians Special has five times the value of a Letterman plug because HBO's viewing market is so much greater. Also, people in Augusta, Georgia, don't stay up late at night to watch Letterman, but they watch HBO. Most cities only have three channels to choose from, and HBO is everywhere, so these small towns and communities eat it up. As a result, a kid with one HBO spot is more promotable than someone who's done five Lettermans. It's more powerful exposure."

Because of the content of comedy and the freedom of cable, a natural marriage exists between the two where nothing like it existed before.

The A.D. period of television commenced in 1982, with the birth of "Latenight with David Letterman." This event reversed the trend that had peaked on May 1, 1972, the day that "The Tonight Show" joined in the great talk show migration from New York to California. When Johnny Carson moved to Los Angeles, he took stand-up comedy with him. From 1963–72, the New York Improv was the only showcase comedy club in the country. The type of comedy that emanated from within was reflective of its New York surroundings: it was ethnic, urban and delivered in first-person (as in David Brenner, Rodney Danger-field, Robert Klein, Freddie Prinze). California comedians were thought of as "fluff," if they were thought of at all, and the attitude toward them was, "What the hell are you doing out *there?*" With the move of "The Tonight Show," came the attitude, "What the hell am I still doing *here?*" By the mid 70s, it wasn't just from the East Coast that trends and trend-setters were originating. The West Coast stream-of-consciousness/observational style, once considered fluff, was now being examined a little more closely; Steve Martin and Robin Williams being two of the most notable examples.

By the late 70s, with the exception of "Saturday Night Live," which was broadcast from the New York studios of the "Golden Age" in Rockefeller Plaza and maintained a strong urban, ethnic flavor, every television outlet for the stand-up comic, whether it was talk shows, variety shows or sit-coms, was in Los Angeles. As a result, network television comedy, still the only medium available to most Americans, took on a decidedly "California" flavor.

In 1982 David Letterman brought a talk show, and a very unique brand of humor to New York. Stu Smiley, who was at that time David's manager at Rollins Joffe Morra and Brezner, remembers that the concept for Letterman's show was always a bit skewed: "All those other talk show sets look so contrived, with the flower pots and everything . . . we figured if David had a flower pot, the flowers inside would have to be dead." And so they were. The success of the show was gradual at first, but by 1983 Letterman had become a cult figure among college students and not long after, he captured the elusive upwardly mobile baby-boom audience that changed him from a cult figure to a "phenomenon."

As a former stand-up comic, Letterman was particularly aware of and receptive to the large pool of comic talent that, for reasons of location or "uniqueness," was largely ignored by network television. Because of this, a comedian like Jay Leno, who appealed more to the younger, too-hip-for-Carson audience, received the national exposure that transformed him from a "club comic" to a "name comic" who, instead of opening for other acts, became a strong enough draw to headline in concert halls.

And so, through cable and Letterman, stand-up was presented to its rightful audience: boom and post-boom babies who, growing up under the threat of nuclear winter and a host of other not-so-promising options for the future, tended to be more cynical than their elders. The greatest attraction of stand-up for the baby-boom generation might be its underlying tone of nonconformity. One element of this is the content of a comic's act; another is his life. In order to make humor, it's necessary to point out "what's wrong with this picture" and that, to a great extent, is what stand-up is all about. As former radicals and flower children, today's baby-boom generation shares with the comedian that impulse of shaking up the status quo and seeing where the pieces fall. But while the baby boomers have, for the most part, decided to trade that portion of their lives in for briefcases and Cuisinarts, the stand-up represents, through his words and lifestyle, one who has not opted for stability. George Carlin feels that the form and content of today's comedy is reflective of its audience's cynical attitude toward life—their feeling of having already confronted the burning issues and finding themselves unable to solve them: "In the sixties, you could do a lot of stuff about race, for instance, because it wasn't resolved yet, but as issues tend to be resolved and lose their glamour and sexiness, they're less likely to be talked about. I think, also, there's less humor of a political or social commentary nature because that type of humor thrives when there's a feeling in the land that that kind of humor means something—that you can maybe affect someone's opinion and down the line things will change. I think people feel now, 'Play the game, make some money, get a nice house, try to keep the kids out of jail and fucking retire.' And people feel that way, including the creators of humor, so there's less of a reason to say something with an idealistic message underneath it." Perhaps, for many of these people, the decision against taking the road less traveled is somehow made less difficult by occasionally watching the travels of those who opted to take it.

Just as the baby boomers have responded to the veiled and unveiled cynicism of stand-up comedy, so have their post-boom brethren been drawn to its anti-social subtext. But, for the latter group, comedy is not simply an anachronistic anthem for an abandoned era, it is a realm of possibility within which a new era can be imagined. Barry Sand, executive producer of "Latenight with David Letterman," feels that stand-up is an appealing break from the despair that usually characterizes post-boomers' contemplation of their future. Their general attitude, he explains, "is probably one of desperation and cynicism—an idea that all the things their parents had, they're not going to get, so they have to joke about the future because they're not as sure of it as my generation was." He feels, also, that part of the comedy clubs' attraction might be a certain type of camaraderie that exists among the audience members and the comics, and the fact they are actually "hearing a guy expressing what's on his mind." He says that college kids' attraction to comedy clubs is based on the same principle as their love for "Latenight": "It's a form of gallows humor, which they respond to. It's like we're on death row and there's something funny about it—sad but funny."

Comic Joe Bolster, who started noticing the tremendous growth in the industry around 1980, also attributes it to a shift in social patterns. But instead of politics, he believes that finance is the key factor: "A huge proportion of the population now is between twenty-five and forty—not at the peak of their earning power, but at the point where they can spend twenty-five dollars for an evening for two people to see original entertainment (not a loud rock band) in nice clubs, similar people around them, inexpensive, people they've heard of. It's not a long night—maybe two hours not including dinner. There is a huge demand for that kind of entertainment." As this group ages, they will continue to appreciate stand-up, but its character will change: "You'll see a proliferation in even more upscale style clubs, maybe forty dollars an evening. At a club like the Comic Strip, when these people are forty-five to fifty, you'll see more of a supper club type place." A notable example of stand-up's increasing upscale appeal is Caroline's Comedy Club in New York. A former cabaret that was turned into a comedy club in 1983 (and opened in an expanded version at Manhattan's South Street Seaport in 1987), Caroline's presents the best of today's comedians in an elegant setting—and the house is rarely less than packed.

That many people (particularly young people) demand entertainment with a message is hardly new; sales figures for early Joan Baez albums are adequate confirmation of that! But while their desire for a message remains constant, audiences' preference for a medium through which they will receive it may vary. Richard Fields, who in 1980 became partners with Rick Newman in Catch A Rising Star, bought him out completely in 1985 and believes "there's a direct relationship between the rise of comedy as an artform and business, and the decline of rock and roll. Rock, today, is burning out the people: the fans, the performers, even the companies; comedy is not. Comedy is also highly accessible—and that's in direct contrast to the growing inaccessibility of rock and roll. Here's an example: we did a 'Catch on Tour,' at the colleges, and with each show, we'd also do a contest to find the funniest student, which was made into an HBO special, and it was pandemonium every time. I realized then there was a real accessibility thing going on. You could really touch the performers; you could even be them. At one school there was a girl whose friends were egging her on, and when she got up, you couldn't believe she'd never been on. It's like in the early sixties, with kids and their guitars hanging around the village, and Bob Dylan and all.

"What happened is that rock and roll became the way to sell Pepsi and blue jeans—it became a multi-million dollar business, and people got fed up; they were looking for something else. As a result of this, a new, unaffected form of entertainment came up—a thing called comedy. The comic comes in with a little manilla envelope, no heavy equipment, and he goes everywhere, including Raleigh and Buffalo. . . . He hangs out at the bar. He's insightful, like the early musicians—not the ones today who say, 'Darling I love you, I want to fuck your brains out, now pay me!' People see the American dream is bizarre, and comedy goes along with that. Also it is accessible, unlike most of the world. Rock goes in with six semi-trailers, the break point is one hundred thousand dollars just to put the act on, the act is surrounded by bodyguards so people don't kill them, the act hates the record company, and all the company wants to know is, 'Excuse me, when's the next fucking single coming out because I have cash flow projections.' Then you have a little comic coming out saying, 'Hey, you know what? I bought a cordless phone . . . and I can't find it!' It's real, it's touchable—it's not automated or push-button. Comedy is the rock and roll of the future, and that's why."

He adds that this accessibility and cynicism of stand-up make it the perfect entertainment for the 80s: "For instance, look at Steve Wright. He's live. What you see is what he is: no bullshit . . . and what's coming out of his mouth are some of the most important things of the decade. I think he's a national fucking treasure. He's perfect for this generation. In Woodstock all you were worried about was getting laid, stoned, and staying out of the mud, but now it's different—we're a little older, and Steve Wright appeals to us. We've been living this bullshit life the past ten to fifteen years . . . I'm paying more now to park my car in a god-damn garage, where I beg them not to steal it, than I paid for my first apartment in New York. I'm from the Woodstock generation, and when Steve Wright comes along and makes a statement like, 'It's a small world, but I wouldn't want to paint it,' I think, 'Thank you, very much. I wouldn't want to have to paint it either, babe, but I do every day of the week.' Today, that's where it's at."

But isn't it possible that, given time, comedy will grow into the bloated form of rock and roll? Fields says that this need not happen if business people learn from the mistakes of the music industry and remember, "No one has to be a goddamn pig." He believes that the comedy business is improving itself as it matures: "The industry is changing; it used to be a bunch of entrepreneurs saying, 'I am, there-fore I exist, therefore you play my club—and if you don't like it, get the fuck out.' But now it's more of an industry. It's having its turf fights and growing pains, but in the end you'll have a solid industry made up of club owners, TV and record people, video and movie people. . . ."

All of these people have a responsibility to check the growth of the comedy industry so they do not repeat the mistakes of rock and roll: "Our growth has to be small. We have a fiduciary responsibility not to burn out the talent we're managing by putting them constantly on the road, forcing them to make their gross higher and higher. We have to create TV shows that don't use them up just so we get a producer's fee. When we build clubs around the country, or take over existing ones as we plan to do, we have the responsibility to bring real talent, not just some jerk playing with his sexual organs and saying, 'Hey baby...'"

But, as in other areas, growth in stand-up very often comes at the expense of quality control. That's "very often," but not "always"... thank God. So while you don't have to look too far today to see "some jerk playing with his sexual organs" onstage, you also have a thousand more opportunities to see an innovative, thought-provoking stand-up than anyone would have dreamed possible just a few years ago.

WHY DON'T WE DO IT ON THE ROAD!

The road is not a new institution in the entertainment industry. It's a slice of the old life—a sneak postview of the way things were in the virginal years before television and movies, when performers came to us in 3-D...without the glasses. "The road" is the term used by today's stand-up comics to describe any paying gig outside of the showcase clubs in New York City or Los Angeles. The road is a traveling purgatory, and a permanent home to most comedians who lie between "dead broke" and "superstar." For the most part, stand-up comics and business people make no artistic bones about it: the road has one purpose as far as they're concerned—to make a buck and get the hell out.

At its worst, the business of the road resembles a shark tank at feeding time; at its best, it's not much better. Its tender age is partly to blame; until about 1978, the road, as we know it today, didn't exist. In that year a comic named Ron Richards began booking comedians from Manhattan's showcase clubs into several Ground Round restaurants in New Jersey. Six months later, he helped out an ex-comedian friend, Jerry Stanley, to set up similar shows in other New Jersey restaurants.

By 1979 Ron Richards was out of the business, and Jerry Stanley was getting very rich very fast. Within one year, he was booking twelve rooms in the north Jersey area, using a group of twenty-five comedians, who were rotated in groups of three. By 1980, the number of comics he was using had grown to eighty. At this time, there were fewer than ten paying comedy clubs spread out across the country, including Garvin's in Washington, D.C., the Comedy Castle in Detroit, the Cleveland Comedy Club, The Laff Stop in Newport Beach, California, the San Francisco Holy City Zoo, Zanies in Chicago, and the Boston Comedy Connection. Most of these clubs, which had been open for only one to two years, paid just enough money to attract and nurture local comic talent. It was not difficult, then, for Jerry Stanley, who could offer comedians $55 a set plus food and travel, to corner the comedy market that was about to get bullish. By 1981 Stanley's comic talent agency, "Showcase Talent Productions," had become the largest comedy agency in the country, with 250 comedians under contract.

Rick Messina also arrived on the comic booking scene very early. Though a minor figure at the time, compared to Stanley, his involvement in the comedy industry was more a case of luck than business acumen: "I got started being in the nightclub business and comedy got hot; before that I used to tend bar in nightclubs and play comedy albums . . . I was the biggest Richard Pryor fan in the world. When this boom took place I just got swept up in it. I felt, at the time, it was a little faddy—I didn't realize there was that much guts to it until later on. In 1978 I knew a couple of guys who were claiming to be stand-up comics—Eddie Murphy, Bobby Nelson, Rob Bartlett . . . but, at that time, there were no places to work on Long Island. We tried it one night a week in a club and it worked so well, I just kept expanding. In 1979 I opened the Eastside Comedy Club and, after that, the comedy boom kicked in—Governor's, Chuckles and other clubs started opening all over the Island."

In the late 70s, word about the phenomenon in New York, New Jersey and Long Island was just beginning to spread among club and bar owners throughout the country. Ears still ringing with the death knell of the disco era, they were desperate for a new angle. In Washington, D.C., in 1977, Harry Monocrusos began casting about for a new concept to attract patrons to his restaurant, Garvin's. He remembers, "I went to New York, looked around and saw they actually had [showcase] clubs that were doing comedy as an entertainment form—which I'd never seen before. I thought okay, these people may be amateurs here, but they're good enough to bring to Washington as professionals. So we picked the best people, like Belzer, and brought them in. Back then, we gave them meals, a room in a nice hotel, and paid something like four hundred dollars a weekend, five shows, for a headliner . . . now it's tripled, of course."

In 1982, two of the largest comedy-club franchises were born—the Funny Bone and the Punch Line. The Pittsburgh Funny Bone was opened by two former stand-up comics, Jerry Kubach and Jeff Schneider, because, says Kubach, "Jeff noticed comedy was getting hot—and I always liked a free beer and comedy—so we said, 'Let's do a comedy/beer place!'" Today, Schneider owns two Funny Bones and Kubach, with his new partner, Mitch Kutash, owns ten others. Another early pioneer was the Punch Line's Chris Dipetta, a former Athens, Georgia, nightclub owner who, after selling his country and western bar, was looking for a new "concept." In 1981, while working as a food and beverage consultant for a local hotel, he decided to try booking local comics into the hotel's lounge on Wednesday nights to help the sagging bar business. "It was pretty much amateurs," he says, "but from the first night, it was packed." Immediately, he and his former club partners began scouting locations in Atlanta, Georgia, and by February of 1982, the first Punch Line was opened.

In the beginning, Dipetta and his partners, Ron DiNunzio and Dave Montesanto, were booking their comedians through Jerry Stanley who, at that time, Dipetta says, "was booking just about all the comedy rooms in the country." And Stanley was earning no small income from it, charging the clubs fifteen percent each for his "booking" fee and the comics ten percent for his "agent" fee. He had also set up a travel agency, through which he and a partner arranged all of the flights to and from clubs, which netted them a ten percent commission per comic. By 1982, Stanley says, "I was getting at least a hundred fifty calls a day from comics, and I was booking sixty acts a week—plus all their travel. At that point," he adds, "I was basically the only one in the country doing this kind of booking."

As more and more clubs began opening around the country, it became increasingly difficult for Stanley to maintain his monopoly. In

1982 Joe Palmisano of Tickles, John Cochran of Giggles and Jerry Stanley formed an organization called "The Association of Comedy Clubs, Owners and Performers." The stated purpose of this group was to insure a high level of quality in all member clubs by preventing plagiarism and other unethical stand-up practices. According to Chris Dipetta, however, "Jerry couldn't justify what he was doing in any other way—so he formed the organization to legitimize it." The organization's rules were, in essence, that if you didn't want to join, you couldn't use Stanley's (the organization's) supply of comedians (which was basically every decent comic in the country)—and if you did join, Stanley got the booking commissions (from both clubs and comics) and the travel commissions.

What happened, however, was that Jerry Stanley's power play failed. Existing clubs and the many new clubs springing up began directly approaching the growing number of new, unattached comics, who were delighted to take any bookings. Because these clubs didn't have to pay a booking fee, they could afford to pay the comics more money, so new comics stopped approaching Stanley and went directly to the clubs.

Dipetta says that some of Stanley's unsavory booking practices also became known, such as "bait and switching": "He'd promise one act, say Garry Shandling's coming, and he'd say he's coming, he's coming, then a week before he's supposed to come, all of a sudden, 'Oh . . . he got a TV pilot, he can't make it—but I have this other guy, so he was able to drop in somebody else who we wouldn't normally take but on short notice we'd have to . . . because he was the only guy booking.'" Dipetta finally caught on to this practice: "I started talking to the acts and saying I heard you got booked somewhere else and they'd say no I'm not." Comic Robert Wuhl, who worked for Stanley a couple of times during this period, remembers being surprised when he found out about that: "He would book me into a club, when I didn't know about it, then cancel me and book in one of his own acts."

Because of practices like this, and the fact that both the industry and the supply of comics were rapidly expanding, it soon became clear that a small group of colluding owners was not the most efficient means of distributing the comic "product" to the club "outlets," and the association folded. The fall of this monopoly made the comedy market competitive, with clubs and bookers bidding against one another for talent; this raised comics' fees, which led to an increase in the amount of comics. What happened then shocked everyone: audiences kept packing the houses week after week, joyously paying cover charges and buying numerous drinks. So, in spite of the higher wages being paid to the comics, the owners continued to make more money. This encouraged them to open more clubs, which brought about "the road" phenomenon we see today, where a comedian can travel around the country, from one club to the next, remaining in relative anonymity, and earn roughly between $30,000 and $100,000 a year.

Chris Dipetta, Ron DiNunzio and Dave Montesanto were, as partners in The Punch Line, the controlling force in comedy in the Southeast. Like their counterparts across the country (the Funny Bone and Zanies in the Midwest, the Laff Stop and Improv in the West . . .), they had licensing or consulting agreements with the majority of clubs in their area of the country (through a company called P.L.T.L.)—in their case, ten clubs. The partners also owned a booking agency called Snikkers, through which they booked about fifty comics a week, at ten percent commission per gig, to concerts, conventions and clubs across the country. (Dipetta subsequently was locked out of the Punch Line offices by his partners, in January of '87, over a dispute about his percentage of stock in the company. After beginning litigation, he immediately began working with Catch A Rising Star's Richard Fields and is currently looking into opening a Catch in Atlanta.)

Like the Punch Line operators, Rick Messina is a dominant booking force in the road circuit. He explains that his rise and staying power are not necessarily the result of being better than anyone else: "[I] basically stayed professional and kept my business clean and so all the other people who are doing what I did in the business were phased out— owners and agents. They were just sleazy characters and I seemed to be the survivor. I think it is because I never tried to get rich off of anybody in the beginning, which is a mistake a lot of people make who do what I do. They produce a couple of shows in a couple of areas and try to make a lot of money in those areas, but most markets are very fragile."

Instead of referring to himself as a booker or manager, he considers

himself to be a comedy producer, and explains the difference: "A producer goes into a market and says this is the market, this is the age of
the audience, and then they take a facility or build one, and they say,
this is the room, this is where we put the stage, the curtains, the
lighting, this is how we run the show, this is the show time, here's what
the emcee and opening acts, middles and headliners do—and the
whole production is outlined down to advertising and promotion.
That's where it goes beyond being an agent. If I were an agent, I
wouldn't be involved in any of that, but I think part of my success is
that I know how to produce and set rooms up, teach people the operations end of it. That's very important because it's theater. A lot of club
owners all around the country think that it's like booking mud wres-
tling or a deejay, and it's not—it's legitimate theater. Many of them
have no theatrical background. They don't know lighting or stage or
anything about creating a theatrical atmosphere—those are either the
short-lived clubs or the embarrassment clubs, where the audiences are
hungry and they keep coming back. But if they run it like mud wres-
tling, it's bad for the industry. So, because these other people were like
that, I became the guy who controlled most of the work in the New
York area."

No standard booking practices exist in the industry, though top
bookers refer to a number of common methods. One of these is called
"taking from both ends," which refers to the agent taking money from
the clubs, as a booking fee, and from the comics, as an agent's fee
(and, in some cases, a percentage of the "door," as well). If the club
owner is also the agent, he'll often receive both of the above fees, plus
all receipts from the door and drink sales. Other agents charge the
comic nothing and make their money by only taking a percentage of
the door, which allows them to lower the comic's base asking price,
and make them more attractive to owners (this is often employed in
cases where one booker "steals" a club from another). The methods
vary, obviously, with an agent's level of control in any given market.
With regard to such seemingly greedy practices as "taking from both
ends," a case needs to be made in favor of club owners. Because the
comedy club business is a new, relatively unproven industry, owners
most likely feel that they should be compensated as much as possible

in the short run, as they face great uncertainty about the long run. As the industry grows and its stability becomes apparent, more clubs will open, forcing agents to adopt more competitive methods of booking.

Richard Fields, owner of New York's Catch A Rising Star, indicates this competition to come in stating his future plans for opening clubs around the country: "There are ones now that are exploitative to the performers; they're not serving the community because good acts won't play there anymore. We're talking to the owners, saying, 'Do you want to do this the nice way, or the not nice way?' The nice way is: 'You've had a nice run, made a lot of money—I'm buying your club now and I'm going to do it the right way.' The not nice way is: 'I'm going to open up across the fucking street from you and I'm going to put you out of business: when the community sees what real comedy is... you're not going to be here anymore.'" (Catch A Rising Star subsequently went public in February of '87 and immediately opened, in Boston, the first of what sources close to Fields say will be twenty-five clubs across the country.)

Among comedy clubs' current booking practices, one of those most often criticized by comics is the unspoken rule against working for the competition. It is, for the record, denied by owners, confirmed by, however, comics, and, off the record, understood by all. Chris Dipetta denies that this practice exists, "because first of all we don't have competition—we're not in the same towns at all. We'll pay the money and no one else does—the Funny Bone doesn't go all out as far as paying the acts. It's different stages, different types of philosophies of clubs." But Tommy Blaze says that this practice, called "cock blocking" or "comedy wars," does exist and is one of the road's more insidious aspects: "If there are two comedy clubs within about a hundred mile radius, you work in one and you're shit in the other. Chris Dipetta books the Comedy Corner in Milwaukee and the Funny Bone is also there—there are about the same number of Funny Bones and Punch Lines and you've got to choose between them."

The "loyalty oath" school of booking is practiced almost without exception by comedy clubs throughout the country. Abby Stein is a founder and former president of the Professional Comedians Association, a group of roughly 400 stand-up comics who have organized themselves in order to better their living, working and earning situations both on the road and in the showcase clubs. Stein, like many comics, feels that in the competitive state of the comedy industry today there is no excuse for this kind of restrictive practice to continue: "At one time, Jerry Stanley was comedy; that was it. But today there is no more monopoly—some owners do their own bookings, other clubs use small agents or ones who control their particular areas of the country —so you'd think there would be more freedom. But there isn't. In cities with more than one comedy club, each one often wants the exclusive rights to a comic; we're trying to spot that kind of situation and stop it." She concedes that certain exclusivity restrictions are necessary for a club's integrity, such as, "If you work here, don't work across the street tomorrow—or if they say there should be ninety to one hundred twenty days between performances in the same town— but this business of 'Either you work for me or that's it' is ridiculous." Stein says that it not only hurts the comics, who lose money, time (commuting to distant places outside a given booker's sphere of influence) and basic freedom, but it restricts the growth of smaller, independent clubs who are denied access to available comedians.

"Why should anyone tell me where I can work?" is the bottom line, according to Abby, who vocalizes the sentiments of all road comics who, in choosing to work, must choose also to keep their opinions about these practices to themselves. The PCA, which is criticized by nonmember comics as being a powerless organization because of its lack of clout with comedy clubs and inability to attract "established" comics, is nevertheless the closest thing to a union that a stand-up comic can find. While the more established comics have unions governing their screen and television work (SAG and AFTRA), they are free agents on the road. Of course, like the 500-pound gorilla who sits anywhere he wants to, the restrictions placed on comics run in inverse proportion to their popularity; if Eddie Murphy wants to play in the club across the street, chances are he'll do it. But for lesser comics, whose bargaining power is cancelled out by countless others who would gladly take his or her place on the bill, the rules of the road are written by management, not labor.

Abby, in trying to set an example for other comics to follow, decided to draw the line. "I'll sign an exclusive contract if they want to pay me five times as much as the other guy, or book me twelve times a year," she says, "but if they want me on their terms plus I can't work anywhere else, I won't do it, and I'd like to educate other comics not to do it. Forget strikes and power. If enough comics said, 'I'll agree to work only here if you pay me more,' then they'd have to do it. Otherwise they wouldn't get anybody."

Jerry Diner, Abby's successor as president of the Professional Comedians Association, feels that one of the greatest obstacles to a good working relationship for comics with owners and agents is the absence of contracts in club bookings: "The comedian has no say in the matter —the club owner is always right. If the comic agreed to do a gig for nine hundred dollars, and the owner says it was seven hundred dollars, the comic doesn't argue, or they won't get hired again." He has since introduced contracts that are called "booking agreements"—"So no one will be scared by the word, 'contract.' If you have something in writing, those people are going to uphold it, as opposed to something that's said on the phone. Before this, people almost never used written agreements—and very few people use them now, which is why there are so many problems."

Tommy Blaze says that he is shocked at how loosely the business is run: "You're paid under the table; you can get cancelled the day before . . . there are comics who show up at a club and the club is boarded up, out of business." Even if a comic tries to impose some order, if the gesture is not reciprocated the effort is useless—particularly because there are no hard and fast rules governing club owners' behavior. Blaze continues: "One time I was booked in Lubbock, Texas, on a Wednesday–Sunday gig. I sent a letter to them confirming this along with a signed contract . . . and I never got it back. Still, I figured if there was anything wrong, they'd call me. I showed up Wednesday and the club was closed . . . I literally got out of the cab, knocked on the door and it was closed. I couldn't get anyone on the phone. I had to find a hotel, pay for it, wait for the club to open—and basically hold my dick for two days in Lubbock, Texas. On Friday, I went to the club and it was open. I walked inside, and right away saw my letter laying on the floor next to the owner's desk—it had never been opened. I never got reimbursed because he said, 'You should've gotten the booking straight.'"

Jerry Diner adds that clubs would also benefit from written agreements because "there have been times when the comics have messed up and we've looked into that and, when there was a signed agreement, we were able to work it out." Association member bookers have also appealed to the PCA when their control of a club was "stolen" by another booker, but Diner says that unless a comic is directly related to a case, they do not have the time or resources to get involved.

Jerry Stanley says that a problem with many club managers is not only the amount of payments ("a lot of these people will give you twelve hundred dollars maximum, no matter who you are") but with the means of payment: "A lot of these clubs get busted for being coke dealers, or for tax evasion. The first thing they do when a comic comes into town is lay a hundred dollar line on the table. A lot of comics say to me, 'I wish they'd just give me the hundred bucks; I don't need the coke.' But they want to suck you in to the whole deal—they want you to party with them. Often, club owners are the personality of the town —it's like the club is their ego."

Blaze feels that, while some club owners are decent, most treat comics like product: "We're liquor, something to be maintained, to be sure it's there on time and does the job. If we get broken, they just find another one." This feeling is echoed by Jay Leno, who in turn quotes another (former) stand-up comic: "It's like Letterman said, 'Most of these clubs are run by people who ran the go-cart tracks and the trampoline centers.' I love that line. Most of them either did that or had some stable of strippers before local ordinances closed them down—so they put up comedy clubs." He adds, "I don't mean to classify them all that way; there are a lot of nice owners, and the nice guys stay in business a long time because you get people like myself or Robin Williams—people who have become reasonably successful who will go back and work for free or for a little money—to help people who helped when we got started. I remember there was a club here in California that screwed over a lot of comics and a lot of us decided we just wouldn't work there any longer. They're still in business, but not like they used to be."

Many comics choose to sign exclusive contracts with booking agents that guarantee them work in all of the clubs that the booker controls. Comedian George Calfa talks about Rick Messina's recent growth: "Another guy used to book Chuckles in Mineola, Long Island, but they got rid of him and gave it to Rick, then the owner of the Westport club, who used to book it himself—gave it to Rick because he's got all the comics. A comic could work exclusively for Rick and do fine. Not only does he book a lot of clubs, but when a club gets cancelled, they call him for a replacement. He has Dangerfield's, Comedy Tonight . . . he just took over Chuckles and Hysterics in Long Island. . . . " In the case of powerful booking agents, like Messina or Chris Dipetta's Snikkers Agency, clubs must employ the bookers if they want access to their "exclusive" comics. And so it grows.

To judge the road in artistic terms would be to miss the whole point; the "art colony" motives (whether real or imagined) of showcase club owners do not exist on the road. As Chris Dipetta says, "I probably work in the bottom rung of the entertainment business, but I know it first of all and I don't try to fool myself into thinking anything else. I also know everyone wants to come out and work on new material, so I'll see them eventually. Depending on how much money a person wants to make, they have to talk to me." And money, on the road, is the name of the game. One comic, who wanted to remain nameless, said, "People like Leno and Wright can make ten thousand dollars a show now—that's not shocking. What's shocking is that I'm a virtually unknown comic and I make about one hundred twenty-five thousand dollars a year."

Joe Bolster explains the various possible work options of the road circuit. "Most clubs range in their bookings from three nights [Thursday–Saturday] to six nights [Tuesday–Sunday], but most are four nights. Pay depends on how much TV you have, and how many shows you're doing, but for a headliner, it's about eleven hundred dollars and up. I make twenty-five hundred dollars a week and that's probably the high end of it for somebody who's not completely a draw. I'm a bargain to club owners. It's always a good show and so that's good word of mouth, but yet they're not going to pay what someone like Guido Sarducci would get, who has a name but may not do quite as fine a show—that may be fifteen to seventeen thousand dollars a week." He gives an example of the money to be made by owners: "The average club seats two hundred fifty people, and you're hired to do eight shows in a week—one Wednesday, two Thursday, two Friday, and three Saturday at eight, ten, twelve... bang-bang-bang. That's when you feel like you're just churning them out. They usually have three sold-out crowds and they're getting cover charge from everybody and a couple drinks. They'd have four shows if they could figure out a way to do it. That's when you realize it's the bottom line, not the punch line. Let's say they had ten shows a week, to make it even. They have two hundred fifty capacity, and they sold out all the shows. That's twenty-five hundred coming in, times ten dollars cover—that's twenty-five thousand dollars at the door. Now double that for drinks and it's fifty grand. So if they gave comics the door, which is traditionally what's been done in show business, we'd be millionaires! But they don't do that. When I played Crackers in Indianapolis, I did eight shows; five of them had in excess of one hundred fifty people. They charged six dollars at the door—right there I'm a bargain. The money I make is very good, but relative to what they're making, I still feel sometimes like I want more."

Messina, on the other hand, feels that comics are probably overpaid on the road, and that ultimately they suffer for it by losing their artistic edge: "The standard gig is anywhere from three to six nights, and the money ranges from one hundred fifty dollars a week to one thousand dollars a week to five thousand dollars a week. It depends on the TV exposure of the comic, whether the comic draws and if he can command a higher ticket price. Ten years ago when David Brenner and people like that were starting out, they couldn't make a living. If they made thirty dollars it was a good night—there was no circuit. That's hurt the business. They used to be hungry, they wanted it so much they could feel it. Now that they can earn a comfortable living doing a half-assed job, they've lost some appetite."

Without improving on his act or getting television exposure, a comic working on the road can be permanently trapped in the level at which he entered the business. Alan Havey says that, in the beginning of his career, he worked as a middle act on the road but abruptly stopped working the circuit when he figured it out: "I wouldn't get brought back as a headliner if I kept middling on the road, and my act probably wouldn't get any better either. So I just stayed here in New York, got a better reputation, got some TV exposure, and worked on my act until I started headlining, which I did before I had any major TV, except 'Merv.' Then, if you do a quality show [Letterman or Carson] and you do well, you can up your price even more. [He subsequently did Letterman.] Then you do the road . . ."

As the money and security increase on the circuit, so does the influx of new comics—each bringing, if not a revolutionary new act, at the very least a new name and face. These new faces are constant reminders to those road comics who, with the short-term security of some pre-booked gigs and comfortable salaries, have lapsed into artistic complacency. They remind them to either motivate themselves to create new material or risk comic burnout. This, Paul Provenza says, is among the greatest threats of the road: "It's easy to burn out fast; that's an occupational hazard, you know that going into it. The kind of comedy that's popular now is a young man's game. It's so immediate, you've got to be so hip to what's happening."

Club owners get very involved in "quality control" when they sense a comic reaching the burnout point, which they judge by the same standards used for the hiring of comics: do they make the audience laugh? Many comics can also fail in owners' eyes because they are too sophisticated for road club audiences. Herein lies the primary reason for comics working-but-hating-it or refusing to work the road. George Calfa, who feels that he's been forced to downplay the degree of real creativity in his act in order to pander to road crowds and bookers, gives an example of a recent run-in: "I just played a club in Milwaukee. Wednesday and Thursday night the audience was good and the owner wasn't there. Friday night he showed up. It was a terrible crowd and everyone, including me, had a bad set. Afterwards, he came up to me and said, 'You better "kill" the next show; that was a real weak set.' I got mad and said, 'Man, this is what I do—you hired me, that's it.' Of course the second crowd was even worse than the first and I'll never work there again. I try not to care, but that whole next day my stomach was in knots. But what can I do? It's not like I go on and try not to do well. It's not like boxing. No one said, 'Hey, George, go on and throw this set.' Even if I hate the club owner, if he's a scum bag, it's still me onstage, and I have to get laughs . . ."

Adrianne Tolsch says that, like any art form, as stand-up has grown, so have the number of derivative practitioners. She cites as the main offenders local comics who frequently emcee, or open, the shows, while the road comics middle and headline. "The only exposure they have is TV or the comics who pass through their towns—so they lift material here and there, and it's really infuriating, but there's nothing you can do about it." Because there is little economic incentive for owners to stop this (why complain when the club is full?), more experienced comics must often tailor their acts to get enough "road laughs" to compete with the "dick joke" comics. Calfa says that club patrons prefer more raucous comedy because they go to clubs more to blow off steam than to appreciate an art form: "It's like stand-up has replaced dancing—if you go to these rooms in Jersey, you see it's the same people that used to go to discos."

In general, club owners and bookers do not deny that this problem exists but, like executives in other entertainment fields, they argue that they don't create public taste, they satisfy it. And they feel that, with regard to comics, it is they who must protect themselves against the downward pull of their less ambitious peers, career stagnation and personal burn-out. Rick Messina feels that the road is a negative, highly seductive experience that blinds many young comics to their own mediocrity. "You take a kid who's making forty thousand dollars a year on the road—he's made it as far as he's concerned. Because he gets so consumed by the fact that he's making a living, he hasn't comprehended the fact that he's nobody. He's unknown and his craft is probably derivative. The road is there to make a dollar, and smart comics use it on their terms."

Jay Leno, considered by many comics to be "the ultimate road warrior," is one of the few comedians who works the circuit because he enjoys it, and who has been able to become a star, while continuing to work the road, despite its countless traps and temptations. Why does he continue to do it? Because like his less humorous counterpart, Mohammed, to whom the mountain would not go, he must go to the mountain: "With the exception of maybe New York, Los Angeles or

San Francisco, when I perform on the road, people always say, 'What are you doing here?' As if I shouldn't be there. . . as if I should be in Monte Carlo at Prince Rainier's house. I am where the audience is—and that happens to be on the road!"

ROAD MONKEYS

In 1980 there were about ten paying comedy clubs in existence; by 1985 there were roughly two hundred fifty. In the space of half a decade, an environment for a new American subculture was created and well stocked with lots of money that lay waiting for the harvest. For those comics in the right place at the right time, comedy proved to be more than funny; it became funny business.

One of these people was Marc Weiner. In 1973 he dropped out of college because of his Sociology professor: "He convinced us to hate the establishment by saying we were just leeches living off our parents —and in order not to be sucked in, we had to get out of the system. So I figured, 'Why be hypocritical?' and I quit school." He then worked as a cook on the Clearwater Sloop (an environmental boat that traveled up and down the Hudson promoting ecology) for several years, eventually getting his Captain's license in 1975. Shortly after that, he left the boat and began performing on the streets of Boston as a clown, after which he studied mime and finally, in 1977, ended up in New York working at the showcase clubs.

His first big break came a year later: "I was juggling a rubber hand and a toilet plunger. I figured if I went 'Na-noo-na-noo' with the hand, Robin Williams would hear about me, bring me on the show and make me famous. The second time I did that, I was performing outside in front of the Metropolitan Museum for about five hundred people. Five minutes afterwards, this guy came up to me and it was Robin Williams with his wife and press man. He said, 'That was great—let's improvise.' So we played on the street and he said he'd be back next week. The next week he came back and he told his managers, Rollins and Joffe, to come see me and they started helping me out."

As the most prestigious comic talent agency in the country, Rollins Joffe Morra and Brezner has nurtured the careers of many major talents in the industry, including Woody Allen, Robert Klein, Robin Williams, David Letterman, Dick Cavett, Nichols and May and Billy Crystal. With the demise of the nightclub business and the rise of their clients to movie star stature, the agency was no longer actively involved in the comedy club scene by the late 70s. Their help for Marc consisted of flying him to Los Angeles for a television pilot, getting him several small film roles and, most importantly, putting his name on the grapevine, where it was heard by a young New Jersey man named Jerry Stanley.

By 1979 Marc was working as one of the twenty-five comedians Stanley was then booking into various restaurants around northern Jersey. While these were some of the rare paying gigs around at that time, they were not necessarily the easiest; an article in the August Morristown, New Jersey, *Daily Record* of that year describes Marc's appearance at the Ground Round as successful, but "his act was heckled so intensively that he could hardly get his lines out... he gamely traded insults with the audience, but as Stanley said, 'his act was pretty much destroyed by the crowd.'" These early road jobs were indicative of what was to come. Outside of the urban, metropolitan centers (which had been the only place comedy clubs had existed prior to this), audiences behaved differently. They didn't want to see experimentation and artistic growth; they wanted jokes, and they wanted them funny.

Some comedians understood this; others did not. Of those who did, Marc Weiner understood the best. In experimenting with different comic styles and props, he found that audiences responded best to his handmade finger puppets. As he began to rely on them more and more in his act, his popularity grew. At the Improv, in 1981, he and Rocco (his star puppet) were seen by Joe Piscopo, who had just been hired as a cast member for "Saturday Night Live." With Joe's help, Marc was hired as a guest performer on the show, where he appeared several weeks in a row. It was during this period that his traveling peaked.

This coincided with the rash of comedy club openings around the country and, according to Jerry Stanley, who was supplying their talent, "Every club I opened, I opened with Marc. Everyone wanted him back—their first taste of comedy was this zany character with the bulbous eyes and cute puppets. So whenever a club owner called me for him, it cost them dearly—I'd get five hundred to a thousand dollars more than for other comics."

But suddenly Marc started seeing something beyond the road: the possibility, for him, of a meaningful life. In 1984, he began observing the sabbath, and became increasingly involved in Judaism. Why, after achieving his life's ambition, did Marc become religious? He explains: "If you're young and single, the road is a party and, when you don't have any morality, it's a lot of fun. But for me, the life was very empty. I'd worked so hard to achieve a certain level and when I finally got there, I discovered there was nothing. What's left? You get to the next level and then think about the next. Being a comedian is totally consuming—you never know when you're going to think of a joke so you're always working. My life was empty. I thought there had to be more of a purpose than that. I felt the only reason I was living was to perpetuate my puppets; it was really sick."

His shift to orthodoxy came with severe career repercussions; according to Jewish Orthodox law, he could not perform on Friday nights, because of the Sabbath. For a while, Stanley made the necessary arrangements which were, if not conventional, acceptable to all parties concerned: "I was booking him with a replacement act for Friday and we would get a percentage of the door. We'd get a guarantee of like forty-five hundred dollars against sixty percent of the door—but he ultimately found that he couldn't be as religious as he wanted to be and still get work. . . ." By 1986 Marc was all but shut out of the comedy club business. In spite of the fact that he had been instrumental in the successful openings of most clubs in the country, he was told that, unless he worked Friday nights, they weren't interested. For the two clubs (Wise Guys in Syracuse and the Cleveland Comedy Club) and, on occasion, television producers, who will work around his schedule, and the colleges that continue to book him, he is profoundly grateful, but, within the next several years, he, his wife Sandy, and their new baby, Avi Shalom Weiner, are planning to move to Jerusalem.

Marc's story is, without the religious element, the story of the "early" road comics—those who grew *with* the industry, as opposed to those who grew as a result of it. Some, like Marc, found that their goals, when viewed up close, looked very different than they did at a distance. Others, like Jay Leno, were able to look beyond the road's baser elements and, focusing on its more positive elements, make it work for them. Jay Leno, who says that he is traveling more today than he was two years ago, explains his philosophy of the road: "I go out for three or four days, stay home for two days, go out for a few weeks . . . I do about three hundred dates a year, I think. I don't care for traveling, but I like the work when I get there. It's like the most satisfying factory piecemeal work you can have; I'm going in, I'm selling a product, and when I'm through no one calls four weeks later and says, 'Those jokes you told me a month ago—I'm having trouble with them now and I want you to come back here and fix them . . .'"

It is also very well paying piecemeal work if you're in demand and willing to travel. Comic Carrie Snow, who used to supplement her nonexistent comic income by emceeing male strip shows, says of the road, "I do it for money, and I've been a real pig lately. I've been booking solid because I'm trying to save a little money. My manager said, 'We're going to take ten percent up until you start making five thousand dollars a week,' and I said, 'Hey, I'll be there.'" Aside from the money, she feels that the road can only be a positive experience to those who use it carefully. She says, "Depending on who you're talking to, it can be the most fun job in the world or a party that's got to end sooner or later; I've combined the two of them. When I was in Fairbanks, Alaska, I copied over my address book. I go to the movies, I read, I rest . . . I even kissed the club cook in Atlanta once!"

The first wave of comics made the transition from showcase clubs to nightclubs; the second wave began working after paying clubs started to open. Some of the latter group have chosen to live similarly to their predecessors, not spending a lot of time on the road, basing them-selves in either New York or Los Angeles in order to perfect their craft in the showcase clubs—earning $25–$30 a set. Others choose to work the road exclusively. After scraping together enough material to be hired on the circuit as a middle, opening act or emcee, they work their way across the country, living from gig to gig, often in an endless state of partydom, spending little, if any, time working on their act. Still others in the group bounce between the showcase clubs and the road, trying to find some way to make both art and a living.

Tim Wilson's entry into comedy is typical of many second-wave comics; it was less of a lifetime obsession than a fluke. Born in Co-lumbus, Georgia, he is a college graduate (though from a school that was "in *Playboy*'s top ten for alcohol consumption"), who held a regu-lar job ("selling glasses in an Atlanta mall") and began doing stand-up by accident. In Atlanta, during the summer of 1983, he was living in a terrible neighborhood with a lot of strip joints, but he heard that one of these places featured stand-up comedians, so he went to check it out. Once he sat down, the comedian onstage began making fun of his shirt, so he went onstage. What happened next, he says, was that "the guy who I was with started yelling for me to do my Richard Pryor imitation of 'Mudbone' and I did. The club owner saw me and thought I was real good, so he started putting me up." And that's how it all started. A few weeks later, he heard about a comedy club with an open mike night and gave it a try. Two months later, he was working the road.

After his first club booking, he quit his job at the mall figuring, "I'd been making two hundred dollars on a good week, selling glasses, so when I found out I could make three hundred dollars for going out and telling jokes for fifteen minutes a night, I thought, 'That's great!' " While performing the next week, he began lining up other jobs and, while it worked sometimes, he says, "I was living day to day for a while. I spent many nights in bus stations with fifty cents and just enough to get somewhere else."

By December he had won a Cinemax comedy competition, held in Atlanta, and his prize was to be put up in New York for three days, wined and dined, and given a shot at Catch A Rising Star. After the wining and dining, he felt like "the greatest thing since bread," but when the time came for him to go up at Catch, he says, "I died the death . . . and that was one of the best lessons I learned. It's not that the people were different, it's that a lot of my material wasn't any good; I just didn't realize it until then."

After this, he worked the road for eight straight months, six days a week, two shows on weekends and, when he started to get a little confidence back, got an apartment in Queens. Once there, he began working out at the Improv and going on the road every two weeks to make money. Since that time, he has moved from opener/emcee to middle, where he earns $700–$1,000 a week. Like most middle acts, he would like to get some TV exposure and become a headliner some day, but says that for now, "I feel lucky to be doing this. There are big Broadway stars who make a thousand dollars a week and here I am, a half-assed comedian, making almost the same thing!" (Less than one year later he made the leap to headliner status, and continues to work the road more than forty-five weeks a year.)

Another post-road comic is Tommy Blaze, who graduated from Syracuse University as a Psychology major. In college he tried stand-up at a club called Chuckles and, after his third attempt, asked the owner what he thought. He was told, "You curse too much— I counted ten thousand 'fucks.'" Tommy says, "I remember thinking, 'what did I do wrong? Richard Pryor does that!' But then he asked me how long I'd been doing this and, when I said, 'three times,' he looked at me, smiled, put his head down, and said, 'You're going to be a major star.'"

The pressures of the real world intervened in the meantime, though, and Tommy took a job with A. C. Nielsen and relocated to Florida where, for a year, he "forgot about comedy and lived like a regular nine-to-five guy"—until he heard there was a comedy club in town. He went over immediately, did his ten minutes and says, "I killed—I absolutely destroyed them." He continued going in for six months, one night a week, and then, after quitting his day job, decided to go out on the road. His first booking, two months later, was for $350 . . . but it cost him $210 to get there. After seven months on the road, he went through hell, several times, but felt like one of the "lucky ones": "It turns out people were giving me work and treating me like a human being a lot sooner than most people are. The only reason for that was that I acted confident right from the start and never told anyone I was new. The first week on the road they thought I was doing this for years."

His attitude about agents and club owners is pragmatic and frank: "They say you've got to show loyalty; I say you're loyal to yourself. It's not like the agents in these comedy clubs are going to be around for fifty years and loyalty will mean something in the long run. They're going to be out of the business in two to three years and then what have you got? This is not a game; we're doing this to make money to feed ourselves. We're not in this business to make friends. The minute Chris Dipetta doesn't have any power, he's out of here, I'm with the next guy."

He says that the best cities to work are those where you can't believe there's a comedy club—in those places, a comic will always "kill." These smaller cities, like Jacksonville, Columbia, Greenville, Charlotte, are the road comic's bread and butter, as opposed to the showcase clubs in New York and Los Angeles which, Tommy believes, are exploitive and overrated ("they do the same shit we do out on the road"). In the smaller towns, he says, "a middle act gets seven hundred dollars and a good headliner can name his price—in the thousands... in New York, a comic is lucky to make fifty dollars a night."

But the road is no paradise, according to many comics who look back on their circuit days with anything but fond memories. One of the most frequently mentioned road atrocities is the infamous "comedy condo." These two words have been known to strike almost as much fear into the hearts of stand-ups as the dreaded statement, "You're not funny—get off the stage!" Carol Leifer still travels two weeks out of every month, but now as a headliner, which means, among other things, that her accommodations will not drop below "standard." Today, she says, "I would never do a place with a comedy condo— that's one of the great advantages of getting more successful. If they say we don't give anyone hotels, I say, 'No thanks.' To me, condos are humiliating. I know what people mean when they talk about some club owners' attitudes: 'It's a great write-off for me to buy a condo, rather than have them go to a hotel,' but they're missing the point of why people go to hotels—clean sheets, sanitation...I once said to someone at a condo, 'When does the maid come?' and they said, 'What maid?' Their attitude was: 'Why should we hire someone to clean the place when it's just you guys?' I'd say fifty percent of the clubs had condos when I was working."

Abby Stein remembers staying in condos "where there were rats... there had also been two break-ins in one place where there was no security; one comic was robbed of fourteen hundred dollars, another of four hundred a few weeks later. Very often this is the situation you have to put up with. Because you're hungry, you want to work, and maybe the same guy who runs that club runs a better club too, and you want to stay on his good side." According to Jerry Diner, clubs in some cities, like Richmond—where so many comics have complained— were forced to provide hotel rooms for comics. He points out that this is an improvement not only in terms of cleanliness, but privacy as well. He remembers, before this, headlining a gig, "where the middle act was this big slovenly guy and opener was a woman—and they were supposed to share a room. I went to bat for the girl and the owner said she knew what she was getting into when she came here. I think he wanted her to stay with him, but she refused."

Comic Fran Capo says that it works both ways; the club owners try to save money by skimping, and the comics react to their demeaning conditions by abusing everything in sight, which the owners react to by cutting back even more on anything that smacks of "frills." She remembers in one condo, "the comic ripped up the mattress and threw it out the window, broke all the furniture, and ran up a phone bill of hundreds of dollars. Several months after that, they stopped letting us use the phones or have decent lodgings...I've seen comics onstage break wall fixtures, pictures—it's rare but it happens."

With the exception of the headliner, most clubs do not provide food for comics. Capo remembers one gig where the comics were told that food was included to compensate for their low fees. When they began ordering, she says, "We were told, 'You can only order from the appetizers.' We said, 'But we haven't eaten all day.' They said, 'Sorry, other comics ate too much.' We weren't allowed to sit in the dining room either—even if we paid. But unfortunately, because everyone's looking for work, no one says anything. So conditions get worse and they'll continue to as long as there's someone else who will put up with it. I think that's why sometimes comics will order the lobster when their food is paid for; because they're used to being mistreated or looked down on all the time, so they try to make up for it when they can."

Lois Bromfield points out that even though the road is big business today, middle and opening acts still have a hard time making ends meet, and "even if you're headlining you still have to fight to make money, fight to get paid and fight for proper accommodations. If you're a woman and you're a headliner and you're making money, then you have to fight so somebody doesn't try to fuck you—either way you're screwed." She has seen a lot of comics entertain themselves on the road by "snorting coke, drinking and getting laid by people they don't know," but that isn't how she prefers to spend her free time. But she is unusual; most road comics do not seem as concerned with combining fun and work as with combining one vice with another for the maximum effect.

Rick Messina compares the mentality of the road comic to that of an immature kid at summer camp. The position of dependence in which most gigs place comics only adds to that mentality: "Say you're a road comic. You get on a plane, you're picked up at the airport, taken to a hotel room, and by that, it's three or four in the afternoon. They say we'll be back at eight to pick you up for the show. You're free from four to eight: you can read, write, sightsee . . . but comics on the road get high, they pick up women, go to malls and watch TV. It's summer camp and it goes on all week. I try to encourage guys I work with to come off the road periodically—I'd go nuts. There's a certain juvenile mentality that flows through a lot of comics. Maybe that makes a lot of them very loveable and funny, but they need maturity too." As an example of how wild road comics can get, he says there's one comic whom he can't book into a certain club because the last time he was there, he shot a hole through the phone book with his gun.

According to Tommy Blaze, Messina's is an accurate picture. He says that, in addition to not doing much outside of the Dionysian realm, many road comics develop what can best be described as the attitude of a spiteful child. On the road "the TV stays on twenty-four hours a day. I don't know why; it's like a good luck thing. When I first went out, I turned the TV off before I left and the guy said, 'No, don't do that.' It's a blatant misuse or waste of electricity, the lights are always on, too. You take hot showers for an hour, just so you can stand there using hot water, you throw shit all over the place . . . it's like being a kid; you never do dishes or anything."

The absence of restriction is often devastating to those comics who lack an internal normalcy gauge. Stand-up Gary Lazer recalls a road comic whose ability to judge the distance between "funny" and "repulsive" was completely worn away after several years on the road: "He had the habit of putting half a gram of cocaine up each nostril before he did his act. One night, after doing that, he went onstage. After a couple minutes, blood started pouring out of his nose and the audience was disgusted . . . then he takes his white shirt sleeve and runs it across his face, so it's covered in blood. The audience is moaning at this point. Then he holds the sleeve up and says, 'What's wrong? Nobody parties anymore?'"

Judy Tenuta used to travel much more, but today she spends only forty weeks a year on the road: "I was turning into Annie Oakley with an accordion—I'd say, 'I'm so glad to be here in Milwaukee' and I'd be in Austin, so I'd have to go, 'I was just testing your geography, pigs!'" While acknowledging that it's virtually the only way to take her message to the people, outside of TV spots, which weren't forthcoming for many years, she does not feel that road is an ideal place to set down roots, let alone breathe easily—particularly when you're at the mercy of other road comics, which is often the case. She remembers: "I was playing Birmingham, Alabama, and they're like greeting me in white hoods, so it's good I'm not too tan, if you know what I'm saying . . . The club owner says, 'Today you're going to another club in Huntsville and another comic is going to drive you.' So the guy arrives and he's like John Hinckley from death row; the first thing he says is, 'Do you have any beer?' Then, about twenty miles into the drive, he says, 'I have a gun, could you put it in your purse in case we get stopped, because on my next arrest, I'm going to jail.' Very nonchalant. I was freaking out—it was like Judy the criminal harborer. He said I wouldn't go to jail no matter what, so I said, 'Excuse me toad, but I'm not doing it.'"

Right after that experience, she had to work a gig with a "burned-out, semi-psychotic comic." In this case, she wasn't dependent on him, which was a consolation, but apparently not much of one: "It was in Syracuse. We came on a bus together—me, him and another guy—and they put us in a hotel. The guy missed the show because he got too drunk (a regular practice with him) so I did extra time, which is fine. After my show, he waits till I'm asleep at two A.M., rings my phone and says, 'I have to talk—can I come in?' I said, 'Hey, babe, you had plenty of chances to talk onstage. Now all of a sudden, when your hormones are slam dancing, when you decide it's time for me to carry your seed, you're real talkative. Forget it toad, this isn't Iowa.' He came anyway and started banging on my door—it was real scary."

Now that she is better known, she says, "I can fly instead of drive, and guys like that usually don't cop an attitude with me anymore . . . the ones who are rude are like that to everyone, generally, and they deserve an immediate bullet. They deserved one from their mothers, actually, and they didn't get it—so they're just going through their life pleading for us to do it. Mostly I get, 'Hey, Judy, is it okay if I smoke this keg of dope in your face?' 'Yeah, it's fine, but did you ever think maybe you should write some jokes and get an act together?' Maybe I'm just being overly concerned . . ."

Paul Reiser's first road gig was in 1980, and, though he'd only begun performing full time in 1979, he was an immediate headliner because the major influx of comics hadn't yet begun. He remembers that one of the hardest parts about the road, in the beginning, was the feeling of guilt—of not working for a living. He says, "One day, I left for Florida, to work with four other comics at the Comic Strip there, to make about four hundred dollars a week—and I couldn't believe it. I couldn't imagine making that much money doing nothing but what I like to do anyway—that I'd pay you to be able to do—it's like being a baseball player. I thought, I can sit in the sun and talk to girls all day, and then go do comedy, then they pay me—Jesus! What's the catch?"

He found out later that "the catch is being comfortable . . . I remember, even on that trip, lying at the pool with a beer in my hand, thinking, 'This is so good,' then suddenly picturing my father walking by the pool saying, 'So Mr. Hardworker. . .' and I'd say, 'No, it's okay, you don't understand!' When you love what you do you feel guilty—you equate the work ethic with misery. I used to punish myself by sitting at the typewriter for three hours to come up with a joke. Now I know I don't work that way. Work becomes something else—it means being healthy, relaxing, keeping your channels open so when something hits you, you're receptive and you can do something with it."

George Calfa does not like the road at all: "I don't go out of town for less than a thousand dollars a week. It's good money, but you spend a lot too." In order to cut down on the misery, he and several comic friends try to arrange bookings together, "so no matter how bad the gig is, we can drink together and have fun. We drink Stoly on the rocks and beer, and laugh—it's great. If I get a call and it's decent money, I'll ask them if they need another act, and we'll go and have fun and make money, no matter how bad the club is."

Alan Havey feels that the road is very often an unhealthy place in which both talented and untalented comics can easily get trapped. He says, "I know people who have no home and they have to work to make money because either they gamble a lot or drink or do drugs, but when you're on the road that much you get so depressed because there's no foundation, no sense of identity—no home, no number—all you have is a calendar and a suitcase. Workwise, you meet very few original road comics. I meet gypsy comics, hear a lot of derivative or stolen material, or both. . . . Basically, if you work with shit, you take on its color."

He feels that the excuse many road comics give, of not being able to turn down the money, "is bullshit. If you let money control where you work and how often, it doesn't work out. There's a difference between really needing the money and doing it because it's there—because you can get two thousand dollars for a week, when you were only a busboy five years ago. Who looks at comedy like a money situation? That seems absurd. The people who go out on the road with shit acts make it harder for everyone because the audiences get used to that. I had an emcee that opened for me and he did this joke about what do they call getting a hard-on in California—and it was like 'pulling a goober' or something... then like, 'and now here's Alan Havey!' It's like, 'What, have you got shit stains in your pants? And now for our headliner...' It's terrible to follow that—to work like that."

For those comics who work the road exclusively, the chances of being "discovered" are slim to nonexistent. Rick Messina explains that many young stand-ups today "would sacrifice media stardom for two hundred thousand dollars in Atlantic City working in lounges. A lot of kids aren't disillusioned about the business—they see it that way from the beginning." Still, some people feel road comics are being exploited by the high-paying road clubs, including showcase club owner Mitzi Shore: "They're raising a bunch of drug addicts and alcoholics... I don't even call them comics. They're giving hope to people that have no right to be on a stage... just so they can make a buck."

Joe Bolster pinpoints the destiny of the lesser road comics: "Either they've given up, or they never had much ambition to begin with, or they had poor role models—and they're endlessly chasing women and doing drugs and partying. They either stall out as middle acts, making seven hundred dollars a week and driving everywhere, or they're quasi-headliners with a lot of dirty stuff in their acts. There are guys out there like that. Their act never changes, they don't work out, they take the easy road on every piece of material—'... a fucking clown!... what an asshole!...'—and they work. They'll always have a place for a person like that, but that's the level they'll stall out on. It's too bad, but talent has a lot to do with it. For some guys, you see their acts and to get that far is, for them, an achievement. They just would not have been in comedy five years ago, but today, with enough persistence, they carve out a place as a middle act and they're in Show Business making a living! For some people that's an achievement, and for them to stop and come to New York would be a waste of time. Other guys could go further, but they get caught up in the money: 'I have to go to the next town to pay for this... and then the next...'"

And so the road continues, fueled by criticism, applause and barrels of money. There are truly tragic stories, like that of the Nashville comic who stopped getting bookings when he stopped getting big laughs. After a show one night, he hid in a closet until the club closed up and, with three bottles of vodka, literally drank himself to death onstage.

And there are success stories, like road comic Jay Leno who rose from emceeing strip shows in Boston's Combat Zone to earning a million dollars a year and playing to sell-out crowds at Carnegie Hall. But most of the stories are about waiting . . . to be a star or to be a millionaire . . . and getting that next paying gig.

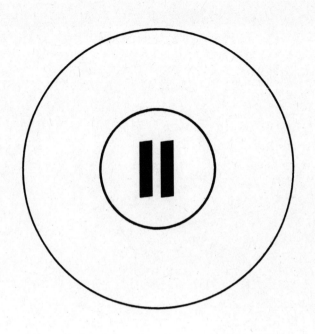

PORTRAIT

OF THE

COMIC AS A

YOUNG HAM

Some careers are things that people just fall into, others are more indigenous to the individual—as opposed to being chosen, *they* choose the person. For example, many a confused youth has "happened upon" the insurance business; something like sword swallowing, on the other hand, tends to involve a higher degree of planning. The act of sticking a lethal object down one's throat to make a living is not by any means an obvious work option and, in this sense, stand-up comedy is very much like it; one doesn't—ever—suddenly find oneself onstage telling jokes to strangers. In the most passionate cases, the decision to become a stand-up is an obsessively premeditated one, and in the least passionate examples it's still far from an accidental choice. The reasons for a person's deciding to become a stand-up may even be traced to childhood.

Comedians' childhoods, unlike those of most grown-ups, are not lived through and discarded; they are, like all other available life experiences, rewritten in humorous terms and performed in front of an audience. This practice makes the analysis of a comedian's youth possible, if done through their work, in many cases, only in an abstract sense. When comedian Emo Philips says of his childhood, "I had a real life force—a wondrous joy and exuberance, which resulted in my being beaten into a coma continuously," his intention is to tell a joke, not the truth. When he continues speaking, about having children of his own ("With my luck, my kid would probably be the anti-Christ. He'd make my head explode, and then go on to lead the world"), the connection between his words and reality is revealed to be substantially less than tenuous.

And yet, in searching for early signs of a stand-up's vocation, one can't help taking the comic's material, particularly when it's about childhood, into consideration. Even if one doesn't view the material as being true, as in the case of Emo, one can't help but think that perhaps comedians' willful alteration of fact might just be their method of dealing with some unspeakable childhood pain. This assumption is not new, of course, nor is it restricted to comics; Freud has helped us all to become obsessed with finding out why we, and everyone we know, is doing what we're doing, because whatever it is, it must be a reaction to something.

The search for a comic's roots is usually fruitless if one uses jokes as an indicator of reality, however. A comic's material about his life may have some connection to reality, but basically an act is just that, an *act*—it's a fictionalized account with a few actual facts thrown in to make the act believable and, perhaps, more relevant to people's lives. Emo says that, as a child, he was "horribly shy," which is probably true, but the reason for saying it is to use this fact as a point of departure: ". . . I was so shy—I would write down 'fire' on a piece of paper and pass it to the teacher. I never said anything at all. Well, sometimes I'd insult the bullies, and they'd beat me up. Then I'd insult them again and they'd beat me up. I never really determined the cause and effect . . ." The same principle is in operation when he describes himself as an "unusual kid," or when he talks about his father: "My family was very nice and loving, except my dad. I'd insult him, he'd chase me with a kitchen knife and I'd go running out of the house; it was a constant scene. My father was like a rhinoceros—he'd charge and then forget why he was charging. The most dangerous thing about the anger was the first ten seconds—if you could escape that you were okay. He looked like Robert Mitchum but had the personality of Moe Howard—and he never drank, either. We'd say, 'Please, Dad, have a drink.' We thought it would be nice for him to have an excuse . . . but he'd just come after us with the knife again."

Instead of "different," Emo says he was "special—avant-garde. I was different the same way, for instance, that the amphibians were different from the slimy little fishes that didn't have the capacity to spend some of their time on dry land. I evolved and they didn't—they're still in the primordial muck." He was smart, but in different ways than other children: "I had certain skills that went unrecognized, unappreciated in our culture; I was very good at drooling—I could drool in special patterns. But no one understood them, so I didn't get credit for that. Once I brought a knife to class and they took it away—I don't think they trusted me. I got in trouble once for making an 8 the wrong way. I said another teacher taught me to do it that way, so they brought her in and of course she said she didn't—so I got sent to the principal. I mean, I thought everyone would take a dead squirrel and trace its buttocks on the blackboard to make an eight. I thought they were unnecessarily prissy."

Hearing this, it's not inconceivable to assume Emo had a troubled childhood. But when one really listens to what's being said, it's obvious that none of it could possibly be true—unless Emo grew up with Charles Manson or in a Stephen King novel. The question of whether or not he had an unhappy childhood would be impossible to answer based upon his act, because what he is talking about has little connection to reality; its primary purpose is to get laughs, and everything else is secondary. He illustrates: "If I tell you, 'My girlfriend's so fat that she weighs one hundred and fifty pounds,' it wouldn't be very funny. But if I say, 'My girlfriend's rear end wasn't that big—only one of its moons had an atmosphere,' that works."

Every stand-up goes onstage as a character to some extent. Some may adopt a persona that's very similar to their own personality, but it's still a separate entity—a person telling jokes as opposed to telling the truth, which no "real" person does. Even observational comics, who base their material in reality, use the truth not as an end but as a foundation on which to build jokes by taking the truth to its farthest extreme. Joe Bolster points out that the styles of stand-up comedy can be divided into ". . . reality and fantasy. Rodney [Dangerfield] does fantasy. Those jokes never really happened, but you're willing to go along with it because the character is so credible. If he says, 'I asked a woman to make french toast and she got her tongue stuck in the toaster,' we know it didn't happen, but he looks like the kind of guy who would know someone who would do that. Other comics like Cosby or Pryor say stuff that may really have happened to them—they're only exaggerating it or following it to its logical end." Regardless of style, a comic's goal is not to report the news, but to make people laugh—and because reality is not as funny as make-believe, it should be assumed that what they are saying is generally closer to fiction than fact.

Comics must also create funny attitudes. "I'm so depressed..." leads to a lot more funny lines than, "Gee, everything's just great," because there's a lot more humor in what's wrong than in what's right. A happy attitude is not as funny as an unhappy one, so unhappiness must either be highlighted, if it's true, or manufactured if it isn't. Like events, people tend to give too much credence to comics' attitudes and because of this, Kip Adotta says, comedians get the rap for being insecure and unhappy people: "Everybody has these feelings—the only difference is that comics talk about them onstage. If I were a vice president at Xerox, I could never go to a sales meeting and say, 'Boy, do I have problems with my old lady,' because I'd lose my job for being unstable. But for a stand-up it's normal to bring these things to the surface. They have to, that's their occupation."

While the combination of unfortunate events and an attitude of "why me?" works for individual stand-ups comedically, it works against them as a group in terms of how they're perceived by the audience. Many people believe that comedians were lonely, isolated, unhappy children that grew up into sad adults who are trying to compensate for their past sorrow by laughing away the tears; it seems like pretty trite stuff, but it hangs on tenaciously. Part of the reason for this lies in several well-publicized, tragic cases of self-destructing comics like Freddie Prinze and John Belushi. And people do analyze comics' material as mentioned above. Finally, this idea persists to some extent because some comedians *themselves* believe that there is a connection.

Although she doesn't remember being unhappy as a child, Carrie Snow says: "I must have been, because I'm obviously drawing on some

kind of pain now." Adrianne Tolsch remembers that she was an isolated, emotionally deprived child ("my mom worked and my dad left a
lot") and that led her to humor and spilled over into her act: "I did a
line where I said I'm an only child because after I was conceived my
mother said, 'We're decent people, we're not doing that again.'"

Two striking examples of comics born out of poverty and misery are
Richard Belzer and Tom Dreesen. Tom, in describing his youth,
paints a portrait that would render Charles Dickens speechless: "I was
born and raised on the southside of Chicago in a suburb called Harvey
—steel mills, factories. I had eight brothers and sisters and we lived in
a shack behind a factory by the railroad tracks—five of us slept in one
bed. We were what they called raggedy-assed, shanty Irish poor. I
shined shoes in taverns from the time I was six years old until I was
twelve. I sold papers on the corner, I set pins in bowling alleys, caddied
in the summer—to help feed my brothers and sisters, since I was the
third child. My mother was a bartender sixteen hours a day, six days a
week." But, unlike his morose Dickensian counterparts, he was not a
victim of his circumstances, but rather a jolly observer: "I wasn't an
unhappy child. When I was six years old, shining shoes in the tavern, I
had an uncle who owned the tavern where my mother worked. His
name was Frank and he was the greatest joke teller I've ever heard—a
great dialectician. I used to watch him and I was fascinated at how he
could stand at the bar and make people roar with laughter. Ever since I
can remember, whenever I hear someone laugh, I'd gravitate towards
them; I wanted to hear what was making them laugh." Today, while he
often thinks and speaks about his "underprivileged" childhood, his material and comic persona reflect not a trace of latent bitterness or pain.

Richard Belzer, on the other hand, speaks much less frequently
about his childhood, but his onstage persona seems to reflect an edge
of anger that years of comic catharsis appear only to have sharpened.
He says that, in addition to being beaten consistently by his mother, he
was raised in poverty and misunderstanding: "I guess I was a bad kid,
but I'm not sure what that means. I grew up in a government project in
Bridgeport, Connecticut, called Marina Village. It was built during the
war for poor families. We gradually moved out of there into a house in
the suburbs when I was fourteen—it was an American success story.

My father became very successful in business, but I remember when we had nothing. . . ."

Hypersensitivity is often the result of painful childhood experiences, as veteran comic Phyllis Diller explains: "What happened to me in my childhood was very simple. I had very old parents and I was an only child, and that alone often produces a very sensitive child, because then things start happening to you that don't happen to a child who's born into a young family, or one with siblings.

"Not only was I around a lot of adults, I was around a lot of dead adults. All my aunts and uncles were popping off, and I was taken to all these stinkin' funerals . . . these real personal funerals where they're lying in the living room in a box. I belonged to the Funeral of the Month Club—you know, I was really thinking about life and death at the age of six. That'll put wrinkles on you! And I'd feel the old stiffs. I'd have to put my little hand on this cold, dead body that I'd seen walking around a week before and so I had all these questions about life and death, like what's it all about, Alfie? Now that's enough right there. Plus, my parents thought I needed to be with little kids to play sometimes, so I had this young married cousin with little kids, and they'd give me to these people for Sunday afternoon and do you know what these people did to me? They'd drive me past the orphanage and say, 'We're going to leave you there,' and my God, I would cry. . . . They thought that was funny. There's a line in my act, which I don't use anymore, where I had a bit about being the world's ugliest baby— great stuff—and I'd say, 'They used to take me to the orphanage and tell me to mingle.' But you see how it came out of my ancient psyche."

Yakov Smirnoff, who was also the only child of older parents, remembers that because of this he was over-protected and not allowed to participate in sports, so he chose comedy instead: "Since I wasn't a jock and girls tended to like those kind of guys—like football players—I wasn't popular. Creating comedy became a way of attracting attention, for me. People would come up and say, 'Tell us a joke.' It kept me from being so isolated."

Comic Rita Rudner says that her childhood was so sad that she still finds it difficult to speak about. "My mother was sick my whole life. She had cancer and it was a very long, slow, painful death. You become a certain way because of things like that. I became extremely focused on dancing, at first; I physically exhausted myself until I was twenty-three. [At the age of fifteen she graduated from high school and went to work in the national tour of *Zorba*, eventually working her way up to a starring role in *Annie* on Broadway before she quit dancing to become a stand-up comic.] And then I mentally exhausted myself thinking of comedy for the next four years." She feels that, for all comics, humor is a direct result of pain: "As far as being a comedian, I think the only reason you want to be that funny is because you're profoundly unhappy. Isn't that awful? You don't see many content people in comedy; they're just not happy—they're depressed. I mean how many gorgeous women could be stand-up comedians? How many models are funny? They don't have enough problems."

Jay Leno says that children often use humor because "what comedy is about is getting a reaction, and when you're a kid *any* reaction is good." But he feels that comedy can also be used to mask unhappiness, based on a personal recollection: "In sixth grade, kids were teasing me about having a hard head for some reason. One day, a kid came over and hit me on the head with a hammer. It hurt so badly, but I remember fighting back the tears—it hurt so much that I was laughing about it. One of the kids said, 'He really does have a hard head,' but I didn't cry. I always remember that—trying to get a laugh out of this situation, that was obviously extremely painful. I realized I could make things funny then . . . but it's not like I wanted to go into the circus and be hit with hammers every day."

Marc Weiner feels, also, that his clowning around in school was probably a way of covering up physical and mental pain. In the second grade, he developed Perthes, a leg disease in which the tissue of the hip disintegrates and must be forced to grow back. The illness left him on crutches for two years. In addition to this, he was an undiagnosed dyslexic. "That made me hate reading, and I became a troublemaker; I think I was hyperactive too." When asked if his parents tried to find an alternative outlet for him, he replied, "Yes, they always tried. They'd say, 'Look, there's an outlet in the wall over there—just stick your tongue in it . . .'"

While these comics make a pretty strong case for a connection between childhood pain and stand-up comedy, A. Whitney Brown brings up an important point: "You could say ninety percent of all stand-ups had unhappy childhoods, but if ninety percent of the population in general had unhappy childhoods, the statistic becomes meaningless." Granted, ninety percent seems to be an awfully large childhood unhappiness rate for a world that has produced only one Franz Kafka, but the point remains valid, nonetheless. Statistics can be easily manipulated to draw conclusions about a given segment of the population; so unless you see the entire picture—beware.

Brown, and many other comics, find this assumption of unhappiness as a prime motivation for humor to be both annoying and insulting; it implies that stand-up comedy is a passive action—a digestion, comic alteration and regurgitation of perceived reality, performed as a catharsis by the comic. It rules out the possibility that stand-up may in fact be a conscious activity that is performed not as an involuntary response, but as an aggressive means to a premeditated end. Richard Belzer agrees, saying, "I've told people that the hardest room I ever worked was my kitchen, because my mother used to hit me all the time and I'd tell jokes to change her mood, so in that sense there is some correlation between childhood pain and comedy for me but I don't like to totally reduce an art form to a psychological reaction or situation, although it certainly may have something to do with it." He states that there is also a theory that painters are only playing with their own feces on a canvas, but why dwell on this aspect of the creative process? "We can reduce any great work of art to a psychological formula and therefore take all the humanity and beauty out of it and everything in between . . . I'm sure we could find some anal-retentive, dehumanizing reason why people do everything. I mean Reagan bombed Libya because he wants to get a hard-on . . . but so what?"

Then there are those comics whose lives refute the painful childhood theory. According to Larry Miller, he was ". . . a good kid with a very fortunate upbringing. I wouldn't change a thing . . . I couldn't ask for more adoring and supportive parents. I loved high school—I had great friends, I was exuberant—I didn't consider myself inhibited about anything. I was a good athlete and involved in all sorts of activities." David Brenner has a similar recollection: "I never had an argument or fight with my parents; mine was a great family. I was very popular with my peers—I was class president from fourth grade to twelfth, I was the gang leader on the corner and I was the most popular kid in the neighborhood."

Perhaps it would be more accurate to say that, instead of comedy developing only as a result of great unhappiness, it is a talent which, if discovered at an early age, can be used by the child as an alternate means of coping with problems. In the case of young Brenner, few things went wrong—but when they did, humor was the method he used to solve his problems. Like young boxers, who discover early that powerful punches solve their problems best, young comics-to-be find that humor is their best defense. Brenner says that while he was a relatively good-looking, very popular kid: "[I] went away for one summer and when I came back, I went from five foot six and one hundred twenty-six pounds to six feet and one hundred twenty-six pounds. . . . None of the clothes fit and I'd broken my nose a couple times that summer, so I had the bump I never had before then. Before that, I had always been funny, but after that, I became funnier."

In Brenner's case he was aware of comedy at a young age because it was stressed at home; his father had been a vaudeville comedian. But in most cases the child discovers comedy on his own. Sometimes this can happen by accident, but most of the time it happens through a child's early recognition and development of some inherent talent— the knowledge that he can be funnier than other kids, and use this talent to his advantage. "I've always had a good head for remembering stuff that got reactions," Jay Leno says. "I remember the first joke I ever got a laugh with; I was in second grade. It's the first time I remember ever getting a laugh saying something that was genuinely funny, as opposed to kid's stuff. The teacher was telling us about Robin Hood and how the Sheriff of Nottingham was so mean—the common punishment then was to boil people in oil. I put my hand up and said, 'They can't boil Friar Tuck.' She asked me, 'Why not?' and I said, 'Because he's a "Fryer!"' It got a big laugh. The teacher said, 'All right now, Mr. Leno!' but I remember she smiled and let it go by. In fourth grade, we were looking at a slide show of Egyptian mummies and at the bottom of the mummy it said, 'B.C. 2050' or something. The teacher said, 'Does anyone know what those numbers mean?' and I stood up and said, 'That's the license number of the truck that hit him.' That got a big laugh."

As a child, Paul Provenza remembers using his comic ability to transform painful experiences into funny anecdotes: "I remember doing routines for my aunts and uncles. I'd tell one story about getting the shit beaten out of me in school. It was sad . . . but I made it very funny." Jay Leno described this comic view of life, held by certain children, as a form of "tunnel intelligence—something like the Idiot Savant Syndrome," or a special, very specific ability to see and re-member things of a comic nature: "I remember obscure things from way back in my childhood and I can remember almost all the jokes kids would tell each other in the fourth and fifth grade—that kind of *Playboy* scatological party humor. Occasionally, when I get in a very unsophisticated situation—in a small-town garage talking to the atten-dants, and they're looking at me like I'm Mr. Hollywood Star, I throw one of these generic, scatological, small-town jokes out, and suddenly I'm one of the guys. I could almost do a half-hour act of those jokes if I had to—they just stick in my mind."

Richard Belzer believes that he was always funny: "At the risk of being corny, I could say I was born funny." Like many comics, he was aware of his intelligence as a child, but refused to direct it through the acceptable channels: "In school I was only as smart as I had to be. I was told at an early age that I was very intelligent, and so why wasn't I getting better marks and why wasn't I a better person? That was the biggest mistake they ever made. It made something click in my mind . . . if I could do whatever I wanted, why should I break my balls in school—when I'm through with school, I'll do whatever I want. So I only worked enough to get by, knowing I was very intelligent. It was like, 'Oh, I can be whatever I want? Great—then fuck Algebra. Thanks a lot.'"

Carol Siskind was always "the nut . . . the kind of kid where, in the car on the way to visit relatives on a Sunday, my family would look at me and say, 'Listen, when we get there, can you not act weird?'" But, like many comics, she doesn't describe her childhood sense of humor as being "silly"; she says, rather, that it was "irreverent." She remembers "I was always like an adult. People have told me that my mother interacted with me like I was one . . . I'd be sitting in a high chair while she talked to me like I was one of her friends." What Carol describes sounds like a case of an adult viewpoint trapped in a child's body, and it is this quality, rather than a high incidence of happiness or unhappiness, that seems to be the most common thread running through comics' childhoods.

Precocious wit, as seen in young comics-to-be, is quite different from the garden variety of childhood goofiness. For example, Bill Grundfest's childhood memories sound more like the musings of an Algonquin Round Table member than a pre-pubescent wise guy: "I was a six-year-old sitting in the back of the room making wry comments about the teacher's performance. Some people were class clowns by making funny noises or faces, but I never had a talent for that—I was always the class wit. My comedy has always been based in the manipulation of words." Unlike many other funny children, who are often silly in spite of themselves, comics, as children, were funny in a more premeditated way. Often they seem to have used their humor as a means of alleviating the frustration of being "tiny adults" trapped in childish situations—a phenomenon coined as the "Schlemiel Child Syndrome" by child therapists Seymour and Rhoda Lee Fisher. While many stand-ups seem to have functioned like mini-adults in their childhood years, comic Steven Wright presents an opposite scenario in which the adult comic functions in a childlike manner: "I think little kids see the world literally—as realistically as anyone can see it. Then, the older they get, they accept more; they get mentally blinder with age. For some reason that didn't happen to me. My stuff is almost in the perspective of a child, but since I'm an adult I get to use the words of an adult. If a little kid heard, 'The line is busy,' he'd be wondering what the line was doing. But an adult thinks, 'Oh, it means beep-beep-beep . . . ,' and that's it. The joke I do about the twenty-four-hour store is like that: 'I went to the store that says, "Open twenty-four-hours," but it was closed. I asked why and they said, "It's open twenty-four hours but not in a row." When adults hear twenty-four hours, they think 'twenty-four hours a day.' That isn't necessarily true. Comedians are like sociologists; everyone's walking around life accepting everything, and comedians are saying, 'Why are you accepting this? It's so weird!' Everything is so strange, but you get used to it. It's so weird for so long that you think it's normal, which is not right."

A. Whitney Brown, who learned to read at the age of four, says that much of his wit came from boredom at school: "In the first grade, they gave us books and while they were talking, I'd read them all. By the end of September, I'd read everything; by Halloween, I'd read them five to six times already. I'd just sit in class waiting to make wise cracks."

A. Whitney describes himself as a loner during childhood, isolated because he saw things in "a different way," although this doesn't seem to be a common trait among child comics. Many said that they felt most comfortable with a few close friends (not unlike most children), and in the case of those who were already developing an interest in comedy, these friends were usually involved in it as well. Jerry Seinfeld recalls that "I always wanted to talk *about* things—to get into things in a different way than what people were doing at that age. The social experience was never as interesting to me—although I certainly felt painfully left out—but I wanted to talk about other things, like Jonathan Winters, 'Isn't it great the way he does this bit?' So I'd make friends with the real outcasts. Because they were grateful for any kind of contact, they'd discuss anything with me—I felt more comfortable around what would be generically called 'the nerds . . .'"

Still others, like Carol Leifer, were content to entertain themselves, alone, while honing their craft. As a child, Carol was very shy: "[I] spent a lot of time alone in my room performing to an imaginary audience." During this time, she became so comfortable with the idea of opening up to "the audience" that today, in front of a real audience, she surprises herself: "Sometimes I feel more comfortable talking to a bunch of strangers about personal stuff than to a friend, it's strange. When I sing in my act, people ask if I've ever had singing lessons and I want to say yes, in my room. That's where all my training was; that's where so much of my rapport with the audience comes from. When I'm onstage, it's me back in my room, but they're there now."

While few comics recognized, as children, that comedy was going to be their vocation, some remember early glimmers of awareness, like their fascination with certain comics, or watching entertainers in a "different way" than other children. "I forgot about this until recently," says Jonathan Solomon, "but when I was little, I was fascinated by comedians. I found this card my father gave me for my birthday when I was ten that alluded to my wanting to be a comedian. I was into Bill Cosby. I'd play this album over and over and I could imitate him perfectly. When I was ten, in camp, my nickname was Cos, because I talked like Cosby all the time and did his routines." Cathy Ladman remembers, "When I was eight years old, I used to listen to this album, 'Nichols and May Examine Doctors,' over and over—I knew it by heart. When my mother came into my room to listen to me do my prayers, I'd do a selection off the album for her." That was a significant age for Jerry Seinfeld too, apparently: "I think it was in me to do this since I was eight years old. I watched comedians on Sullivan—I watched Winters and Skelton with a different look on my face than other people did; I was absolutely transfixed by them. It was always the thing I wanted to do, but I never thought I would. It was like watching people on the moon, and you think, 'I'd like to try that,' but you don't think you will. It was that deeply embedded a fantasy." Larry Miller says that kids often aren't aware of their differences; he thought everyone reacted to watching movies the way he did, "transfixed by the magic of them, and wanting so excitedly to tell everyone, 'Listen to this piece of music! Watch this scene!' I thought everyone lived like that—and of course they don't."

Steven Wright, whose unique, surreal approach to stand-up has created a new comic genre, remembers watching comedy as a child but, "I never analyzed it—ever. I just liked it. And I didn't think that's what I wanted to do until I started watching 'The Tonight Show,' year after year. I don't know why I focused in on stand-up comics, because I was a fan of all comedy in general, but I did. I focused in on the concept of one guy out there alone. When I was fifteen, I decided that's what I wanted to do; that was my dream—to be a stand-up comedian and eventually go on Carson."

While he didn't begin writing jokes as a young child, he recalls an early fascination with them: "In second grade, for Show and Tell, you could go up in front of the class and say anything. I used to watch the

'Jackie Gleason Show' with my father every week and so, when I was six years old, I went up and told a joke from the show: A cop stops this guy because he's going up a one-way street and he says, 'Didn't you see the arrows?' and the guy says, 'I didn't even see the Indians.' I said that, then I went and sat down." His actual joke writing didn't begin until high school, he says: "One of my earliest, weirdest jokes is one I have on my record. I thought of it in tenth grade—about the guy who tried to learn Spanish by listening to an album in his sleep, but the record skipped. So the next day, he could only stutter in Spanish."

Paul Provenza remembers a specific incident in childhood that crystallized, in his mind, the power of comedy as a means to obtain attention and love. "I was about ten years old," he says, "and our family went to the Dunes Hotel in Miami and Tubby Boots was playing. I don't know how many hundreds of pounds he weighs—disgustingly fat. He used to play a stripper and he was so fat he had these huge tits, which he'd put pasties on and make them twirl around. He'd been around for centuries, working everywhere from strip clubs to the Catskills to these kind of shows in Miami. At night I'd go and try to get in and the bouncer would make me leave, but one night I hung around outside the door. It was a glass door and there was a black velour wrap around the whole room, and on the door. Every time the door would open I'd peek in and see what was going on, and hear the laughs and the bouncers would be trying to block me from looking. I was so fascinated by the whole nightclub thing. So one night, the bouncer left for a minute and I quickly snuck in and went under the velour—I stood between the velour and the wall, worked my way around and got to see a good portion of the show.

"At the Dunes, everyone ate in the same room, the show room, from a big buffet table. Tubby used to eat all by himself at a big table covered with food—he was like a freak show. Then, when I saw his act, I remember getting the feeling that this guy, who was so disgusting and always alone—like if he lived on your block you'd hurry when you passed his house—could go onstage and people would cheer and applaud and tell him he was great. I thought, 'Holy shit—there's something strange going on here.'"

While he doesn't recall any specific fascination with watching stand-up, Paul Reiser says that his childhood interest in comedy was channeled through school work. In the third grade he remembers rushing home eagerly to work on compositions because he knew they would be performed before the class. "I'd put some jokes in—some inside stuff only my friend would get. That was really my first stand-up comedy." He says that then, as now, he responded well to things that were fathomable to him—like homework that either involved humor or had some finite boundaries: "Like, okay, so I read these eight pages and answer these four questions? Great—that'll take me up to four thirty, and then I can watch 'Superman.' Okay, fine. But if it was something beyond me, I'd get lost. That's still my general pattern. I'm very systematic and obsessive about trying to maintain order, but then I lose it. I don't keep a room clean, I'll be sloppy, then clean it all up, starting from scratch—new notebook syndrome."

Whether or not young comics functioned well in school, virtually all of them were intelligent children, and knew that they were regardless of how parents and teachers viewed them. Carol Siskind remembers she was a "good girl who didn't give her parents any trouble," but her good grades were offset because she was always clowning around and "wouldn't get on the honor roll because I'd doubled the cookie recipe to be funny, in Home Ec., and gotten an F." David Brenner agrees that, while most comics were probably disciplinary cases (he was expelled over two hundred times), they were also intelligent. "You've got to be bright to make fun of something—there are a few who are really dumb, but I think comedians are generally of above average intelligence." He says that he hated school, but continued through college because he came from a family where it was important: "I was very tenacious in college; that's why I graduated with good marks—and I had a photographic memory in school. But I have always disliked formal education—from the first day of kindergarten until I walked out of the university, I hated it. You know why? I was always chastised for being funny—what I'm making all my money on, how I'm taking care of my family and friends. All the wonderful things that have happened in my life come from the ingredient I got thrown out of school for."

Alan Havey remembers a creeping sense of disillusionment that first bred anger, but eventually metamorphosed into something quite different: "I goofed off a lot and made terrible grades and I felt I saw things differently than other people did. I knew that school wasn't important, or being raised a Catholic—there was more to the universe than God or heaven and hell . . . I sensed it at an early age, and a lot of my anger comes from that, from having adults push things on me. Adults don't have that knowledge you're told they do. I knew I was funny and that I'd be funny, even though teachers told me, 'You can't be funny all your life.' But even then, I knew they were wrong." His childhood memories, like those of many young comics-to-be, revolved around a then vague concept of having watched his young world from a third-person omniscient point of view. In adulthood, this viewpoint came more clearly into focus, and eventually took on a name . . . comedy.

C O M I C S
A N D
P A R E N T S
O R . . .

"Congratulations Mr. and Mrs. Jones...It's a Comic!"

Like poets, popes and serial murderers, stand-up comics begin life as children; the question is, what happens *then*—what in the world makes human beings turn into stand-up comedians? In the search for answers, we can argue about the relative roles of nature and nurture— the possibility of genetic predisposition—and the incidence of "only child syndrome"... or we can go directly to the self-proclaimed possessors of (almost) all worldly knowledge—mothers. What these women lack in scientific jargon, they more than make up for in holy vows of omnipotent comprehension: "What, you think I don't know everything? You think I was born yesterday?" And so, confident that they'll provide us with answers to our question of "what makes a stand-up comic (sh)tick?" we place our trust in them, and await their insightful replies.

Bea Bass and Blanche Lewis are hard-working women, eloquent speakers, and, as mothers of stand-up comedians, qualified experts on the question at hand. Like all experts, they carefully review all relevant data, formulate hypotheses, conduct experiments, and, finally, draw conclusions based on the results. Unfortunately, as often happens in even the most carefully controlled sociological experiments, the two experts came to different conclusions: Bea Bass discovers that her son,

Paul Provenza, is the best comedian in the world, while Blanche Lewis finds that it is *her* son, Richard, who is the best. (Both emphasize, also, that their sons are not married and "*very* eligible.")

Bearing in mind the fact that Sociology is not a perfect science, and that mothers are not a particularly objective species, we must rephrase the question (emphasizing that we *aren't* looking for qualitative answers—we just want to know what their kids were like growing up), and hope for better results. We should also tell the women that we'll be interviewing their sons, so they won't be tempted to make outrageous claims like, "He played Caesar's Palace at the age of seven." When this has been accomplished, we clear our throats, shrug our collective shoulders, and begin.

Bea Bass describes her son, Paul Provenza, as having been glued to the television from the day he was born, "though he didn't watch it with the usual eye . . . he was actually observing," and, almost immediately, it became apparent that his viewing habits revolved around comedy. "When he was about six years old," she says, "he started doing 'Crazy Guggenheim'—with his little hat on crooked and his face all twisted up . . . after that, there were all kinds of impressions. He did them to get into the spirit of comedy and then, when he got older, his own personality started to come out."

Blanche Lewis's story begins even earlier; she describes her youngest son as a beautiful little blond child, who was born premature, weighing only four pounds. "His father ran a kosher catering business," she says, "which Richard talks about in his act. He says when he was a preemie at the hospital, laying in the little bassinet, he remembers seeing a man with his nose pressed up against the glass of the nursery. The nurse picked up his head, and he heard the man saying, 'I want you to be a caterer—a kosher caterer.' So he goes back to his little bassinet and says to the other little preemie, 'What's a kosher caterer?' and the other one says, 'How should I know? I'm an Italian.' I think that's such a funny story." She smiles pensively, then adds, "It's made up of course!"

Bea Bass believes that her son's childhood obsession with comedy was, in part, his way of coping with the difficulties brought about by a physical impairment. "Because of a weak muscle that made his eye turn inward, Paul had to wear a patch for several years," she says, "and I'm sure kids were cruel to him. But he just focused his attention on other things. He got involved in activities where he didn't have to prove himself with other people. If you're playing ball, you're playing with a team . . . and he just wasn't able to do that."

Paul concurs with this analysis, saying that he turned to comedy as a solution to the problem of being a "super geek." (A super geek?) "Yes, a total geek. You can imagine what the patch was like, and on top of that, I only wore crew cuts until about the age of thirteen—not terribly hip in the late sixties—because my grandfather was an old world Italian barber and my father was in the National Guard. I'd always tell my grandfather, 'I want it like the Beatles' . . . and demonstrate the cut for him. Then he'd go, 'sure,' take out this thing and go, 'brr-r-r-r,' and that was it—a crew cut. He'd say, 'Look at that! Just-a like-a the Beatles!' I'd be very hip now—shaved head, eye patch, pants above the ankles like Michael Jackson . . . but then it was awful."

Blanche Lewis says, "I wish I could say in the first grade Richard wanted to be a comedian, but it wouldn't be true. What I do know is that he was cute and everyone adored him." She explains that most of the material he writes concerning his childhood has some basis in fact, however, so he must have been thinking about it a little bit. "For example, in his act he says that I made him wipe the dog's feet off when he came inside, which is true—but the part about the dog developing a nervous bark because of it is not true." She adds, "He was always a funny kid. He used to tell me, 'Mom, you look like a million bucks . . . all green and wrinkled,' but he never expressed any desire to be a comedian."

Paul Provenza, on the other hand, remembers, "When I was eight years old, I knew that I wanted to do stand-up comedy." In reflecting upon his friendships during this period, he explains the bittersweet connection between childhood pain and humor: "I had a couple of friends then—we were all misfits who ended up together because nobody else would have us. We would sit around together, having our little group therapy sessions, and what happened was that we all ended up developing the same defense mechanism—a sense of humor."

The two comedians' young lives continued along the same basic paths; Paul became increasingly obsessed with comedy, while Richard remained indifferent. At the age of sixteen, after years of writing jokes and monologues, Paul decided to audition at the Improv in New York. Appealing to his mother's love for music and educational experiences, he told her that he and his (much older) cousin Bob were going to the club to watch a friend record a live album. So, armed with an alibi, a six-minute routine, and cousin Bob, he set out to become a comedian. Bea says she didn't find out about any of this until long after it had occurred, "Not that it would have made any difference, though, because he would have done it anyway."

Paul's memory of that night is etched as clearly in his mind as his own name. "At that time the Improv used to stay open till everybody left. Soon it got to be about three-thirty, four A.M. and there were about six or seven auditioners left. . . I'd been there since nine P.M. Jay Leno was the emcee at the time—he was the first comic I'd ever seen live [other than Tubby Boots] and, even then, he was great. The way he worked was he'd open the show, then use an offstage mike at the back of the room to bring on each auditioner. I went back and talked to him and said, 'I thought you were great . . . and-uh . . . I have to go to school tomorrow—is there any way I could go on soon?' He said, 'sure,' and put me on next—at four A.M.—which was a big break then. I remember everything about it—the sweat, from nerves, the light—that's really all you can see. And my head—I was kind of watching from a point behind me. I remember seeing the silhouette against the light, thinking, 'Something feels right here,' even though I wasn't getting any laughs. It was scary because whatever it was that I had to do onstage completely escaped me. I had no idea what I could do, but I needed to be there. It's like saying, 'Yeah, sure I can scuba dive,' then you get in the water and think, 'Wait a minute, I don't know what to do,' and you're gasping for air."

While the experience wasn't a negative one, it was apparently too much too soon for the adolescent comedian. He continues: "It didn't feel bad afterwards, but it wasn't what I thought it would be. Everybody who goes on for the first time thinks, 'Johnny Carson will see me and I'll be on "The Tonight Show" next week . . . paramedics will be taking people out who are dying of laughter . . .' That's what you want.

I didn't set foot onstage again, to do stand-up, until my freshman year in college."

Blanche Lewis explains that the early rumblings of comedy didn't begin in her son until he finished college. Before discussing Richard's comic beginnings, however, it's important to note that the child of whom she speaks is no ordinary comedian. He is Richard Lewis, the man whose name is synonymous with the word "neurosis"—whose brain is a rushing stream of consciousness spilling out in waves of paranoia that ooze through the minds of audience members like power tools through melted butter.

Richard is a dizzying mixture of Hamlet and Henny, as he stalks the stage unpeeling the layers of his life in abstract comic soliloquy— grasping at props that don't exist, running flailing hands through his flying hair, and, stopping to strike an impossible pose, responding to questions that exist for him alone. So how did he get to be neurotic? Blanche explains that the manic person we see onstage is not the "real" Richard. "I mean, he's not the calmest person in the world either, but he's not like *that*. I don't know how he developed himself into that character—I guess there had to have been some neurosis way back. How could anyone *suddenly* become so neurotic? [She laughs.] Well . . . whatever it is, it's working, and when he reaches his goal I'm going to make such a party."

Obviously not all comic's mothers are as supportive and understanding as Bea and Blanche, but neither are these women anomalies.

For Carrie Snow, her mother provided not only love and support, but a sense of urgency about her career: "She tells me: 'Please make it soon. I hate those award ceremonies where people look up to the sky and say, "Mom, if you're watching..."'" And parental "encourage-ment" is not restricted to her career; her marital status is also up for grabs: "My parents put an ad in a Jewish newspaper in San Francisco saying, 'Our movie star daughter is too busy to look for a husband, so we'll look for one for her.' My mother wore a white carnation and went to a prearranged spot—they didn't tell me until after they'd done it, and they think they're so fucking funny now, Yuk-O-Rama." While she doesn't know exactly how it happened, her love of comedy came from both parents: "They're the ones who taught me how, without knowing it. We used to listen to Shelley Berman and Allan Sherman albums at home, they took me to see Jerry Lewis in Las Vegas—they exposed me to all this, and then they act surprised." She also feels that, by instilling confidence in her, they allowed her to pursue a nontraditional career, which stand-up is—*particularly* for a woman. But this didn't come without a price; she explains, "My parents never told me there's anything I can't do. They also said a job worth doing is worth doing well, which is why I can do this—and also why I'm so neurotic. I don't realize there are things out of my control . . . like life."

Other comics were able to become stand-ups in spite of getting no encouragement on the parental front. Steve Mittleman's parents couldn't help largely because they lacked the necessary tool— a sense of humor: "Growing up I was mentally abused. In my family I was the comic relief. I think in many ways, my parents are the dullest people I've ever met; they have no minds of their own. My father was a printer and all he ever talked about was the alphabet; my mother repaired typewriters. I was funny at home, but my brother and sister were my audience mainly, not my parents." He gets along with his parents better now that he's achieved some success in comedy, but, "before that, it was hell. They weren't supportive on my terms, which I wish they'd be—being supportive on their terms means being behind me once I started doing well. Sometimes they don't know when to call—when your kid is on a national TV show, you call, right? They wouldn't know that sometimes. I just have to accept that they don't know better, and that's something you have to do in life, even if it hurts."

Their lack of support is not only related to his career, Mittleman says. It was something he experienced throughout childhood: "I hated living at home so much. When I was eighteen I joined the army on the delayed enlistment. I never went in though . . . instead, I went back to college, got my grades up and transferred my next term. I hated living at home so much. To be a Jewish middle class kid from Queens and join the army is unheard of, so you can imagine. I'd be the only Jew in the army—it would be like being a black in the Israeli army."

Cathy Ladman (who was involved with Steve for three years) explains that, though always a funny kid who made people laugh, she had great difficulty in becoming a stand-up because of insecurity that

came from "years of being fucked up by my parents. I was very restricted when I was growing up, which is why I graduated from high
school at sixteen—to get the hell out. My father was very strict, over-
bearing, determined to have us make it on our own—I was *not*
spoiled." Giving a recent example of her father's inability to give her
credit, she says, "I went out to Los Angeles and became a contestant
on 'Wheel of Fortune'—so I'd have enough money to live on out
there. This shows how little support I got when I was a child . . . I was
losing the whole show, and in the last ten minutes I won everything—
it was unbelievable, so much fun. But the night the show was broadcast, my parents called me at eleven o'clock EST and my father said,
'You know, you were losing the whole time—if I was going to bet on
the show, I wouldn't have bet for you. I was starting to doubt that you
were going to win.' I said, 'Dad, the show was taped, I told you how it
turned out already!' "

While Joe Bolster believes that his becoming a comic had something
to do with trying to get his parents' attention, it was not so much a
result of their behavior as the fact that he was the oldest of fourteen
children. "There is a pretty obvious psychological analysis—with thirteen kids following me there was that constant battle for attention, and
comedy is certainly a 'hey, look at me!' business." He describes his
family as a metaphor for the baby-boom generation, "In 1967 we had
to turn the attic into a second floor, so at its peak, in 1971, there were
sixteen people living in the house. Now there are four so the second
floor is closed off. It's like a museum: a little rope across the stairs, a
tumble weed blowing through . . . abandoned rooms—only four where
once there were sixteen. Then it fills up at Christmas." He says that he
talks about this in the act, but it's so incredible that often people assume it's just a cheap contrivance to get laughs: "They think it's a
device like fat mother-in-law jokes—but it works well in Princeton
[where he grew up], because everybody knows it's true."

With regard to parental attachments, Bob Goldthwait feels that
comics have a stronger bond with their mothers than their fathers. He
says, "They're all momma's boys—ask them about their momma, they
love her." He says the father is usually a figure that comes and goes,
but Mom is the one they talk to at 4 in the morning at the coffee table.

He recalls, "I was sitting in a bar once, loaded, and I brought up the topic of Irish moms in Boston—lots of tears... and the guys are drinking and crying, because everybody loved their momma. They even do Mother's Day shows in the clubs in Boston."

Tom Dreesen views it a different way; instead of feeling closer to their mothers than other people, he believes what stand-ups have in common is a certain alienation from their fathers: "This is something I've come across... my father never said he loved me. He never put his arm around me, he never played ball with me—I'm like my mother, who would hug stop signs; I hug my son all the time. But my father never told me he loved me, and I never thought about it too much, until once I asked a comedian if his father ever told him, and he said no. I've asked old and young comedians and some say, 'I didn't know my father.' Some say, 'Oh yeah, he loved me.' But I ask, 'Did he ever tell you?' and they say, 'No.' Letterman said no, Johnnie Dark never knew his father, George Miller's father left him when he was three... maybe it leaves a void that needs to be filled—and laughter could be the love that fills it."

Other comics describe their relationships with their fathers as being very strong, however. In fact, David Brenner gives his father full credit for his stand-up career. He says in one respect his sense of humor was physical: "I have to attribute whatever funniness I have to my genes, mainly. My father's extremely funny, and I got his genes...." In another sense it's philosophical: "Comedy was a highly regarded commodity in my family." Finally, there is the fulfillment of his father's unresolved destiny: "He was a vaudeville comedian—a song-and-dance man. When he was nine years old, he ran off and went to vaudeville. He was in the show business part of the navy after that, in World War I doing shows, and he got a contract to do a Hollywood movie. He got on the train and came back to Philadelphia and his father was the leading rabbi of Philadelphia and he said, 'You can't do this. It's against our religious beliefs, working on Shabbat, Friday night, and Saturday matinées—it's against everything we believe in.' And, unlike Eddie Cantor and Al Jolson and people like that, who said to their rabbi and cantor fathers, 'Forget it, I'm going into show business,' my father listened to his father and never went onstage again. It's a sad story in a way because my father could have been a great comedian—and I think that's been verified by the success of my career—and it's one of the reasons why I did it too. It validated my father's talent, because he really is funnier than I am. If I went this far in my time, he would have gone all the way in his time."

He inherited not only the desire to do stand-up, but also his style from his father: "He used to say—the premise of his act was, 'I'd like to catch the guy.' Like, 'You know, I'd like to catch the guy who puts the fuzz in your pockets at the cleaners.' As his son, I turned it around and said, 'I hate pocket fuzz—you get it back from the cleaner and it's still there. Who puts it in? Where does it come from? You take out your comb and it's hanging out and people are laughing.' If you put 'I'd like to catch the guy' in front of almost everything I do, you'll see it's my father's comedic mind I'm doing, not mine. It's ingrained in me— being a little kid, crawling around, hearing this madman in the house all the time, 'I'd like to catch the guy who invented the hammer! Why is the hammer... bump-a-bump...'"

Paul Rodriguez credits his father with planting the seeds of comedy in his mind, but in a more indirect way. He instilled in him the importance of *language*, as opposed to physicality, in affecting people's lives. As a member of a teenage gang in the barrio, he would fight if he had to, but his basic means of survival was "to make the tougher guys laugh and be my buddies, and want to protect me because it was fun being around me. I carried a big joke, not a big stick... words were always first, and that comes from my father. He never physically beat me, but his tongue would kill me. When he got mad, he could make me feel like such manure that I'd never do the bad thing again. His words would put such pain in me—such guilt and misery I'd never want to hurt him by doing that again. The day I got caught with pot in my pocket, I gave him the same line everyone gives, 'I'm holding it for a friend,' and he said, 'Son, I'm ashamed that you'd give me such an unimaginative, bullshit line—I thought at least you'd do better than that. Why don't you have the courage to say, "I bought this with my own money," and let me get angry with you...' I felt like such a schmuck! Verbal torture—that was his method. You can get over a quick beating, but those words—they stay in your mind. And I remembered that."

Once children decide to become comics they also must go through a process of learning to ignore what their parents might think of their act. For Alan Havey, the process was alternately difficult and liberating. The first time his parents saw him perform he "was unbelievably nervous, thinking of saying certain things in front of them . . . but afterwards, they said they were proud of me, and that approval helped; it was a big worry I got out of the way. It was satisfying on another level too; I thought, 'My mother's coming here to see me and I get to talk about masturbation—sexual stuff.' I'm over thirty years old and I get to be real naughty in front of my mom, like, 'Too bad, you have to listen to it and I'm getting paid for it and there's nothing you can do now—ha-ha-ha . . .'"

For years, Bob Goldthwait carried the baggage of his mother's opinions with him, not only onstage but everywhere. "I would do interviews and I wouldn't worry about how I looked, but what my mother was going to think when the story came out. Being a drug addict and stuff, that was good publicity for me . . . it sells more tickets according to the Ozzy Ozborne school of publicity. But I thought, what will Mom think? A lot of comics get started in the same city they're from, but I moved. My parents had no idea what I was doing for a living, and that gave me so much freedom. Now I can say anything I want onstage and feel no repercussions."

He understands why his chosen profession is sometimes difficult for his mother to accept and feels that being the parent of a successful stand-up is gratifying on one hand, because your child is a success, but difficult on the other hand because of its socially unacceptable overtones: "I think being my parents is like being Alice Cooper's parents—one half of them is really proud, and the other half is very ashamed at the same time. That's how they are." But as he becomes more famous, he becomes easier to accept—and so he must constantly remind them of who he is: "Fame is like a big eraser. It's strange, now that I'm famous, in their opinion, all the shitty things—all the wreckage of my past—is erased. I never was the son they worried about or yelled at because I flunked everything and only hung out with my friends. I'm the son they're proud of now. I used to tell them it's more important for me to socialize than it is for me to do school work, because I'm going to be doing this for my living. Now it's like I was never the kid who got arrested—now I'm the wonderful son. I like to remind them, now, that I still suck."

Emo Philips says that he no longer has to worry about his father's approval because "He's dead—he's pushing up the daisies—went to the big cabbage factory in the sky . . . but he saw me perform, and he predicted that if I went into comedy it would result in an early death. He was right; he's dead. He lived to see me get some nice recognition from the newspapers though, that was nice." As for his mother, he says, "I did 'Miami Vice' and I took her to Miami to meet Phil Collins. She got a big kick out of it, but she didn't know who he was. She pretends she's not excited by this stuff but she is."

Regardless of their feelings of gratitude or resentment about their parents' contribution, most comics can not resist immortalizing them in their acts . . . by transforming them into comic material. A Barry Sobel "bit" exemplifies the way in which comic parents are deftly changed into monologue components: "My dad would always use the phrase, 'That's how they get you.' We used to go to this place called the Sirloin Inn, where they gave you a salad bar and everything. I'd say, 'This is a good place!' and my father would go, 'No! It's a clip joint! That's how they get you! They give you the soup, the salad, all the bread—by the time the steak comes you can't eat it . . . that's how they get you! You can't eat the steak!' So I said, 'I don't get it—you mean they serve it to someone else after you have a couple of bites?' And he would say, 'What, do I look like I know the steak guys? What do I look like?' Another thing he'd say was, 'This hour? You're going out at this hour? Where do you go at this hour? I know—you go to a crazy place at this hour—you go to a sick place at this hour!' If I went to use the phone, 'Who do you call at this hour? Don't you think I know who you call at this hour? You call crazy people at this hour—sick people: Hello—come on over and kill me! They come over, you're out with your crazy friends, they come over and kill us—that's how they get you! That's how they get us!' He was the kind of dad who would go to the bathroom every night at three A.M., trip over the same coffee table and blame my mom, 'Booby traps! She puts them there to kill me! That's how she gets me!'"

And such is the case with every comic parent. Whether making a contribution to their child's act through genial genes, love and kindness, lack of support or martyring their personas to create a funny bit, à la Sobel, they *will* contribute to it in some way; it's just a matter of "how they get you."

YOUNG COMICS IN LOVE

Relationships among comics are as varied and unpredictable as jokes or, more accurately, punch lines. Perhaps the most unique are those which move beyond friendship to love. In these unions there exists the traditional conflict between career and relationship, but with the added problems of the partners existing in the same highly competitive world. Initially, many comics are drawn to one another because of this shared lifestyle: they're both *there* and available. In the clubs, the secret desires and fears of comics are kept under the surface, but silently recognized and acknowledged by the other performers waiting their turn at the bar.

The number of married comic couples is small primarily because of the highly unequal distribution of sexes in the profession—many men to every woman. Of those who are involved, a small percentage marry, and of that group, few like to talk about it. A romantic explanation is that these many relationships begin as extensions of the kinship among comics; a more realistic view is that, in spending ninety percent of their waking lives in clubs, most comics are going to be spending a lot of time with comics.

Hours also are important. In the showcase club, the typical stand-up's work day begins at 8 P.M. and ends sometime after 2 A.M.—if they don't hang around the bar. Jonathan Solomon, a New York comic, says, "When you're talking about weekends, this puts just about ninety-nine percent of the earth's population out of the comic's dating range. The lifestyle is fifty-fifty—part of it is great, the other part is hellish. The business of working when everyone else is enjoying themselves sucks—social life-wise, it's hard. The last girl I went out with for any length of time was a rock-and-roll singer, who had the same hours and state of mind, so it was great. But if I'm attracted to someone who works on Wall Street, forget it. I've had relationships where we saw each other for dinner, I'd fall in bed at two after she'd already been asleep for three hours. She'd wake me up to say, 'How'd it go?' Then get up at nine and I'd have to get up also—it was awful."

Alan Havey says that, while in the beginning it is harder to perform, "and to keep your self-esteem, respect and confidence going on at two A.M. before people who are exhausted," the late hours make it easier to have a relationship than later on, when a comic starts getting earlier spots onstage: "When I was less successful it was easier on my relationship—we could go out to a movie, dinner, come home, make love, she'd roll over and go to sleep—and I'd be out the door going to work. That was fine for her, but when I started working more, getting good spots, she didn't like that. It cuts into everything, but it's worth it."

The image of the stand-up as a lonely crusader, battling the windmills of convention, takes on a decidedly less romantic tone here; for many, every convention battled adds up to another dateless night. And that's between the hours of 8 P.M. and 2 A.M.—days are even harder for some. Waking at noon, the comic's day runs on a separate timetable from the rest of the world. Their breakfast is the civilian's lunch, their winding up is the world's winding down. Every hour is a countdown to club time, where in the absence of one-on-one affection, they will run to bask in the love of an audience for a twenty-minute set.

Jonathan Solomon says that his friend, John Hayman, does a bit about what it's like for a woman to date a comedian: "They pick you up at five o'clock but he won't be too into it, because he's only been up for an hour. Then you have dinner while he has breakfast and he'll talk about what he's going to do that night and what happened last night when you weren't there. Then he'll go pace around the club talking to his friends and you'll sit in a chair and watch. If he has a good set, he'll be totally wired and won't have time for you; this goes on for about five or six sets and he does it again. At two o'clock he wants to hang out with other comics and you can sit by his side. If you have a joke maybe people will look at you—then he'll go home with you and then you won't have sex because you're too tired."

This is often the unfortunate scenario of a comic/civilian liaison, but the circumstances can be even worse in a comic/comic match. Because of the high degree of self-involvement associated with the profession, the idea of a comic dating a comic is almost redundant. But, in some cases, intense personal involvements are the natural extension of equally intense professional attractions—and occasionally, when this happens, comedy gives birth to love.

In still other cases, love has been known to spawn comedy. Carol Leifer is a comic love child, the product of a boyfriend's love for stand-up, and her love for the boyfriend. It began innocently enough at Binghamton College where she and comedian (of late, movie star) Paul Reiser dated and played opposite one another in "funny guy and funny girl" roles in the theater department. In the summer of 1975, when showcase clubs began opening around New York and one of the Improv regulars, Freddie Prinze, was just making it big, Paul decided to give stand-up a try.

His decision was less of a heartfelt one than a result of an elimination process. "I had no tradition as an actor," he says, "like Olivier or something. So I thought, what job is there where you can go onstage and get laughs and there are no other people and you don't have to wait forty minutes until your number comes up—and you don't have to sing and dance." He found the answer and that summer auditioned at Catch A Rising Star with five minutes of material. On returning to school, when people asked what he did that summer, he said, "Oh, I was a comedian," and continued, casually, to class. The idea that he had made a life choice didn't occur to him.

The experience stayed with him though, as did the identity of "comedian" which he loved even more than performing. After his third year at school, he did a couple more sets at Catch and forgot about it until graduation, when he decided to spend a year performing to "get it out of my system." During this summer, while working days in his father's office and spending nights at Catch, he introduced his girlfriend, Carol, to stand-up. Carol says, "I started to do my act during the summer of my junior year. He told me about going to Catch and doing the audition nights and said, 'Why don't you do it? It's fun.' I did and I enjoyed it. Then they said, 'You can work here now.'"

Hooked immediately, Carol left Binghamton and finished her degree at Queens College, commuting to Manhattan at night to perform, back to sleep in her parents' house on Long Island, and to Queens during the day for school. Working out at the Comic Strip during her senior year of college, she waited and went onstage every night for the late-night spots, beginning at 2 A.M. While her dedication had a lot to do with stand-up's immediate appeal, she is honest to admit there were other things at work: "Not the least of which was going out with Paul, who was a year ahead of me at college. He was leaving school and it was also an opportunity to be with him." Though the relationship ended several years later, Carol eventually married a comedian, Ritch Shydner, and both she and Paul continued working as stand-ups, ending up as two of the more successful in the business.

Cathy Ladman decided to become a stand-up at the instigation of her first love, Jerry Seinfeld, who went on to become one of the most popular comics working today. She urged him to become a comic as well but, at fifteen years of age, neither began making any serious preparations. Ten years later, Cathy had worked in advertising, cosmetics, teaching, and was looking for another job. So depressed about not doing what she wanted with her life, she had to avoid watching all comedy—it upset her. One night, while lying in bed she turned on "The Tonight Show" and heard Johnny Carson say, "Let's welcome Jeff Seinfeld!" Thinking it was a mistake, that he meant Jerry, she kept watching and was right—it was his first "Tonight Show" spot. She remembers her feelings as a mixture of amazement and regret; he had done it and she hadn't. But that night, though they hadn't spoken in five years, she called him in California and made arrangements to meet when he came into New York the next week.

When they met, she told him how she regretted not following up on their teenage plans, and how she was now taking an improv course to prepare herself for the stage—and he said, "You're one of the funniest people I know; you'd make a fine comedian. Just do it." That was four-and-a-half years ago and today, Cathy says, Jerry is one of the greatest admirers of her work.

After a year of doing stand-up, Cathy met comic Steve Mittleman "either in the bar at Catch A Rising Star or on a crosstown bus on the way to another gig." When he asked her out on a date, several months later, she had to refuse because it was the night of her first paying gig. They got together eventually, however, and began a relationship that lasted three years.

The common, all-engrossing lifestyle that helps draw and hold together both members of a comic/comic relationship can also present problems that drive them apart. The most insidious of these problems is career inequality—namely whose is happening and whose isn't. In the case of Cathy and Steve, her year of experience and no credits in the business were no match for his six years, one Letterman spot, commercial work, and a top prize in the New York Laff-Off. This type of intense, inter-career competition may sound strange to the outsider, even unhealthy. But in stand-up, where such details as moving up from a 1 A.M. to a 12:30 A.M. spot at "the club" are the central goals for which one lives, career comparisons, regardless of their context, are a logical extension for two people in this hyper-competitive business.

The difficult theme of career inequality was a recurring one in their relationship, as Steve remained more established throughout their relationship. Like many comic couples, they tried to work together but on the road, with Steve as an established headliner, Cathy had no option but to work as a middle or opening act. At first this was ideal, though she felt that being perceived as Steve's appendage held her back emotionally. Then, after two years, she started getting offered work as a co-headliner with other comics; at this point, working with him held her back professionally. She cites examples of several comedy couples who work together, but in each case it is the woman who is dragged along as part of the contract: "I feel I'm too talented for that; if I had to get jobs that way, I wouldn't want to be in this business." Steve and Cathy split up after three years for the reasons outlined above and another one that she says was the most important of all: "I always felt like I had trouble making him laugh—and that was very difficult."

Because the great influx of women into stand-up came several years after that of men, the relative career positions of the sexes are generally tipped in the men's favor. This was the case with Cathy and Steve but, she says, the problem was compounded by the fact that he could not grasp why the different points of their careers upset her. "He didn't like me feeling so competitive, but I didn't like feeling like an appendage. I tried to be supportive of him, but I didn't have the capacity to do it completely. I'd say, 'Honey, it's great you got that . . . but I want one, too.' I felt like I wasn't pulling my weight in the household, and I resented that."

If it sounds like this occupational rivalry is more intense than that of "civilians," that's because it is; but there's a reason. In any relationship where both partners work, there will likely be competition; if both work in the same field, the competition will probably be even more intense. In stand-up, however, where the occupation is a not indirect extension of one's ego, the stakes involved in the "who's ahead" game are much higher. The "you make more money" victory of a "normal" job competition is easier to accept than the "you are better liked" victory of stand-up (which then translates into more money anyway). The same principle operates in comics' friendships, but they aren't taken home.

The problem of being the "opening act" of a relationship is not restricted to women; it is a burden that falls on whoever is the less experienced of the couple. Adrianne Tolsch is a tough New York–based comic who has been in the business for almost ten years. As the emcee at Catch A Rising Star, her duties included booking the night's show from the talent pool (once, she says, the phone rang seventy times in a single afternoon), scheduling and mixing the acts—like a deejay—so they fall smoothly against one another, booking singers, handling the audience, introducing acts, getting the phone, getting laughs and keeping everyone happy. And yet, one night she had time to fall in love. In terms that lie somewhere between the boundaries of "lover" and "foreman," she describes their first encounter. "I was emceeing Monday nights and Bill [Schefft] came in to audition. He was scruffy and raw, but very funny. I gave him a few pointers about material, writing, and I said, 'Get a shave. Clean up!' And I think his second time, he passed. He had been working in a club in Staten Island on weekends for a year or so. He watched the comics every night, all night, and he was a good emcee with good administrative ability, so he could put a show together. That's how he started, then his act caught up with his emcee ability, which happens sometimes. Now he's on the road writing and emceeing. We've been living together almost two years and he's ten years younger than me—so we got a lot of flak from people."

For the two of them, the positive benefits of mutual support outweigh the negative aspects of comparison and competition. Adrianne says that the best part about a love relationship with another comedian is "suddenly, you're not alone." She describes getting onstage as being the easy part of life, where there are rules—where you can get verbally abused, but never seriously hurt, because you're ultimately in control: "It's the everyday part of life that is difficult, because anything goes." She adds that, because of their close involvement with one another's careers, she and Bill can give each other helpful advice that other comics either couldn't—or wouldn't be able to. "Bill is wonderful about helping me. He remembers everything I've ever said onstage. For the taping today [of a TV special on comedy], I couldn't think of any good anecdotes about being an emcee... but he reminded me of this bit about Mr. Zimmerman, who was the oldest auditioner we ever had at Catch. True story... Mr. Zimmerman was eighty-four years old—he went onstage and did one-liners until his teeth fell out and ruined his timing. It was so cute."

The onstage aloneness of the stand-up is an illusion; it is, for many comics, the time when they feel the least lonely. Offstage, where they're in closer physical contact with humanity, aloneness often becomes a reality. Alan Havey explains, "Comedians are notoriously lonely. It's the lifestyle—traveling, working late at night—it's hard to maintain a relationship. You're working in bars—flirting, around people with alcohol, on the road. And ultimately, you work alone also. You have friends, but you work alone... A lot of comics have trouble with relationships—with the odd hours and the constant travel you get used to being responsible for yourself and when someone else is involved it's tough." Being alone is not only the preference of some comics, but often their only alternative.

While this can be tough for men, it is often tougher for women comics. Why is that? Because in general, it's easier for a strong, witty man to meet women than for the same kind of woman to meet men. As Carol Siskind says, "Doing this makes it very hard to have a relationship—I hope I'm not a ball buster onstage; I try to be approachable, and I have met a few guys doing this who don't seem threatened by it, but it's a weird thing for a woman to do still. I need to meet someone who's very secure about what they do."

And if the female comic's problem of mixing love and jokes is difficult now, it was an even greater dilemma when Phyllis Diller began performing in 1955: "It was extremely unusual for a woman to be a comic, never mind supporting her family. But my husband was having a terrible time making a living. He was not fitted for that—for being out in the world. He's a man who suffers from agoraphobia." She says that, apart from the hours and travel, "it's also not good in a marriage for a woman to be extremely successful when the husband isn't." In her second marriage, her husband was in the same business as she, but things became equally difficult because, she says, "he wasn't as successful as I. A man cannot take that, unless he's very secure, and what makes him that secure is to be a success . . . so it's a bottomless pit . . . but I certainly couldn't bring myself down—that's phony." She feels that, while the situation is different today than it was when she began in the business, women still have a harder time dealing with success than men, "Their egos are much different than women's—are you aware of that? I think it has a lot to do with sex. Women's original role was as homemaker—they weren't supposed to do anything else—so remember, it's going to take millenniums to get away from that idea."

Fran Capo solved the problem of career conflict by getting her husband-to-be immersed in the business. She says, "I told my fiancé that before we get married he had to go up onstage so he'd know what it's like—how hard it is. So he did and did great. I was real depressed. But then I said, 'I did great my first time, too—try it again.' So he did and he bombed—and I said, okay, now you can stop. Now, we book clubs together. Last week one of our acts didn't show up so he had to get up and start telling old jokes—and he got by. We write together, we manage the Comedy House together, we have a business where we blow up balloons at home for this guy's balloon business. He says, 'I used to be normal—now I'm staying out at clubs all night and blowing up balloons all day . . . and I like it.' We were extras in a movie so I made him dress like a punk, holding a doll with a knife through it. I took a picture of us and he sent it to his mother in South Carolina and said, 'This is the girl I'm going to marry.' She was thrilled."

Being a "ball buster" is something male comics don't have to stay up nights worrying about, on the road or off it. In fact, according to many comics, it is guys with the aggressive acts that are approached most frequently by women after the show. As Jonathan Solomon tells it: "With road comics, the thing that keeps them going is trying to get laid . . . but that exhausts itself eventually, I'd think. There's a certain state of mind that the women just love—the subtext of the act is 'fuck you' and I'm not a fuck-you act. Women who want to sleep with me come up and say things like, 'You're the nicest guy I've ever met—I want to date you,' and once in a while it occurs, but not a lot. With some guys—I don't even know what they're driven by." He feels, also, that the thrill in these kinds of relationships burns out quickly—particularly if the comic is sober: "By sometime in your early twenties I think I and most other mature comics realize you can sleep with various people and that being settled you begin to lose interest in it and then there's the flip side, which is you have to wake up with them, and I'm not good at that at all. Also, I don't drink anymore, or do drugs—and to stay interested in some girl with the intelligence of a small novella, you need to be doing something until four A.M., or you're going to go to sleep. I wish I could do that, but I can't."

This principle doesn't operate for women, on the road or elsewhere. Carrie Snow says that aside from being scared off by the word "comedian," many men cannot accept the tremendous ego that comes with being a comic. She says the same is true of actresses, which is why so many marry doctors . . . "because they're such egomaniacs and they're gone a lot; just like firemen—I'll marry one or the other." The question of dating other comics is out, for her; she feels that the community is too insular and her mistakes would follow her from one club to the next.

Paul Provenza says that many comics on the road date waitresses (another option not open to women) partially because, in working at the clubs, they have a real understanding and appreciation of the comic psyche, but primarily because they're *there*. Waitresses, as a part of the comedy club, also represent an element of stability for the rootless comic who has no ties to solidarity in any given city. According to Alan Havey, "a lot of comics get involved with waitresses because they're in clubs and they understand, and they have the same hours. That's how I met my girlfriend." Dating waitresses is comforting, says Adrianne Tolsch: "It keeps them inside the established community there, around the club. It's like hanging out with the owners—they're used to dealing with comics . . . behavior precedents have been set already." Jerry Diner says that a lot of waitresses go out with comics and "some owners dig it, others don't," but there are comics who sleep with a different waitress in every city. Chris Dipetta says that, currently, out of the fourteen waitresses he employs, "two have been swooned away by a comic at one time or another. With certain people it's constant, with others they fall in love every week. One comic's looking to see how many waitresses he can possibly muster up, what he can do in a week—with others, they see one and just fall in love with them and want to be with them all week. The guys are on the road, they're away from home for a week, they don't have anyone to talk to. Naturally they're trying to score, but at the same time it's pretty lonely out there—it has a lot to do with being lonely." Other than "girl in every port" set-ups, relationships are very difficult for comics to maintain. They must be adapted to this strange, uncertain lifestyle, where new parameters must be drawn nightly. Ultimately, the comic must face the fact that unless the partner is either unusually understanding, independent or a comic, any relationship will be limited.

The definition of "limited" can range from Provenza's "You don't get to see the person you love all the time" to many road comics' "Last night was fun, what's your name again?" Again, the latter types of relationships (or relations) are more common among men. The option of going into a bar alone, simply to meet and talk with people, doesn't exist for women in most cities—especially during the after-work hours of a comic. Adrianne Tolsch says that, in most of the country, you're dealing with provincial ideas about women, basically that if they go into a bar it's to be picked up. "Someone will come up to you real polite and say, 'Hey, little lady, can I buy you a drink?' If you say sure, it's 'Hey, Zeke, I got me a hooker!' That gets to you."

In the realm of "normalcy," there are comics who marry civilians, but this is more of a phenomenon than a rule. Some comics say marriage is uncommon among them because they are inherently rootless creatures, that the footloose element which attracts them to stand-up governs their relationships as well. Others say that they are drawn to stand-up because of an inability to maintain a one-on-one relationship, and that for them, the love of many is a substitute for the love of one. Abby Stein says that, for her, stand-up was a way of making up for the love she didn't have as a child, that it became a substitute for a relationship—until she met her husband. Today, like many women, having made the decision to marry, she is faced with the problem of career versus family. For now she is backing down from stand-up, "because you have to almost not have any life. I want a husband and a family and there are things I want as a person in my life." As a mother, her options would be further limited by road work: "People say, 'But you can do both—you'll have the baby and take it on the road,' but who can and who wants to. I don't want to live in a hotel room, and you can't make a living doing stand-up in New York alone." She never wants to give up stand-up completely, she says, but neither will she continue to do it for a living.

The conflict between stand-up and a stable relationship is not confined to women, though perhaps it may be more accentuated in their case. Tom Dreesen, who today has made over fifty appearances on "The Tonight Show," separated from his wife several times, before he became successful, because of his inability to make a living in stand-up. The problem of constant travel didn't exist during this time (the early 70s) because comics' only option was to stay in New York or Los

Angeles and work the showcase clubs; instead they faced the problem
of making no money, which is often equally detrimental to a relationship.

In Dreesen's case, he had been working small clubs in Chicago,
catching cheap opening gigs here and there for several years, barely
supporting his wife and children. Finally, he decided to risk everything, move to Los Angeles and become a star. Things didn't work out
that way. After a few days his money ran out and he spent a month
sleeping in the back seat of an abandoned Nash Rambler. In the morning he would go to a gas station to wash up, then hitchhike around
during the day looking for work. He ate one meal a day at Kentucky
Colonel (where they had a special—"Corn and Cluck for Under a
Buck"—"two pieces of chicken, corn, a biscuit and gravy for ninety-
nine cents") and had no luck at all. Finally, he says, his wife realized
he wasn't coming right back and wrote him a "Dear John" letter: "She
loved me and hoped I became a big star, but she didn't want to put the
kids through this anymore—not knowing from week to week whether
or not we'd have grocery money." Months later, he finally got on at the
Comedy Store, where he was seen by Carl Reiner, who cast him in a
TV special called "Take Me Out to the Ball Game" with his son Rob.

For this performance, he received $500, which he used to regain his
family. "I took that money and went to Canada and did a TV show
there that allowed comics on, and I took the money from that, took it
to Chicago and worked with Fats Domino at Mr. Kelly's for two weeks,
and got enough cash to bring my family out here, get an apartment,
draw unemployment and go work out at the Comedy Store (for free) to
try to make it."

While the general incompatibility of personal relationships and
stand-up is, for some comics, a severe drawback, for others it's a valuable fringe benefit. Emo Philips says, "It keeps my relationships nice
and shallow. A hotel owner never tells me, 'Emo, I want you to mow
the lawn, or put in the salt blocks, or shovel the snow off the front
step...' So it's a nice existence, and I've really adapted to it very well.
It doesn't matter to me whether I'm traveling or in the same place. I
honestly don't care." While he has a "close friendship" with comic
Judy Tenuta, Emo insists that she is not a girlfriend in any sense he

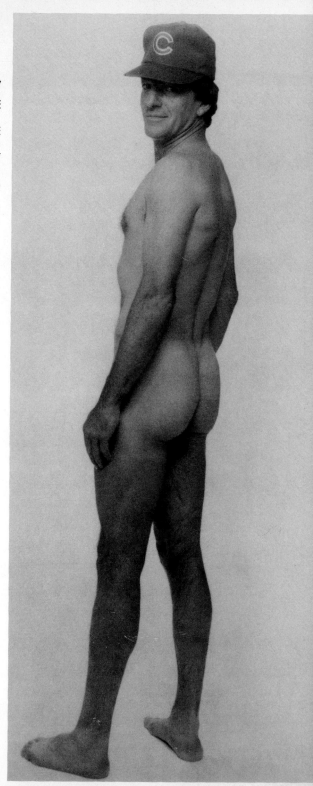

TOM DREESEN, "YOU CAN HAVE EVERYTHING I'VE GOT, BUT DON'T TOUCH MY CUBS HAT!"

JONOTHAN SOLOMON
WRITING JOKES

KIP ADOTTA IN NEW YORK

Credit: Dave Shelton

BILL GRUNDFEST

JERRY SEINFELD

FRAN CAPO AT "SUDS,"
NEW YORK CITY

RICHARD BELZER
ONSTAGE AT
CAROLINE'S,
NEW YORK CITY

Credit: Dave Shelton

A. WHITNEY BROWN ON
"SATURDAY NIGHT LIVE"'S
WEEKEND UPDATE

A BBY STEIN

(P)AUL
RODRIGUEZ
AT CAROLINE'S
COMEDY CLUB,
NEW YORK CITY

Credit: Dave Shelton

(S)TEVE
MITTLEMAN
BACKSTAGE AT
JOAN RIVERS'S
"THE LATE SHOW"

 HYLLIS DILLER

AT HOME

 LAN KING

O TONY
DEPAUL
ONSTAGE AT
THE HOLY
CITY ZOO

Credit: Steve Depaul

O JERRY DINER

E MO PHILIPS

Credit: Cathy
Cheney

J UDY TENUTA, THE PETITE FLOWER

Ⓐ DRIANNE
TOLSCH

Credit: Elizabeth
Wolynski

ARRIE SNOW

TOM PARKS

Credit: Bosco

CAROL SISKIND

Credit: Jean Strongin

R ITA
RUDNER

Credit: Dave Sh⟨

P AUL PROVENZA
WITH HIS MOM, BEA BASS,
AND DAVID BRENNER ON
THE SET OF "NIGHTLIFE"

Credit: Dave Shelton

B OB GOLDTHWAIT

BACKSTAGE WITH

PAL DEE SNIDER

AND OMNIPRESENT

CASE OF TAB

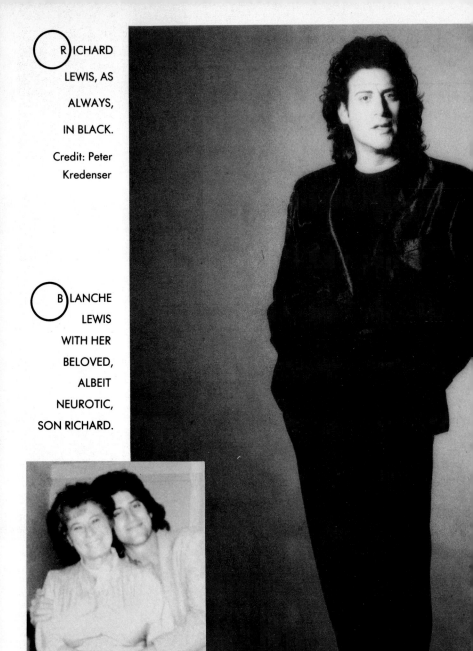

RICHARD LEWIS, AS ALWAYS, IN BLACK.

Credit: Peter Kredenser

BLANCHE LEWIS WITH HER BELOVED, ALBEIT NEUROTIC, SON RICHARD.

would like to explain, saying, "You must remember, we're free—we're earth people... I think she's one of the most naturally funny people I've ever met. We never actually had sex or anything, but we went out—she's such a fun person, everything about her is so wonderful, so full of life. She has a Zorba the Greek zest for existence; I'm more like Sartre. He actually did fine with girls—he'd say, 'Sure I look like a frog, but I wrote *Being and Nothingness*.'"

While he says, "I'm a very affectionate person," he claims to have no desire to settle down with anyone in the conventional sense; like many road comics, he doesn't even have a permanent address. Significant relationships, for him, are friendships that change daily. "Everyone is my friend," he says. "I really don't like to keep friendships alive if the person isn't right there. I like everyone as much as anyone else."

Many comics mirror Emo's distaste for attachment, but draw the line at his apparent commitment to celibacy. While realizing that no comic is an island, many come as close to being detachable peninsulas as is humanly possible—particularly the "road warriors," who literally have no homes. Others accept the side-effects of life in the up-and-coming lane as temporary barriers to stable relationships, and work toward the success that will bring fame, money... and love.

"At this particular time in my life I've got everything I ever hoped for, except that my love life isn't where I want it, and that's only because I don't have the time. But that's my next project," explains Yakov Smirnoff: "I want kids, a two-car garage, a dog, the picket fence—but I don't want a divorce. That's why I'm thirty-four and I haven't been married. I feel it's very important to know what you want in life. As far as my career, I knew what I wanted and even though everyone said I was crazy, I did it. It doesn't matter what happens next because I'm happy now, so it can only get better. I have plenty of money, I do what I like to do and I'm in control of the situation. I want that out of marriage—to know that if some gorgeous woman passes me by, I won't look and say, 'I wish I was there.'"

His parents, whom he brought to this country with him from the Soviet Union, have lobbied, very strongly in the past, for him to marry. Five years ago it was a major issue, but now he has become adamant about making his own decision: "If they drop hints about one of my dates like, 'Oh, we like her,' I say, 'Fine, you want to adopt her? Go ahead. But that's not my future wife.' I'm prepared to wait."

Richard Belzer, now on his third marriage, believes that stand-up comedy does not preclude stable personal relationships, or love; it's simply a matter of the right time and the right person. Having moved to Los Angeles partly as a concession to his wife and partly because of his own career, today he is very happily married and the stepfather of two daughters. In describing the current state of his life, he leaves no doubt as to its quality: "To be honest," he says, "I didn't know Jews could be this happy."

HECKLERS
AND
HORRORS

Whatever the psychological elements that combine to bring a stand-up to the stage, one can be sure they're damn powerful; to keep an otherwise sane person running back to that elusive "point" every night, against all odds, they'd have to be. But once he gets to that mythical place, cause and effect pale under the glare of the keen stand-up mind at work. Onstage, a comic listens to the beat of the room—a fine-tuned sensory outfielder, he waits for the imperceptible signals of the group, identifies their pattern, and throws back whatever the group is unconsciously begging for, be it honey or vinegar.

The mood of an audience is determined by various factors, including the room in which they sit, the type of people they are, and even the day and time of the show. Adrianne Tolsch describes the de-evolution of a club crowd on a typical Friday night: "The early show is usually a good one; people are still wide awake and, because it's a weekend, in a good mood. By the second show, because people have been either working or going to school all day and it's now twelve thirty in the morning, they're probably more tired than they realize, and they may have also been drinking since quittin' time." She says that, with few exceptions, "that's the worst show, anywhere in the country—you can almost guarantee it's whip and chair time . . ."

Before a comic takes the stage, he must try to identify as many potential problems as possible and come prepared to act on a combination of conditioned responses and an instinct for survival. Saturday, first
show, is supposedly the easiest one of the week; the people are rested,
relaxed and ready to laugh but, according to Adrianne, on out-of-town
gigs, during this show, a woman is still like live bait. "Take Savannah,
Georgia," she says, "the town smells like a fart, because there's a
sulphur base in the water. It's incredible, and seeing a woman onstage
in a comedy club—in a nightclub—does not thrill them. A lot of
towns are Baptist, conservative—they find it threatening and they
don't think it's funny. A lot of times, the smaller the town, the more
trouble. I had a lot of trouble in Columbia, South Carolina, but sometimes you just have to do those gigs. I get my laughs here and there,
but it takes longer to warm them up. I have to couch my material differently, put on a different front. I try to make it evident I'm there to
entertain, not antagonize. I say, 'Those of you who have never seen a
lady comic before, I'm here to entertain you, not to make you uncomfortable,' but then I may say, 'So let's start with this guy's shirt . . .' I
hate doing places like that. I do it for money—and I like to travel."

For Abby Stein, these kinds of jobs—which the comic knows in
advance will be an hour-long descent into hell—are never fun, but
one does get used to them: "It becomes like, 'Did you have a bad day at
work?'—like any ordinary job. But you know in advance, a lot of
times, that it's going to be bad. You know that there's absolutely no way
you can do a real show, but you take the job because you need the
money. I'm talking about things like one-nighters in New Jersey—
these are zoo type gigs." This kind of thing "gets to you," agrees George
Calfa, ". . . making your living playing gigs you don't want, after begging people for them on the phone, but what else are you going to do?"
In addition to playing them because they need the money, comics also
play them in order to get to the next level on the comedy ladder. In
order to prove themselves to owners and bookers, a comic often has to
play *all* of the clubs in that person's control—starting with the worst.

Calfa remembers one incident, while playing a one-nighter in up-
state New York, where he was heckled en masse: "The crowd was so
bad it was like a horror movie. They were shouting, 'Get off, get

off . . .'" So he decided to battle rudeness with obnoxiousness. "I kept saying, 'The only way I can get off is if you give me a standing ovation.' Finally they did, so I came back and said, 'This is the first standing ovation I ever got—I'd better do an encore.' I thought they'd kill me." But regardless of how many of these situations he faces, when he thinks about how many awful things *could* happen, he is amazed at how little actually does happen. He says, for instance, that instead of just verbal heckling, "people could throw things a lot . . . or physically assault the comic."

But that isn't to say that these things never happen. Often, the combination of a comic's artistic license onstage (his ability to say anything to anyone) and some people in the audience's inability to take a joke is the catalyst for these kinds of attacks. Once, at the Comic Strip, Calfa narrowly avoided being taken apart. He remembers, "I was saying something to these thuglike guys in the corner and when I got offstage, they said, 'Now you're going to have to pay!' So I ran onstage and grabbed the mike stand to defend myself . . . but then some people came in and helped me—it was pretty scary." Another time, he says, "I was working to a great crowd, but there were these four guys who were disruptive, so I started saying stuff to this guy. He said, 'I'm gonna kick your fuckin' ass!' and the other guy who was stupid, but not as much, said, 'No, Joey, that's what a comedian does, he's makin' fun of you, that's the whole comedy thing, and the audience laughs, you know.' I stopped and said, 'Please, listen to your friend, Joey.'"

Other comics have not been so lucky. Alan Havey was once stabbed with a pencil by a crazed female patron. Tom Dreesen remembers, in the days when he was part of a double act with Tim Reid (who later went on to become Venus Flytrap on "WKRP in Cincinnati"), "One night, one drunk walked by, put a lit cigarette out in Tim's face . . . I jumped up and threw a punch at the guy, and the whole place was up for grabs: tables and chairs knocked over—the guy picked me up and broke the table in half with my legs . . . and he was holding me so tight I almost suffocated. It was a real donnybrook. That's one of the worst things that's ever happened." He says that comics are particularly vulnerable up there because the light is directly in their faces, so they can't see where a potential attacker is coming from. Jonathan Solomon says that he was once attacked by a drunk man (who was also 6'4") and nobody came onstage to help, which made it particularly upsetting. Another time, he remembers, in Washington, a man threw a drink at him onstage. But, he says, "because I'd been on the road a couple of weeks already and I hated it, this worked out fine. It gave me an excuse to end the show, put down the mike, chase him into the lobby, and get into a fight, which immediately liberated me from about two weeks worth of hostility."

Paul Rodriguez relates a story that describes the alternately vulnerable and invincible position of the stand-up onstage—the clash between his open invitation to violence and the impregnable nature of his comic persona: "I do my act in Spanish, too, and I was at a club called Pantera Rosa—the Pink Panther—which lets you know what kind of club it was . . . a lot of Charo look-alikes with sagging breasts, and after them it's 'and now a funny comic straight from the Barrio . . .' So I'm up there and, at the time, the El Salvador death squads were in full swing, and I was discussing this onstage. I was saying how ironic it is that the bloodiest country in Central America is named after Jesus. Suddenly some drunk Salvadoran comes onstage and punches me square in the face. Before I realize what's happening I punched him back, and I got lucky, he fell to the ground . . . and it was like a comic rim shot—I just moved on to the next joke without missing a beat. It was like, 'Boom! . . . but seriously folks, how about these wacky Salvadorans—this is the first time I've been heckled by a death squad.' The audience went from shock to laughing again—it was crazy. I was proud that I didn't lose my rhythm—and what's strange is my face didn't swell onstage. It's like up there I'm immortal, secure, quick—when I come offstage I become weak and mortal again . . . and I don't know if it's adrenaline, but right when I got offstage my face started to swell . . .".

Generally, however, any comic's physical encounters onstage can be counted on one hand—more often, one finger. But these incidents make the rounds through the stand-up grapevine, and serve to plant the knowledge firmly in a comic's mind that the worst thing they can possibly imagine happening, *can* really happen. And, of course, there are certain kinds of verbal insults that rival physical abuse for the amount of pain inflicted. While there is some relief to be derived from not being told, "Your act sucks—get off the fucking stage!", it fades quickly when one hears instead, "You're a fat, ugly pig—get off the fucking stage!" Insults about appearance are almost exclusively aimed at women.

Carol Siskind says that, for this kind of torment, "New York is the best training... those clubs are open until four A.M. Do you know what it's like to go up on Friday night at three thirty A.M. when people have been drinking since five o'clock that evening? They can be animals—guys comment on what you look like, what you're wearing..." But this kind of behavior is not restricted to the Big Apple: "I worked in Virginia and there were some real piggy guys there. I heard them talking about what I was wearing and saying things like, 'She's not bad...' or 'She's not very attractive.'"

In these "personal" situations, Carol says, she acts as she does in any heckling episode: "I try to ignore them... or I state my position right away. Recently I was headlining in a club; before me, the middle act had been heckled so badly he got offstage after five minutes. So when I got up there I started by saying, 'Look, I'm gonna tell you right now, I'm not paying any attention to you... there are regular people who pay to have a good time and they shouldn't have to listen to this shit.'" If this attitude doesn't work, however, she is forced to get just as personal with the heckler as he has gotten with her... which she does by working him into her act: "I do a thing about being horny... it's the bit about that Harvey's Bristol Cream ad, where I say that commercial has nothing to do with drinking, it has to do with being horny. I tell them, 'I don't know if men are ready for this. They like to think being horny is their idea—they don't know we think about sex as much as they do, but the thing is, being horny is the same for all of us. You know when you're horny, you know when you have it bad, when everyone starts to look good... the guy who picks up trash in the morning, "Look at the way he ties that hefty bag..."' So, when someone's giving me shit all night, I do this bit and say, '... even the garbage man... even that schmuck over there—that asshole sitting over there,' and it gets an enormous round of applause."

Like all comics, her responses to hecklers are usually not ad-libs, but cold, calculated antidotes to what she knows can easily slip from innocent fun into a malignant problem. To develop this kind of heckler-deflecting skill takes years; like writing and timing, it is developed with the benefit of those lovable comic twins: time and pain. Adrianne Tolsch says that, like stand-up in general, the key to dealing with hecklers is to remember, "It's all about control." She learned this early after an episode in which she was heckled and froze: "A guy yelled something at me, so I hurled a non sequitur at him. He said, 'You suck!' and I said, 'It's not that I have enough insurance!' and he got hysterical. I realized, it's not what you say, it's how fast and forcefully you say it . . . it's that control thing." Now, she says, "I love when people talk to me—especially hecklers, which are my favorites. My whole background is of being a bigmouth—of improvisation."

Carol Leifer says that, before she developed a set of appropriate responses, one of the hardest parts of performing was the fear of being heckled. She remembers the first time it happened. "I put my middle finger down and said, 'Can you hear this?' The guy said no, and I turned it upward and said, 'Here, let me turn it up for you.' That's all I knew how to do—and it didn't help." But since then, she's learned how to take care of herself, mainly by assuming an attitude of "You're so trivial, what you're doing has no effect on me . . . sometimes I get guys whistling. They think, by doing that, they're going to make me really angry, so what I do when that happens—and it's so humiliating to the guy—is to say, 'Wait a minute. Did you just actually whistle? Boy, doesn't this guy have a way with women?' So he feels really stupid—when his intent was to make me angry." She points out many subtle things that can be done to shut up a persistent heckler. "Say it's a table of loud, drunk guys. I ask them, 'So, where are the girls tonight?' and they're immediately embarrassed. Then I say, 'I guess they're still out parking the car, right?' It becomes a case of, 'You're heckling me because you're obviously frustrated.' If they're real jerks, I say, 'No women with you tonight? I wonder why . . .' (to the audience), which gets a big laugh and makes them feel stupid so they shut up." Carol Siskind says that she wrote some jokes to deal specifically with hecklers when she discovered, in several small towns, that "I was the first woman comic a lot of people had ever seen onstage, and sometimes they said unbelievable things to me!" In addition to other tactics, she used a plea for sympathy, saying, "You're the kind of guy who comes here when deer season is over. You want to go home with a comic strapped across the hood of your car and have it in your den: 'Improv, '86.'"

George Calfa remembers that in the beginning, he prayed nobody would say anything to him, and if they did he responded with, "Yeah? Well, fuck you!" That was his only solution. Now, however, after years of practice, he says, "I just don't take shit from people. I've realized that you have to get the audience on your side instead of the heckler's. Because if they side with him, you're dead." Based upon this principle, he has developed an anti-heckler system that works with a high accuracy rate, and says, "Now I don't fear anything; if someone says, 'You're not funny!' I stop and say, 'How many people think I'm funny? Clap your hands.' So people clap and I say, 'Well, I guess you're wrong. They like it—you're just too stupid to understand what's going on.'" The only catch is if the audience doesn't clap, in which case, he says, "you're dead . . . but there are other tricks to get them with you again, like saying, 'This crowd paid money to see comedy, not to hear you,' and they're like, 'Yeah! We paid money to hear him!' Or I'll say, 'What's your name? Vinnie?' and then, 'At the count of three, everybody yell, Vinnie, shut the fuck up!' And you get two hundred seventy-five people going, 'Shut the fuck up, Vinnie,' and that's power, it works—this guy is dead. It's like some scene out of the Middle Ages, 'Burn Vinnie, burn Vinnie . . .'"

Views on why people heckle a comic differ from one stand-up to the next. Carol Leifer feels it's the result of a need for attention—a need to be heard and acknowledged by the performer. Paul Reiser believes that "it's a very egotistical thing to go onstage and say, 'I have something to say; listen.' And that's why there's heckling. It's a challenge to that statement. 'What do you have to say that's so important?'" He believes there are two responses people have when they identify someone as a funny person, and both responses are equally constraining: "Either they expect you to be funny, or they don't allow you to be funny, and either one is a real insult to me."

Abby Stein explains that some kinds of hecklers can help a show (though she says she'd always prefer there not to be one): "If they just yell one thing, it gives you the chance to say something funny, but if they're a drunk, incoherent person they'll usually just step on your punch lines." Richard Belzer says that hecklers can range from mean-spirited drunks to people who just go out to have a good time and want to feel a part of the show: "They are all people who want to make contact with the performer, on all different levels, and I've seen them all. You can tell right away, by a person's attitude, intonation, what they say, if they're just mean, or drunk, if they do or don't know what they're saying. Not every heckler is a mindless person. And of course some think they're making a contribution . . . they're the ones who you want to grab by the throat. They're the kind of people who would knock the skull out of Hamlet's hand during a Shakespearean play—they break the third, fourth and fifth wall, and make their own wall."

Belzer's ability to identify and deal with all types of hecklers does not come from some innate gift; it's the result of working as the emcee at Catch A Rising Star every night for five long years. This kind of experience is crucial not only in allowing a comic to hone his responses, but also to know when they are—and aren't—appropriate. Carol Siskind explains: "If someone up front is heckling you—if they're not in the center of the room where everyone can hear them, it's very insidious because it eats away at your ego but no one else knows what's going on. So the choice to deal with them could ruin the set for the whole audience—there's that moment when you have to evaluate that." Many comics have made the wrong decision and "dealt with" the person. Because the crowd hasn't heard the heckling, they assume the comic is picking on the person gratuitously . . . and turn on him.

Emo Philips believes that identifying different kinds of hecklers is a talent that comes with experience: "I can usually spot whether or not people are drunk, or suffering from some nerve damaging disease—after awhile you get a sixth sense about how these people act." Having mastered this means of heckler-labeling, he feels he can use them as positive additions to the show. "I like hecklers; they show that the audience is alive." It's all a matter of how one handles them: "Once I was onstage and a fight broke out," he recalls, "so I emceed it," but he adds, "last night, a drunk woman came onstage and that was sort of scary; I don't mind whatever happens as long as the people are conscious." Generally, however, he says it's rare to have a drunk person jump onstage, so he just takes Nietzsche's approach: "That which doesn't kill me makes me stronger," but adds (in the case of Nietzsche), "I don't know if having your brain eaten up by syphilis is the best form of exercise."

Steve Mittleman says that sometimes he has made the right decision —other times, he wishes he hadn't responded at all. Once, he remembers, "a guy yelled, 'You look Jewish,' and I said, 'Oh? You look prejudiced.' It got a scream in the first ten seconds." Another time, however, he moved too quickly in responding to an anti-Semitic statement: "I was in Toledo, Ohio. My brother and his wife drove in from Chicago, and it was the first time they had seen me perform. The crowd heckled the act before me unmercifully, but she kept encouraging it by taking shots at people, particularly one guy. So then I go up. I'm doing my set and I mentioned the National Rifle Association and this guy to the right of me yells out, 'Shoot the niggers.' I look over in shock, and then another guy, to the left of me, yells out, 'Shoot the kikes.' I totally broke character and said, 'Listen, don't ever say that again, we're all people . . .' and I went into a whole preaching thing about being Jewish and whatever, and said, 'And you shouldn't knock black people . . .' After a while the police came and took the 'kike' guy out, and the other guy, at my right, kept quiet. I did another fifteen minutes or so and cut it short and got off. After the show this group of guys comes up to me, they're wearing yarmulkes, and they say, 'We feel kind of bad—we were yelling stuff out, but we didn't say "shoot the kike," we said, "shoot that guy." We would never say "shoot the kike!"' They were from a Jewish fraternity in Bowling Green . . . Then, as if I wasn't humiliated enough, I asked my brother what he heard, and he said, 'I heard, "shoot that guy!"'"

Since that time, he has taken a different, novel approach. "I had a heckler recently at the Comedy Store and instead of ripping him apart, I said, 'Sir, I just want to share the fact that I really love you and care about you.' He kept quiet and had no idea what to say to that. It was the total opposite of what he wanted, which was total attention. He wanted to manipulate the show in his corner, he was insecure and probably drunk and threatened, either for the people around him or himself, and he wanted to be the star of the show. I pulled it off because my voice was straight—and because I really meant it in a way."

People often truly believe that heckling the comic helps the show. Every comic who has worked for any amount of time has had the following experience: after a show in which they are heckled mercilessly, the heckler approaches them afterwards, as friendly as can be, saying, "How'd I do? Did I help you out?" Mittleman remembers that he used to rip these people apart, saying: "Do you have any idea what you did to this show, not for just me, but for everybody else in the audience? You wrecked it!"

Regardless of how much blame an audience has to bear, many comics feel that heckling has a lot to do with the comic as well. Paul Provenza says that many "rockets out the ass" acts (comics who spew a stream of gratuitous expletives, yell insults at the audience, use ridiculous or vulgar props) set a rodeo atmosphere in the clubs. Provenza believes this "promotes hecklers who think they're helping the acts. They get drunk and start screaming back—and it's not helpful! This is comedy—a man or woman talking about something that's important to them . . . it's not a tractor pull."

Joe Bolster says that while he is not confrontational, many acts are and, "once you start tearing someone down, you're open to having anything come back at you." He avoids being heckled not only because he doesn't "zing anyone in the audience" but also "because my act is so fast that even if you wanted to say something, it would be difficult to find the time to do it . . . a heckler would have to have incredible timing to interrupt. Occasionally they must be dealt with and you think, 'Okay, it's a drunk table, this has happened before, here's how I handle it.'" But he adds, "I never turn on them; I say, 'What's going on? You having a good time?' and try to involve them in the show." He estimates that, for him, a true heckling incident happens in one show out of ten.

Even though Carol Leifer has an inbred resentment of hecklers, she says, "I see some comics who should get heckled. Their attitude is very cocky—'You're the audience, you don't know anything, I know every-thing, so just shut up.' I don't think of the audience that way, and I don't think of my act as mean or surly—that's why I resent hecklers." A comic can also avoid heckling by becoming successful, Leifer points out: "If people know you've been on Letterman and HBO, you have credibility before you get on; it's like, 'Add on fifty points.' When you're nobody, people are just waiting for you to be bad."

While infrequent, there are incidents of comics heckling comics. When Steve Mittleman was eighteen, before becoming a comic, he went to the New York Improv and, after having a few drinks, yelled something out at the comic. It was the only time he did anything like that, he says, and because of it, "I know it's humanly possible for *anyone* to become a heckler." Jerry Diner, 1986 President of the PCA, uses heckling as a weapon against comics who steal others' material: "That's what I fight when I'm on the road . . . The reason I *can* fight it is because these comics are afraid of me because when I say, 'If you do that material I'll heckle you,' they know I will, because it's my only weapon. I can't beat someone up, but I can heckle them. I don't say, 'You suck,' which is what most hecklers do. I will take the material they're doing, and twist it around so that I'm funnier than them, and everyone sees that it's happening in the audience."

Bob Goldthwait once experienced a case of inter-comic heckling that was neither innocent nor for a good cause. He recalls, "I was onstage screaming 'Down with America!' and stuff like that, saying: 'I'm not a Communist . . . I'm not anything. But I hate politicians—they're just comedians who don't have acts. They have big egos and think, "Geez, I need a job and I don't have an act . . . I know, I'll be the president!"' Then I said, 'It's unbelievable; if I talk about Reagan up here I'm a pithy intellectual, and if I talk about my dick I'm crude. To tell the truth, I can't tell the difference between the two. But I think I'll go back to talking about my dick, because it wasn't as scary in here then . . .' After that, I heard this Southern voice, that's been heckling me all night, yell, 'Yeah, well why don't you go back to talking about your dick, you were funnier then.' So I said, 'Oh great, the Czar of Comedy is here,' and started crying and said, 'Oh sir, I don't care if anybody else in the audience liked me, I just wanted you to like me.' And I was really crying—I can do that whenever I want, because I'm always ready to cry."

A few seconds later, the heckler walked up onstage and, Goldthwait says, "it turned out to be [he names a well-known comic]—and he's loaded. He gets a cheap slut round of applause because everyone knows who he is. So I let him take the mike, and he didn't say anything. I said, 'Oh, you got a night off from Vegas so you thought you'd come blow me some shit? If you want to get on the stage, why don't you go sign up like the rest of us poor slobs.' Then I said, 'I thought most dinosaurs were dead now—why don't you go to a video store and hock your video rentals you whore fuck!' By this time, the crowd's going bozo, when suddenly a glass, thrown a good fifty feet, smashes onstage. Dee Snyder was there, and he gets up and yells, 'You fuck!' But the crowd didn't want anyone to help, they wanted to see what was going to happen. I said to my manager, 'When someone pulled a gun, is that when you were going to help?' So what happened was it started becoming fun. I got the audience back, they were laughing, and I said, 'I don't want this to be fun. That man just threw a glass. He didn't care about you and you guys could have been hurt, and so could I. Think about what this means. Goodnight.'"

In addition to confronting merciless hecklers, stand-ups have to face various general horrors that run, if not rampant, then with fair consistency in their line of work. Because of the live, immediate nature of their business, they have all the pleasure and pain associated with the word "impromptu." Comics' reminiscences of their lives onstage are rife with stories that would curl the hair of less hearty performers.

Paul Provenza remembers the night he had to perform after the following announcement was made to the audience: "Ladies and Gentlemen, we have some horrible news for you. John Lennon was shot and killed today in front of his apartment in New York City. Now welcome, please, the comedy of Paul Provenza!" Other, lesser, difficult situations have arisen for him, but none so far has compared to this. Most comics have been forced to go on after some star makes his annual (or even regular) guest appearance at a showcase club—stand-ups' reminiscences abound with horror stories of following Robin Williams, who was on a roll, Eddie Murphy, whose sharp language and mere presence left the audience in a Von Bulowesque coma, and any number of other tough-acts-to-follow.

Paul experienced a uniquely disheartening situation of this kind: "I was at the Improv and Rodney Dangerfield came in to do a guest set right before I went on. He absolutely killed—and I had to follow him. I didn't feel so bad at the time, until someone came up to me afterwards—a sketch artist. He drew a little cartoon of me, as a very small figure onstage, and this looming figure of Dangerfield hanging over me, devouring me. He said, 'I know how you must feel,' and he gave me the picture. I told him thanks, but I didn't feel that way until you gave it to me."

Perhaps the only thing more frightening than battling against a drunken audience, for a comic, is going onstage drunk. Paul Rodriguez describes the experience as thinking you're great on the surface, but, "no matter how high or how drunk you are, you know, deep down, that you're fucking up . . . one New Year's Eve I was at a party drinking, and everyone started saying, 'Come on—tell some jokes,' so I went up . . . and made a fool of myself, and I said, 'I'll never do this again.'" Paul Provenza's ultimate comic nightmare came true after he got drunk *accidentally* before going onstage: "Recently, I was working in Vegas with Diana Ross and an old friend was visiting me. Between shows, I took him to this place called the 'Bacchanal Room' in Caesar's Palace—it's a fixed-price place, like ninety-five dollars a meal. The first show was at eight thirty, I was offstage by nine, and the next show started at eleven thirty—so that gave me two-and-a-half hours to eat dinner. It was like this eleven course meal—and some woman in a courtesan outfit with a jug on her shoulder kept filling my glass up . . . Well, I'm not a drinker, but it's a special occasion so I'm having wine, and never having seen an empty glass I didn't realize how much I was having. Finally, we're about eight courses into the meal and it's eleven twenty-five. The stage manager comes over and says, 'What's going on?' So I stood up and almost passed out. But I raced down, got onstage, and did the whole show—hanging on to the curtain behind me. I was terrified, but no one knew because I was on automatic pilot. In the back of my head there's a dialogue taking place with myself, 'This is the end of my career—onstage with Diana Ross at Caesar's Palace —and I'm going to piss on myself.' There's a rumor of a comedian who did that in Vegas once—and I thought I'd end up like him. But it went off without a hitch."

Paul is probably speaking about Kip Adotta. (Although he would not give a name.) A persistent rumor circulates among comics that in 1980, Adotta performed drunk, in Las Vegas, and wet his pants onstage. The catch is, Kip claims that this incident never happened. If he's lying, it's a sad legacy. But if what he says is true, this makes the story more unfortunate, and horrifying, than if it had happened. He explains the incident this way: "I'd done 'The Tonight Show' dozens of times, Douglas, Merv—I'd done five hundred national TV shows at that time, so I had credibility . . . but no one ever asked me about the incident; they just assumed it was true, and because of that, I was blackballed from every TV show, every important venue in the country.

"What happened is that I was opening for someone in Vegas and the fellow I was opening for had the hots for my lady, and every time I was onstage his bodyguards were all over her saying so-and-so wants to party with you. She said, 'Kip and I will be glad to party with you,' but they said so-and-so doesn't want Kip. One thing led to another and I finally said, 'This will not happen. I'm here to open your show; I'm not going to play cards with you, serve you drinks or have you sleep with my women. You don't pay me that much.' The next night, I was fired under the guise that I had wet my pants onstage, and the next day I was out of the business. 'The Tonight Show' wouldn't return my calls, the 'Merv Griffin Show' wouldn't—I couldn't get hired anywhere. But no one ever asked me what happened; they just assumed I'd actually pulled my pants off and peed onstage—and the rumors grew, that I had defecated onstage—my God! But no one has ever asked me. They'd just say (sweetly) 'How are you, Kip?'—like I'd just gotten out of a mental institution and they were wondering if I was stable."

Citing the example of Jackie Mason (who was blackballed from television in 1964 for supposedly making a vulgar hand gesture on the "Ed Sullivan Show"), Kip says that he is not the first victim of this kind of thing, nor will he be the last, as long as people are so quick to condemn without knowing all of the facts. "Human beings don't change. Different generations come along and make the same mistakes, thinking they're more sophisticated, but people are just as petty and ruthless as they've always been. People are blackballed today just like during the McCarthy years; no difference. The same people who make a TV special about that era and say how awful it is will turn around and blackball people from that show." Like Mason, he began working the club circuit instead of doing television—and, as happened with Mason, he became quite financially successful doing it.

Today, he says "it's all behind me, the storm has passed. At the taping yesterday [for "Comedy Tonight"] about six people came up to me and said, 'You look terrific, how are you? You look terrific...' I wanted to show them, 'No needle marks...' What no one knows about Kip Adotta is that, in the meantime, I've raised three fine children, I'm forty-one years old, I've had a long history of business and family before this... but I didn't talk about it in my material. I have a twenty-three-year-old, a nineteen-year-old and a seventeen-year-old. They were hurt by this—'Your dad is a drug addict, he has no control over his bowels...' of course it hurts... but I've survived it."

There is no shortage of comic horror stories—inflicted by either themselves or others. Jonathan Solomon says that even simple things like exhaustion can be deadly to a stand-up—particularly on weekends in the showcase clubs when comics race from one club to the next to capitalize on higher weekend rates. If a stand-up is not well rested, after he performs the same act three or four times he can begin to repeat himself—telling the same joke twice in one set, which tends to nudge the crowd closer to hostility than they may already be. He gives another example of exhaustion, which must rank as one of the most extreme cases: "I know one comic who actually fell asleep onstage once. He had his shoulder against the wall and he asked someone a question... but during their response time, he just fell asleep."

Fran Capo says that hellish experiences were commonplace in the beginning of her career. She gives a typical example of an early road/ zoo gig, "I was working with my partner, Alan, and this woman calls us to emcee at a club—she says it's real close—a few minutes away. It turned out to be a three-hour drive, and all the time Alan's yelling,

'I've camped closer than this!' We get there and it turns out we have to follow two transvestites—the first one is this obese guy in a mini skirt with hairy legs, and he's singing, 'Kiss me when I'm sweet sixteen . . .' By the end, he's rolling on the floor, but he was so fat he couldn't get up. Finally he pulls himself up and gets off. Then another transvestite comes on and does an act where he's supposed to be making love with a snake, and everyone's acting like this is perfectly normal! I'm thinking, 'How do you follow a transvestite and a snake?'

"Finally I get onstage and this guy yells, 'Are you for real?' I don't answer—and he goes nuts. He jumps onstage and does cartwheels in front of me and then flips. Then he gets down on his hands and knees and starts barking like a dog. I look over and the owner's yelling, 'You're doing great!' I said, 'But he's barking!' That was comedy hell. Another time I got booked to emcee an amateur night. When I got there, 'Dynasty' was on TV and everyone in the place was watching, so the owner says he's going to leave it on. There's a pool table, 'Pac Man,' people yelling . . . and when I get up there a guy yells, 'You should be in the kitchen not onstage!' Someone else yells, 'Females aren't funny.' Then a woman in the audience stuck up for me and this guy punched her—so they start fighting. In the meantime, I bring up the amateurs, and they were horrendous; a fat bald guy with pizza stains all over his T-shirt gets up and eats and sings at the same time— food falling all over—and the crowd was going nuts, they loved it! I was afraid to say anything because that guy would have punched me. Alan was supposed to go the next weekend and I warned him, but he thought I was exaggerating so he went. Apparently it was worse."

Many comics say that these kinds of indignities, suffered at the hands of road audiences, while uniquely heinous, are part of the territory. Still, most comics never forget their all-time worst episodes; Bob Goldthwait remembers his: "I was in Canada, and this gig was the biggest horror show of my life . . . I had to go onstage after a stripper, who was bombing, and when I got up, nobody could understand what I was saying. So I'm really getting heckled: 'We don't need a Thanksgiving turkey now, eh? We have a big one in front of us . . .' I mean big, long, non sequitur heckles—very strange. It was one of those real wild clubs—they had bar stool racing, where they modified two bar stools and put motors on them, with steering wheels and everything, and they'd race them around the club. That was Tuesday night. Then Wednesday night, wet T-shirt contests, then Thursday night, comedy. Oh, the food was lousy, I was so depressed, and on the sign, they had flashing, 'Tuesday: bar stool racing, Wednesday: wet T-shirt contest, Thursday: comedian Bob Goldflake.' When I saw that, I started crying. Every gig at this place was worse than the one before it; the owner said to me, 'You're the first comedian we ever had who made everyone be quiet.' Every comedian I know, I ask, 'Have you ever played Cantaloupe's?' [the name of the club] and every single one who did cried at that gig. It's closed now . . . thank God."

Alan Havey says that often private performances, though an easy way to pick up quick cash, can be risky because one has no guarantees about the actual performing conditions. He gives as an example a recent "private roast" in Queens, saying, "When I got to what was supposed to be an 'elegant' restaurant, there was no mike, stage or lights, and I was told I had to follow a stripper. I said, 'The stripper goes after me, or forget it,' and they agreed. Then, they gave me notes on the roastee, and said, 'Take twenty minutes and work these into the act.'" At this point, he says, a comic must make the best of the situation and improvise, "which I did . . . and it worked great. Afterwards, people asked me, 'How did you know so much about this guy that you could do this so well?' You know what kinds of things I said about him? 'You're a fucking asshole, pal!' and apparently, I was right on the mark."

Most comics feel that heckling and other horrors are simply the downside of live performing . . . and they're far outweighed by the upside. Joe Bolster considers that it's "just a hazard of the business— you're working with people who are drinking and they know you're live, right there—and things can happen . . . but that's the risk you take in order to do what you love." Unlike the movies or TV, stand-up is real life—it's immediate, and with the advantages of that, come the responsibilities: "Someone can drink too much, take too many drugs, get sick, even have a medical problem . . ." He gives an example one step beyond this, in which the comic (himself) actually *caused* a medical problem. Afterwards, he was struck not only by the immediacy of stand-up, but by the sheer power of the art to alter a person's physiognomy: "Once I was working in San Antonio and I made a woman laugh so hard she started hyperventilating. She was kind of panting, so I thought she was kidding. She was right in front, and I started making faces right in her face... and she's gasping, but I still thought she was joking. Finally her boyfriend said, 'My God, stop! You've got to stop! You're killing her!' Then I realized it was serious and I didn't know what to do—so a waitress came with a paper bag and the woman blew into it. It was the ultimate in comedy—literally 'killing.' It was almost a joke, like 'Hey, how was your show?' 'Oh, I killed! A woman in the front row couldn't stop laughing and she choked to death! Great show!' You see the power you can have—I actually created a medical difficulty because of my jokes. Once a woman came up to me after a show and said, 'You were so funny, I pissed my pants,' and she opened her coat and was drenched to her kneecaps. I said, 'I'm glad you didn't shit—and thanks for coming!' What do you say in a situation like that?" Nothing. Except perhaps, as in the case of all hecklers and horror stories, thank God it wasn't worse!

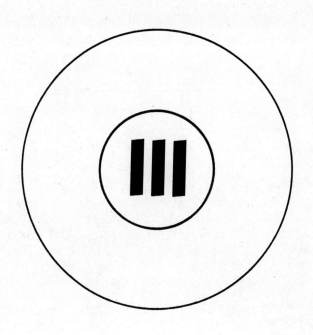

PUNCH LINES AND BREAD LINES... BEGINNERS' TALES

For every person who works as a stand-up comic, and faces the terrors of heckling and other horrors, there are thousands more who wanted to, but somehow never got the chance—or the nerve. Uncertainty alone will scare off most potential comics—in any other profession you don't get those big laughs, but neither do you have to face the terror of a hostile crowd, followed by the even greater terror of not earning a paycheck. Aside from innate talent and blind ambition, nerve is the most important factor in beginning to do stand-up; without it, no one can outlast those first crucial minutes of onstage purgatory, where the comic-to-be stands fighting to prove that he's worthy of the harrowing journey on which he's about to embark, which will leave him suspended, nightly, for countless years, somewhere between heaven and hell.

Most comics did not take the decision of whether or not to go onstage lightly; in fact, many became comics only after trying everything else... only to find that unspoken desires do not disappear simply because they're ignored. Some repressed their desire to perform, choosing instead to pursue a "real" career, but this desire resurfaced suddenly at a point of crisis in their work—specifically, at a point in which they had to commit themselves completely to a career in the real world. At this time, many described what hit them as a sudden jolt of awareness, after which they became acutely aware that they were missing out on something essential to their happiness; namely, standing in front of a faceless mass, martyring themselves for a single chuckle.

Abby Stein's moment of clarity came when she was poised at the peak of her career and found herself suddenly confronted with a life-altering decision: "To buy or not to buy?" Working in the garment center since the age of sixteen, when she left school to support herself, Abby was running a company there, and had worked her way up to a point where she had the option to buy it. This was the catalyst: "I panicked and thought, 'What am I doing? I'm signing away the rest of my life, and I don't even like doing this.'" Several weeks later, she quit her job and remembers, "I didn't know what I was going to do, but I knew I had to try something. I took six months off and took a comedy writing course, then I saw an ad in the paper for a course in stand-up. Doing comedy was always a fantasy for me, but I thought, 'Adults don't do things like that.' Anyway, I went and there was an actor in the class, a retired hospital administrator who was seventy-five, an obese housewife who'd gotten it as an anniversary gift, and a salesman. We'd sit around and watch tapes of comics and dissect them. But the thing is, you can't teach stand-up... although, for me it helped. It made me see I was funnier than anybody else in the class. When they got up to talk they were boring, and when I got up I was funny. So the teacher said, 'Why don't you go up to Good Times and try it.' So I went and auditioned and died a terrible death—horrible. But it felt like coming home, it felt right. And that was it."

After graduating from Cornell, Carol Siskind waitressed, worked with disturbed kids, ran a shop on Martha's Vineyard, worked in a youth center, and finally ended up working in her cousins' stationery store. Two-and-a-half years later, they asked her to "come into the business" with them and at this point, she remembers, "it suddenly dawned on me—there's got to be more out there." She started taking acting classes, then began auditioning, where she met a girl who told her, "I'm a stand-up comic." "I swear," says Carol, "in that instant, a light bulb went off in my head." A couple of months later, the girl invited her to a little cabaret where she was doing a show at midnight.

She told Carol, "You'll see—you'll want to go on." When she got there, she could barely stay awake but, "there was something in me that really did want to do it... and I went on. I had no act. I had just spent a week on Long Island at a party and I told the story about it, and people were laughing. I got offstage and the girl said, 'I can't believe you don't have one joke and they're laughing at you.' And that was it; I was hooked."

Before David Brenner became a stand-up comic, he was the producer of a television variety show in Chicago. Between acts, he would goof around for the staff and one day the piano player said, "Man I've worked with every comedian, and you're funnier than any of them. You should go on a show, what are you doing producing?" His friends, also, began encouraging him to perform, and he started wondering if he could be "professionally funny." At work, he says, "you know there's a fine line between a niche and a rut—very fine—and I felt I was going to slip into the rut area soon." When that happened, he quit his job, figuring he'd take six months off to make a career choice and, during that time, "I figured, while I'm thinking about it, I'll get up and goof around onstage... I only did it because I didn't want to be idle." He decided to give himself a year, after which he'd quit and go into another "real" career. But after a year passed, he extended it six more months, "to do TV, then quit." A year and a half after he began, he made his first appearance on "The Tonight Show" and, overnight, "the whole world opened up." He obviously never thought about a real career again.

Some comics trace their beginning in stand-up to a single traumatic experience. Andrew Smith makes his living by writing—for film—*The Main Event*, starring Barbra Streisand and Ryan O'Neal, *Quicksilver*, starring Kevin Bacon and himself—and television—he was head-writer for "The Merv Griffin Show," and "Saturday Night Live." Although he has performed as a stand-up, the terror of bombing kept him from actively pursuing stand-up as a career, and writing became a sublimation. "Writing is the 'Andy Smith Show' for me, there's no question about it. When I write scripts or sketches, all those fast lines and that repartee is what I'd like to be able to do, but I can't seem to get it out." Several years ago, the death of his mother represented something that "dwarfed all other terrors by comparison." Having led a tragedy-free life up until that point, he thought that the worst thing that could happen to him was to face the embarrassment of failing onstage; he was not able to see the relative insignificance of that until his mother died: "That's the worst thing that's ever happened to me. When something that awful happens to you, suddenly the terror of failing is dissipated; you say, 'Hey, man, I've been through hell now, so this is bullshit,' and that gives you a certain cockiness—a daring that you don't have if you've had too good of a life. It makes you realize that the fear of bombing is petty compared to the sorrow of losing a loved one."

Shortly after her death, Smith made his first appearance on the "Merv Griffin Show" in many years (as head-writer on that show in the early 70s, he had occasionally warmed up the audience) and said, "It was the first time I'd done any performing in a long time. I felt I had that control—I controlled the audience, I controlled the panel. I knew exactly where I was, what I was going for, where the jokes were. I thought I was the best I'd ever been, and I wondered then if it had any connection with my mother: maybe it's like being through a war—either you're destroyed or it makes everything seem simple by comparison."

The death of Paul Provenza's father forced him to confront his own mortality—to weigh his options not according to what was and wasn't proper, but according to what would make his life a meaningful one. He explains: "My father died when I was seventeen, and it had a lot to do with everything that happened; if he had been alive, he would have either charmed me into the decision he thought was right, or forced me into it. He tried to convince me that I needed stability in my life, and we always fought about that; we never really got along and towards the end of his life we were at each other's throats all the time. I was struggling to become who I was and he was struggling to maintain his dominance—lots of arguing, screaming and yelling—very Italian.

"He was sick for about a year before he died, and in that time he really changed his perspective on life. Mr. Stability all of a sudden started to tell me things that were very different from before. He was a big supporter of the Vietnam War, at the time, but he said, in retrospect, that if they had tried to take me he would have shot my toe off so they couldn't have me. I found that out later on—for the first time in my life he was emotional and I'd never seen that side of him before. He gave me a lot of strength. It was actually a beautiful time in a strange way, the culmination of everything that had gone wrong.

"He had only worked for two companies in his life, and I remember the shift from one to the other was very traumatic for him at the time. But when he was sick, he said, 'If I had my life to live over again, it would be three years—tops—in any one job, then I'd go somewhere else. I'd keep moving and let nothing hold me back... you can do anything you want to do in life; don't be saddled with things just because you think you should be.' I remembered thinking, 'This is why he was so domineering at home—he's lived his whole life for other people, not himself, so his family was really all he had.' I also started thinking about how everyone in my family has died of either a heart attack or cancer every fucking month as far back as I can remember—three of my grandparents died of cancer—aunts, uncles, everyone. I thought, if all indications are clear here, I've got a short time to do whatever it is I want to do—it's not morbid, just reality—and what I really wanted to do was comedy."

Kip Adotta had been a hairdresser in Rockford, Illinois, for seven years, by the time he was twenty-five. Though he always had an interest in comedy, he never considered it as "real work." When his wife passed away suddenly, he says, "I realized life is so short—why am I so worried about what other people think? If I go become a comic and people say, 'Who does he think he is?'—so what! I could be dead tomorrow!" Like Paul, the death of a loved one forced him to confront his own mortality, but it also gave him a valid excuse for doing something out of the ordinary: "Because she died, it gave me the opportunity to get a little crazy—to be, of all things, a comedian. The family said, 'He's a little off, but he'll straighten up when this passes...' and I depended on that. I moved to Los Angeles in 1972, got a job parking cars, and started working at the Comedy Store."

When Richard Lewis's father died he was left with a "tremendous void," and his desperation to fill it in some way compelled him to finally go onstage after years of being frustrated by selling his jokes for other comedians to perform. He remembers: "My father died and two months later I was onstage in Greenwich Village—it catapulted me there. I was going to do it eventually, I think, but it got me there much faster . . . and for the next few years my life was consumed with stand-up." He says, also, that perhaps his father's passing made it easier for him to fail because "there was nothing for me to lose—as far as being embarrassed or ashamed if it didn't work out."

This liberation by tragedy can best be summed up as, "What have I got to lose?" These six words are probably the most frequently spoken by those who make the decision, finally, to become a stand-up comedian, and they are words that reflect the conflicting feelings about stand-up held by most comedians—it's the thing they want most in life, yet the hardest thing they can imagine doing. Only by reaching, or pushing themselves, to the end of the line—by exhausting all other possibilities—can many comics transcend the fear of their own failure and the terror of being judged by a terminally sane world.

Once free of these restraints, many find that they fall into stand-up almost naturally. Paul Reiser says, "There's a theory about art, that you don't have to 'do,' you just have to remove the blocks and allow it to happen. I didn't really try to become a comic, I just stopped saying 'no,' and it happened." Often their reminiscences take on a fatalistic tone, as if becoming a comic was not a professional choice, but the fulfilling of a destiny. "One day I was going to be a dental hygienist, then I was going to be a lawyer or get an M.B.A.—but I never worked as hard at or cared about anything this much . . . until I became a comic," Carrie Snow says. "For me, I feel it was meant to happen." It is, for many, as if all of their prior experience had somehow been leading up to the fact they *are* a comic. When it happens, at last, they feel great relief; the search is finally over.

Joe Bolster remembers a similar enlightenment: "I was watching David Brenner one night on 'The Tonight Show' and in the middle of his monologue I just suddenly went, 'That's it! That's what I'll do!' It's like that 'Eureka!' thing with Archimedes in his bathtub, when he lay down and realized his body displaced the water in proportion to his weight, and he cried, 'I've got it!' It was like that for me—everything I've done since then came out of that tenth of a second when it hit me.

It struck me that all he was doing was talking about funny things and I'd been doing that, in an amateur way, all my life."

After graduating from college and traveling around the country for several months, in June 1979 Steven Wright returned to Massachusetts to find a job. It was on his return that he heard about a Boston club called The Comedy Connection: "Deep down, I'd always wanted to try stand-up, so I said to myself, I've got to confront this fantasy now. I didn't want to wonder about it and be forty years old, selling insurance in Wyoming, wondering what would have happened if I'd tried. So I decided to force myself. I say 'forced' because I was so introverted that to go in front of the audience was the last thing in the world I wanted to do, but at the same time it was my dream to be a stand-up. So I went to the club and watched four guys who were hilarious—and I thought it was going to be much harder than I'd even imagined. But two weeks later I wrote about two minutes of material and went down to the audition night. I went onstage that night for literally two minutes, and I taped it. The first joke I did was: 'I once was talking to a very French-looking girl. She was a bilingual illiterate—she couldn't read in two different languages.' The audience laughed at about half of my jokes, and when I walked off I was really disappointed that they didn't laugh at all of them; I didn't realize it was crazy to expect that. Then one of the comics there, Mike McDonald, told me that, for the first time, it was pretty good for them to laugh at half. So I walked home listening to this two-minute tape and it was an unbelievable feeling! I was twenty-three and it had been my dream since I was fifteen to do this . . . and eight years later I heard these people, on tape, laughing at something I said. It was my fantasy—I had made an audience laugh. Instead of thinking they didn't laugh at half, I thought, They laughed at half! Then I went back the next week and added a few more lines and did that every week—adding and adding."

Some comic-meets-comedy stories reek with the romance of fate and destiny. A. Whitney Brown's is a good example: "I could trace my comedic career back to a single second when I was eighteen. I'd been a hippie for three to four years, living on the streets, and one night I was hitchhiking in Morrow Bay, California. At about seven o'clock, a police car pulled up and I got arrested for having a roach clip. It turned out I was clean, so they took me back out to where I was picked up. Then, at about midnight, a '49 Plymouth Sedan, with suicide doors, pulled up and these two guys said, 'hop in.'

"The guy who was driving was celebrating the other one's birthday, so we went out drinking and afterwards he invited me to stay on his ranch. It turned out this guy lived in a truck where he had a medicine show that he was going to take out and work at fairs. I knew how to juggle, but not very well, and he played an accordion and had a little dog. He said, 'Hang with me, and we'll go work together,' and that's how I started. If he hadn't picked me up, I'd never have gotten into show business... maybe everyone has a moment like that—where there's a little twist, and everything they do afterwards stems from that one little thing." (A couple of years later, the man, who Brown says was "brilliant," put a gun to his head and killed himself. A. Whitney continued to work with the dog, Brownie, on the streets, but they had to split up the act when he started working in clubs—no pets allowed. Today, he says, Brownie resides happily in Vermont.)

Like Brown, comic Tom Parks traces his beginnings to a single incident: "I had no emotional investment in becoming a comic... what happened was that I went to a show one night and saw a comic performing. I was with a date and said, 'I think I could do that.' Well, she looked at me, and in the right tone of voice said, 'I think you could, too.' At that point, I thought, 'I'm going into show business—I don't care.' Literally, that's what happened—I did it to impress her." The way he went about entering the business is not the kind of story that lends itself to the usual image of a romantic, starving artist: "I got a directory of colleges and started calling them for work. I lied and said I'd been working a lot—but I hadn't. My college degree was in P.R. and advertising, so I knew what it took to sell a product—and I realized that I was just a product. So rather than concentrating on material, I got together a great promo package and it looked like I deserved the money. Then, once I got there, I worried about being good."

Not to be outdone by anyone's claims of connections, Fran Capo began her career by invoking the name of God. "I kept praying, 'If I'm meant to be a stand-up give me a sign!'" she remembers, "but nothing happened. So then I said, 'Okay God, if you make it really convenient

I'll take that as a sign.' Then one day, I went to school and the main door was locked; I went to the back door and there was a sign on it that said, 'Comedy Auditions' at a place two blocks from my house, and I thought, 'That's my sign . . . I guess if I don't try it now I'll go to hell.'"

Lying somewhere among these near-religious revelations, erstwhile epiphanies and tales of fate are several instances of logical, deductive reasoning. Jerry Seinfeld was very unhappy until he knew what he wanted to do in life. When he discovered comedy, he considered the high rate of failure in the business, but figured, "If you do something you honestly enjoy, chances are you'll have a happy life regardless of whether or not you succeed—because at the very least, you'll like what you're doing every day." Alan Havey followed similar logic, but instead of being suddenly confronted with comedy, he arrived at it through the process of elimination. In college, Alan lived in a trailer which, he says, "scared the hell out of me." Working his way through school, he was at different times employed as a janitor, gas station attendant, dishwasher and elevator operator. When he moved to New York to become an actor, he says, "I met other actors who had been lawyers or whatever—they could go back to that. But I wasn't anything; I was a person who wanted to be an actor." In looking for something that would not render him completely dependent, "it occurred to me that being a struggling comic is much better than being a struggling actor, and it is. This way I work all the time. I can always get up in front of an audience, whether I'm getting paid or not, and get that release— and it's my work; I can take total responsibility for it."

While it may take a great deal of soul searching and courage to arrive at the decision to become a comic, it can be small potatoes compared to the anguish of actually becoming one. In addition to overcoming one's own limitations, a stand-up must become immune to the opinions of the "normal" world around him. Becoming a comic is not generally accepted behavior; it is the kind of occupation that people react to by saying, "But you could have been a lawyer . . ." more often than they say, "You're a comedian? Congratulations!" For Cathy Ladman, the decision to become a comic was complicated by her fear of disapproval, especially because she had always used humor as a defense mechanism, "against not being praised. I was never good enough, you know? I was always very anxious. I remember in third grade we'd have to write five words in five sentences every night and by the end of the year my teacher had fallen behind in the curriculum and we had to do ten words and I thought, 'My God, how am I going to do this? I have to go to sleep at eight o'clock!' I started worrying in second grade, that's young! I was never taught, 'Go out and do it—don't worry if you fail.' I was taught, 'You'd better succeed.'"

After college, Cathy continued to do the "right" thing; she taught school in Philadelphia ("I grew up in a middle class Jewish family in Queens, where you were either supposed to be a teacher or a speech therapist, or an accountant, since that's what my father is"), but after a year, she decided to pursue her dream. She quit her job and moved to Los Angeles to become a stand-up, but says, "I lasted four months and didn't go near a comedy club. I didn't know anybody—it was the worst. I sold my car and flew back to New York, moved back with my parents—horrible. I'll never forget that day—February 5, 1978. I was snowed into my parents' house for a week, and the first thing my father did was shove the classified section in my face and say, 'What are you gonna do, where you gonna go, huh, huh?' I was like, 'Please, I still have jet lag and emotional trauma—I need a day.'" But three years later, after a series of unfulfilling jobs, her desire to perform became so strong that it overcame even the fear of disapproval—and she became a comic.

Alan Havey fought against the impact of others' opinions: "When I started, I met with a lot of condescension—raised eyebrows: 'You do what?' Especially when I went home, before I moved to New York, people thought I was crazy. My girlfriend's parents told me, 'You're an idiot.' It's like, stay here, live in a trailer park, get a Craftmatic Adjustable bed and watch your belly grow . . . I think that's sick." Alan is not immune to disapproval, but his fear of becoming "normal" far outweighs his fear of criticism. As a child, he began to notice that people didn't have much passion in their lives, and that scared him. "I didn't want to grow up and work nine to five and just raise kids; I'd be miserable. When people aren't happy, I think the reason they aren't is because they're not happy with their work . . . because they've settled.

You have to always challenge everything, or you'll end up in a trailer park."

Whether this aversion to the status quo is an innate characteristic that contributes to one's being a comic, or one that is developed as a person becomes a comic, it is a trait that has kept many a depressed stand-up going. No matter how late or low-paying a gig may be, the alternative is always worse: "I could be working nine to five." Jay Leno, who seems never to have been depressed, says that this sense of independence is one of the best parts of his job. "In the sixties, all my friends were blowing up the Bank of America—and now they work for the Bank of America. They all make a product that they hate or they're selling something they don't believe in. With what I'm doing, the worst that can happen is that people don't laugh. Nobody's going to get cancer of the pancreas, in years to come, from me telling them these jokes. When I see these TV commercials where the guy's going to impress his boss—or they're going to the boss's house for dinner and he's got something on his collar—I don't have to do any of that. I'm my own boss—if I want to work, I do; if I don't, I won't." He seems to value the freedom from hypocrisy that stand-up allows him, as well, and though it sounds as if he is a rebel, he is reluctant to use words like this to describe himself or other comics, saying that these terms are relative: "In Massachusetts [where he grew up], it's very straight-laced —people said, 'You're a comedian? Why don't you become a doctor or lawyer?' Then I come to L.A. and it's, 'A doctor or lawyer? Why don't you become a dancer or a comedian?' Here I'm considered very straight."

Some comics began in stages, stubbornly clinging to the belief that they could still become "regular" people with "real" jobs, promising themselves that each performance would be their last. Jonathan Solomon says that he viewed stand-up as a rite of passage, a milestone in his growth, to be passed and remembered fondly. But each time he seemed to pass it, he found the elusive milestone had expanded further into the horizon: "I always thought it was temporary," he says, ". . . the first time I went on, I wanted to get one laugh, then I'd never do it again. Then I wanted to pass at the Improv or the Strip—and I'd retire. Then I wanted to have one prime-time set, and I'd stop... then I just never stopped."

Paul Reiser edged toward his destiny by willing himself to move in one direction, while actually moving in another. Between 1975 and 1978, he auditioned at several clubs during breaks from college, then spent the year after graduation "kind of performing—to get it out of my system," while working in his father's office during the day. Though it was never discussed, he says, it was always assumed he'd go into his father's health food business ("My mother would have loved for me to be the next Horowitz [he had studied piano] and my father would have liked me to be the next him...") so in 1979, he decided to quit stand-up and go into his father's business. But once established, his bond with stand-up could not be broken. "I tried to walk away..." he recalls. "I told the clubs, 'Please don't give me spots even if I call!' Then, after about four months, I realized that this was not something I could get out of my system. It was a real eye-opener in my life—that I have a calling and I've got to go with it."

One of the hardest parts about beginning, for Paul, was trying to explain his obsession in terms that would make sense in spite of the fact that he had no immediate success. "For my father, I had to make it analogous to a business. You don't turn a profit right away, you build customers, you set up an identity, and slowly it grows...I couldn't explain why I was drawn to the clubs like a moth to the light."

Jay Leno never intended to become a professional comic. "I always assumed I'd be a funny salesman—telling jokes to get my product across...Andover, Massachusetts, isn't the kind of town where people go into show business. If you knew a guy who went out with Sandra Dee's cousin, you knew somebody in show business." But, like Paul, he didn't realize that a bond had been formed. When he started after college, in 1973, "it was what I liked to do, but I was never like Stalin —setting five-year plans. I figured, 'I'm out of college and have my degree so why not?'"

What Jay explains as a casual attitude toward his career, in the beginning, could just as easily be defined as intense, singular dedication. He says, "I used to work out at the Improv—I'd drive there from Boston every night, five nights a week, just to try and get on. I was working

for Rolls Royce at the time, and I'd sneak one out at night and discon-
nect the speedometer and just piss down to New York. Or sometimes
when a Rolls would come into New Jersey, I'd have to drive it back to
Boston. But first I'd go to the Improv with it, which was great because
Budd would look out and see me in a new, different Rolls every time.
He started saying, 'Go right on, you must be pretty successful.'"

In the beginning, most comics agree, the most important things are
getting stage time, watching others work, and earning a living. For
some, the best way to achieve all of these goals is to get work in one of
the showcase clubs. In the Los Angeles Comedy Store, Mitzi Shore
says that she has always given work to young, promising comics so they
would have enough money to continue performing: "Yakov [Smirnoff]
was a carpenter here. He came here from New York and he was bad—
but he had something. He said he had no money but he could be a
carpenter. I have things all over my place he did—in fact, he was the
first one who started to help me fix up the Belly Room; he was a
carpenter here for two-and-a-half years." She also maintains a sort of
comic hotel up the hill, behind the Comedy Store, ". . . a big white
Spanish place where I house a lot of comics. At one time, there were
six or seven there, now there are five. It's like a college. Robin [Wil-
liams] was always in and out of there—Sam Kinison, Tom Wilson—
they lived there and worked here as doormen, runners, carpenters
. . . to get extra money."

In New York, where living space is a luxury even for club owners,
nothing like a comic hotel is ever likely to exist, but many comics
have, at various times, supported themselves in the clubs. Larry Miller
worked at the Comic Strip seven nights a week bartending, playing
piano and drums, and waiting for a spot onstage. Although he didn't
make a lot of money, he was able to save it because he never left the
club. "I ate cheese burgers there every night, wore the T-shirts from
there, drank for free—that was my whole life—and it was good, it was
my thing. I had my days free—all the money in the world. I was
making, say seventy-five to one hundred dollars a week, all cash, and I
was there every night not spending anything, so my rent was one
hundred and fifty dollars a month, and that was it."

When Carol Siskind began doing stand-up, in 1979, she auditioned at the Improv until she was passed, then got work there answering phones and taking reservations. She says, "I'd be there from three in the afternoon until eight at night. But on the weekends, I'd go at eight and work the door, seating people, until three in the morning, then go onstage at three. I was happy—I was getting an hourly wage and it meant I didn't have to work at the stationery store anymore, but the best part was, I could be around comedy." On the nights when she wasn't working the Improv phones, Carol performed at least two sets in other clubs ("I mean dives!"), ending up back at the Improv in the early morning to get her precious stage time.

Jay Leno makes the crucial point about new comics: "They're brimming with inexperience, but out of that comes this tremendous energy level, like, 'I hung around the club for eight hours and the guy let me get onstage for three minutes. It was great!'" He likens this almost blind enthusiasm to an old Democratic Convention joke about a guy waiting to make his speech: "It's eleven at night and the keynote speakers are up—people are standing and cheering—this goes on and on, until finally it's four fifteen in the morning and there are two people left in the hall, with like a thousand empty seats. One guy's in row five and the other's in row twelve. The row five guy finally has his turn to speak and he's sitting there thinking, 'I can't go on—no one's here . . . wait a minute! I *am* going to speak—I put this thing together, spent so much time on it, and this man is here to hear it!' He goes up, gives a real firebrand speech for twenty minutes, and when he finishes the guy in row twelve applauds. He starts to leave, but then he walks over to him and says, 'Let me ask you something—you've been here since seven tonight, you sat through the whole thing—why did you stay to hear me?' The guy turns to him and says, 'Oh—I speak next.'" He says that the same thing is true of comedians—most notably himself: "That's happened to me, too, at the Improv. It would be like four A.M. and you wanted to go on so desperately. There would be three guys there, so you get up and do your act—then you realize they're just comics waiting to go on, too."

For comics in the showcase clubs, beginners' enthusiasm is often tested to its limits by endless hours of waiting and watching—waiting to get on, and watching those who do. But watching is not something to pass the time; it's part of a comic's training—part of the dues package that must be paid. Rita Rudner remembers, "It's like starting in the mailroom, you have to sit there and wait for so long, there are so many others with established authority. But while you're sitting there, you watch—that's how I figured out what made people funny." Jerry Seinfeld says that he, too, learned his trade by observing other comedians: "I'd sit in the audience and listen to the nuts and bolts of jokes—what worked in someone's act and why. I learned maybe it didn't work because a word in the set-up was unclear or maybe it was the timing . . . but I'd sit and watch for hours every night after I did my set."

In order to work out at a showcase club, a comic must be "passed." This involves waiting in line for a number on audition day, and, if you get one, performing a five-minute set that night for the owner or manager. If, after this, you get a call-back, it means that they like you but want to see more material—so the next time you do another five. If after that (or before that) the set meets the club's standards (which can happen any time, ranging from the first audition to never, depending on the performance) the comic is "passed"—which means he's allowed to hang out at the bar every night and wait to be given a spot onstage.

Almost without exception, a beginning comic works only in one club because to get stage time, he must be available at the bar all night, waiting. Several clubs hold comics to an unstated policy that "if you work another club, don't bother coming here." In L.A. it's a commonly known fact among comics that if you work the Improv, you're not welcome at the Comedy Store. Budd Friedman says he has had several cases where comics told him that if they worked the Improv, they risked "offending Mitzi"; some chose to work for him, others went with Shore. Mitzi, however, says that there is no competition, as the two establishments aren't comparable: "The Improv is not a place to develop stand-ups; he develops drek there . . . dead comics. It's a place to hang out—no one's developed there. This is a cultured place, an art colony." (For the record: many comics agreed with Mitzi, but just as many found the Improv to be the superior club/art colony, and said the Store develops drek.)

As always, politics are just as important as talent. Abby Stein remembers: "I started at the Improv but eventually fell out of favor when there was a change of management—you just hope the person who likes you stays in power. After that, the Comic Strip became my home club, and they've been very good to me throughout the years." Some comics, like Cathy Ladman, choose to work outside of the major showcase clubs for this reason. She says, "They want you to give your life blood, hanging out there forever, and to me that didn't seem like the way to do it. I didn't want to stay in a bar all night when I could be doing a set somewhere else. As a result, I haven't become one of their first string comics, but I know it's someplace I can audition in when I need to and I have other places in the city I can work, too, instead of pacing up and down a bar all night. It's a hurtful, oppressive place."

Alan Havey remembers how difficult it was climbing up the greased pole to earlier club spots: "I got passed at the Improv in 1980, but then quit for awhile. I took off for three months one time, then three months another—it was just too hard and too depressing. I'd go in there night after night and not get on—or maybe get on at two in the morning when there was no one there to prove myself to. The only way to prove yourself is to go on earlier, but you can't get on then—so you just wait and wait... It was awful—there were times when I just couldn't get on before one thirty in the morning. I was good, but I just needed an audience. It depends on the club owner and the politics."

If a comic can't get passed or doesn't like the atmosphere of the major establishments, there are other options: he can bust his comic butt in the lesser known clubs around New York and Los Angeles or, more recently, those in towns like Boston, Chicago or San Francisco. Fran Capo broke her act in this way: "It's better to work and get stage time someplace else than just hang out at the bar all year waiting to get on with five minutes. I see the same ones at these clubs all the time, saying, 'I never get on!' Then why do you hang out there?" But for most comics, the prestige of working the major showcases combined with the fact that these are the places where casting agents look first, keeps them hanging out... or waiting in line for the chance to hang out.

Joe Bolster says that beginning to do stand-up is particularly difficult because there is no real program or method of training: "If you want to be a lawyer you go to law school—if you want to be a doctor you go to medical school—but there's no logical means by which you become a comic. There are no schools, coaches or trainers." When Bolster began, in 1978, there were few places to work, and most of those that existed were found in New York or Los Angeles. In those days, like today, the competition at the top showcase clubs was fierce. He describes trying to get on at the Improv: "Every Sunday night was audition night there. You'd line up outside and they'd give out forty numbers. I can remember several times being one of the first forty people there, but then when the doors opened, suddenly guys would jump out of cabs and elbow me out of the way—they'd appear from out of nowhere... and the next thing I know, I'm eightieth in line. I thought, 'If shoving people is the means to getting onstage, I can't do this.'"

Several months later he heard about a place in Philadelphia that was booking different kinds of acts on Wednesday nights; apparently they had lots of singers, jugglers and magicians, but they needed comics. He went there, got on the first night, and became a regular, traveling from New Jersey (where he worked during the day for Bill Bradley's senate campaign) to Philly three to four nights a week. He realized, however, that "comedy is like baseball, you have to do it enough to get into a groove—you need to do it five nights a week at least," and soon after, Rich Hall (who had worked with him in Philly) told him about the Comic Strip in New York and arranged an audition for Joe, which, he says, "I passed and became a regular."

Carol Leifer remembers waiting on line at Catch A Rising Star, in 1977, to get a number: "You had to get there at two thirty in the afternoon to line up—and I got a number... at that time, Catch on Monday night was a real happening thing; I remember it was crowded —very hot—and I did great. I killed. I remember walking offstage and Rick Newman [the owner] shaking my hand and saying, 'You're really good.' I was flying, thinking, 'In two weeks I'll be on "The Tonight Show"—I'll have to quit school...' It wasn't until the next Monday, when I went back, that I realized what it was all about. I didn't do well, the audience was surly and awful, somebody kind of heckled me and I just jumped on him."

For a comic to "kill" the first time and "bomb" the second is not an unusual occurrence; in fact, it's very common, as in the case of Leifer —and George Calfa. George worked for the New York Transit Authority, before going into comedy, in order to have his teeth fixed—and, he says, "the day my teeth were finished, I quit." He remembers calling the Improv first, because it was the only club he'd ever heard of, and being told, "'We give out numbers at four in the afternoon on Sunday,' so I said fine, I'll get there at two and get a good number. When I got there at two, there were twenty-five people who had been waiting there since seven in the morning for a number." Someone in line told him that other clubs, like Catch, had audition nights every Monday—while the Improv was just once a month—and that the Comic Strip had a lottery, so you never had to wait on line (if you pulled a number you got to perform, otherwise, you came back the next week).

He remembers, "I went to the Comic Strip, got a good number, and my friends came down. It was August, a packed house, and I was getting laughs, I was really getting laughs—and it was my first time on!" He was also passed the first time, which is unusual, so he came back the next night to start hanging out and says, "I got there about nine thirty, and it was about two thirty in the morning before I got on. There were four people in the audience who were sitting in the back —and I went on. I used to do some things with props, so I kept having to turn around to get the things, and at one point, I noticed it was really silent... but I kept working. Finally, I realized they had walked out silently. I was performing to nobody, but it was so dark I couldn't see. I was in the middle of a bit and I looked out and saw there were no waitresses, no people—nothing. After that, I was just doing late-night shows, hanging out a lot, and waiting to get on."

After deciding to become a stand-up (again—after failing in California), Cathy Ladman worked to develop "five decent minutes" and when she had them, she says, "I wrote down in my date book, 'Go to Good Times,' [which, she says, was "a disgusting club—all mirrored, people didn't know where they were looking, terrible audiences, no pay, the worst"] or else I wouldn't go. It was July 27, 1981, a Sunday night. I went down by myself, took a number and did well—I did very well." But, like many others, she went back the next night and bombed. Instead of giving up this time, she continued working out at little clubs around the city, and finally auditioned at the Improv in October, where she wasn't passed, at the Comic Strip, where she wasn't passed and, in December, at Catch. At this point she was beginning to get discouraged again, but remembers: "My nephew was just born a few days before that and I was so excited about it, I thought, 'How can I be worried about getting up on a stage when this new little human being is in the world?' Somehow, it just put everything in perspective for me and, as a result, I had a fantastic set, and passed auditions there."

Fran Capo, too, says that (after her requisite sign from God) she killed the first time. While an audition is usually five minutes, she happened to begin at a small place that was desperate for performers, so she was asked to prepare ten. On the day of the audition, however —right before taking the stage—she was told to do a half hour, and says, "To this day I have no recollection of what I said up there, but it worked because I got a standing ovation." The next night, confident she could do the same act, she tried again . . . and bombed. She remembers that everything seemed to go wrong: "My mother was so excited the first night, because I was so good, but on the second night she got so nervous she got drunk and fell off her chair . . . after the show, I went into the bathroom and I wouldn't come out until everyone left. But I got over it and I've been doing it for four-and-a-half years now."

But all comics do not kill on their first spot. Alan Havey remembers his fear and hostility on that first night, and many others after it: "You fight, you get your courage up, and you go on . . . but it just doesn't happen, so finally you look into the audience and say, 'I know why I'm here, but why are *you* here?'" Paul Reiser remembers the disappointment of his first performance—which was also confirmed on tape: "My sister drove me in to the city and recorded the set. You hear all these loud dish-clattering noises, and you hear me very faintly in the background. You also hear her laughing, very conspicuously, but no one else is . . . then you hear these businessmen, who didn't see the tape recorder, and one says, 'I'll say one thing for this kid—he's got balls.' No laughs—just, 'He's got guts.' That always cracked me up."

In order to get themselves onstage for the first time, some comics were forced to anesthetize themselves. "I remember I had a martini and I walked around the block and almost wet my pants," says Richard Belzer, though he adds, "I went onstage and did remarkably well for a novice." Kip Adotta remembers, "It was at the Comedy Store of course and it was horrifying . . . I got through that first time on sheer adrenaline—and five vodkas." Others, who faced their first audience stone cold sober, may have wished that they'd been anesthetized—or perhaps knocked unconscious. Steven Wright recalls: "It was absolutely, horribly terrifying. I wouldn't even stop for them to laugh—I didn't know how to pause. I just wanted to get on and get off. I was shaking —even after the first time—whenever I went on." But it was this initial terror that gave birth to his comically dense, deadpan style: "I didn't want to be standing there when they weren't laughing. That's why I tell so many jokes in such a short amount of time—the silence would make me too nervous. I didn't realize that until years later—it's why I tell like five jokes a minute—a long set-up would make me too nervous."

Jerry Seinfeld says that his first time he froze completely: "It was at Catch . . . I had gotten there at two in the afternoon and picked the number one. I had rehearsed my act over and over for weeks. I had papers laid out on my bed, with the jokes, and I kept reading through them, practicing the gestures. But the first time you get up and see all those people looking at you, it's an overwhelming experience." For Jerry, this marked the only time that, as a performer, he was aware of the process as it took place: "As you get on in comedy you forget—you don't realize what you're actually doing; it's just that place you stand, and that act you do . . . like being on TV—you don't think about how there are millions of people watching you, expecting you to be funny. You can't."

But this awareness was an overwhelming liability for him: "I got up and all I could remember were the subjects that I wanted to talk about . . . so I just stood there and went, 'the beach . . . cars . . .' I did about three minutes [of subjects] and I got off . . . and the sad thing is, I'm not embellishing this story to make it funny." His friends, who were in the audience, tried to cheer him up, he remembers. "They said, 'The audience liked you—really!' but of course I was inconsolable. I walked out into the street and just kept walking for miles and miles."

But he was determined to become a stand-up, and like almost all determined young comics was willing to work anywhere, under any conditions—and did. He says, about those early days, "I did shows where people didn't even know I was on. I did a show once at a disco in Queens about eight years ago—real Saturday Night Fever type of disco—and they turned up the music and said, 'Okay, now it's comedy time.' The dance floor was jammed with people, music was blasting, and the microphone cord was eighteen inches long . . . it was so short, I couldn't even turn to face the audience. But at that point in your career you're afraid to make waves, so I just yelled my act into the crowd; no one heard—complete bedlam. After I was done, I went over to the owner to get paid and he said, 'Oh, I didn't even know you were on . . .' there was that little response." He performed in places "that weren't so much nightclubs as restaurants with a table missing . . . they'd say, 'We took a table out over there—just stand there and talk.' They'd have a sixty-watt yellow light bulb over your head, so you felt like you were in a french fry heater or something, and that's how I'd do my act."

Carol Siskind also spent her early days in hot pursuit of audiences. Like many comic novices, she would perform for anyone who sat down long enough and/or did not threaten to kill or maim her: "I used to travel around with two guys and we'd work out in Central Park. We'd perform with the open guitar case—anyplace, as long as we could work. We went to these pimp bars where hookers hung out. If there was a piano with a microphone, we'd all lean into it, talking to whoever was there—the mafia—who knows! One night we passed one of those places that says, 'Reader/Advisor' and went in and said to the woman and her daughter, 'Hi, we perform. We'd like to do a show for you.' She said, 'Okay,' and pulled open a curtain—you always wonder what's going on in the back of these places . . . and there are like thirty people there. They sent out for sandwiches and we performed. We performed at parties—if I knew someone who was having a party, we would go over and do a set—in apartments!" She says, simply, that her goal was to get good, and, "One thing I realized early on is that the only way you get good at this is by doing it."

When Emo Philips began performing in 1976: "Every night was amateur night because no one was any good." The field was wide open because there was very little money to be made—and so there were very few comics around. This also meant that, since he was in Illinois, the gigs to be had were few and far between: "When I started I used to drive twenty miles to do one club, where I'd get on at nine with five other people on the bill. Then, I'd drive another thirty miles and go on at two A.M.—this was Tuesday thru Saturday every week for a year, with no money." While the money wasn't great, the personal rewards were . . . not either: "Nobody ever laughed—but I just kept doing it. For the first six months I was just facing the back wall . . . I thought the rapture had come, but I was used to total rejection so it didn't bother me at all, which is nice. I never had any cataclysmic thing happen that made me want to do stand-up. People used to laugh at me whenever I walked down the street, so I figured if I did comedy, maybe they'd stop laughing . . ."

While the stand-up situation is, and always has been, tight for comics in New York and L.A., Yakov Smirnoff says that where he began, it was even more difficult—in the Soviet Union. He started working in resort areas for $4 a show while attending art school and eventually worked his way up to the popular variety gigs. Though he says he was happy compared to a lot of other people there and his popularity was skyrocketing, he couldn't really take off because censorship prevented him from doing the spontaneous material which is his forte. All jokes had to be submitted to and approved by "The Department of Jokes" (a hyper-Orwellian sounding institution but, nevertheless, one that does exist) once a year, which ruled out any spontaneous, audience-inspired humor.

Yakov emigrated to the States, at the age of twenty-six, and settled in New York, where he enrolled in bartending school. After finishing, he was placed at Grossinger's (as a busboy) and, though he didn't know about the resort's status as the home of countless legendary comic acts, he says, "When I walked in and saw the big fifteen-hundred-seat room,

I said, 'I'll do whatever I have to do to stay here.'" Though he was earning about $1.50 an hour, "I didn't mind; I could watch comedians every night and see what made people laugh, and I did." After six months, he remembers, "they let me do lobby shows; it was called 'Daytime Entertainment with Lou Goldstein,' which was Simon Says and stuff like that." He began performing by translating his jokes from Russian to English: "I could hardly be understood but I had to start somewhere...." The strange atmosphere was not particularly conducive to a young, developing comic: "It was very weird—senior citizens groups who were afraid to laugh because their dentures would fall out. One woman was laughing real hard one day, so I thought I was doing well; I realized she was having a seizure when they wheeled her out—I guess that was the first time I killed."

Like many comics, however, Yakov learned that the style in which he performed was something he should outgrow—in his case, as quickly as possible. In L.A., where he moved to pursue film and television work, he discovered that the performers he had studied at Grossinger's were called Borscht Belt comics, and as a result he was "a typical Catskill comedian; I was 'Take my wife, please!'" At the Comedy Store, he was told, "You're doing old-style comedy. Go watch Richard Pryor and Robin Williams—watch Letterman... but don't watch Henny Youngman anymore," and so, for the next year, he learned how to tell stories, instead of battering the audience with machine gunned punch lines—and eventually developed his own style.

Yakov's mimicking of other comics' styles is unique only in his ignorance of the fact that he was developing into a dated comic. Generally, mimicking of successful, established stand-ups is a common practice among beginning comics. In any club at any given time, one can often observe at least one new stand-up who is "doing Johnny, Eddie or David." In many cases, this "borrowing" is not really a conscious decision to imitate, but instead, a means to discovering one's own style. As Paul Reiser explains, "When I started, I did what everyone does—bad impressions. A lot of comics start by doing either specific impressions of other stand-ups, or using mannerisms that have been heavily influenced by other comics—because they have no identity of their own."

If the comic is a hack, he'll continue aping others' styles until confronted, but if he's an artist, he'll begin to experiment and develop a style of his own. David Brenner says, "I see a lot of me. I started the whole observational thing, but besides that, I've seen people physically do me—the hands, things like that." He recalls the first thing comic Garry Shandling said when he met him was, "When you see me onstage, do you see yourself?" and Brenner told him, "Yeah sure—my hand movements, the thank you, the smiling . . ." but emphasizes this was during the early part of Shandling's career. Ultimately, this all proved to be unimportant because Garry "is an artist, he found himself—and today he's his own man . . . but the guys who didn't, who are doing warmed over David Brenners, will never smash through."

Regardless of a comic's style in the beginning—and in spite of details, like whether he kills, bombs or just fades into the spotlight, the process of "becoming" is a long one in the life of a stand-up, and no matter what his motivations are, or how painful the process is, it's never as hard as beginning. Carol Siskind says, "I remember Jerry Seinfeld saying to me once, about the first set he did that was really good, 'Oh, I've got this down now. I know how this works.' And of course you don't, not for awhile. There are so many levels and plateaus—the biggest stars in the world have bad nights. But you do learn a technique, like anything else. What happens as you work more is that the bad sets get better—and even if you have a horrible set, it's not ever going to be as bad as it was in the beginning."

STAND-UP AND GET OUT OF MY WAY

Stand-up comedy is a competitive business—there are only so many club spots, so many TV spots and, in the opinion of some comics, only so many jokes. Comics' feelings about the amount of competition among themselves varies from "it hardly exists" to "we're all cutthroat bastards (and bitches)!" A strong advocate of the former viewpoint is Jay Leno: "People think this is a real back-biting business, but I've gotten more work from other comedians than from anyone else." Describing his early days at the New York Improv, he says that "people like Robert Klein, David Brenner, George Carlin, Cosby would come in and say, 'I like your jokes, you're funny—there's a club I used to work—call this guy and tell him I recommended you.' That happened to me a lot so now I try to do that—call the Letterman show to tell them about people . . ." In the early 70s, the New York Improv was still the only showcase club in Manhattan and according to Richard Lewis the atmosphere there was conducive to comics supporting one another because there were about twenty of "them" versus the rest of the world. He describes it as a "brotherhood . . . everyone used to listen to and help each other; we'd go out to eat at four in the morning. Of course I had to go back to Jersey and get up in an hour and write brochures, which turned out to be pretty psychotic."

Lewis used to drive David Brenner home at night, after the club closed, and Brenner would give him advice about everything from his material to his career. "He was so good to me—he guided me, told me not to go to the Improv for about five months, but to work on my act in other places." Having taken over the mentor role, Brenner took Lewis to his own mentor, George Schultz, who owns the comedy club Pip's in Sheepshead Bay. "That's the man they call 'The Ear,'" Lewis says, "he hung out with Lenny and Rodney, and he opened his club before the Improv [it is still operating today]. Pip's was a paying gig ($30 for the weekend), which the Improv wasn't at the time, so I went out there and opened the show for Brenner, and George took me out by the bay afterwards and said, 'If you eat, sleep and fuck comedy, you're going to become a big star.' That fit into my obsession—to this day, he's been one of my closest friends."

David Brenner has been supportive of many up-and-coming comics since his rise in the early 70s and believes stand-ups should help one another, particularly once they have become successful. "How would it have helped me not to be? What's the difference? Will anyone take a job away from me? Where it's such big money what's the difference. Even if it did affect your business, what's ten percent less? It's an ego problem with some people—but I think they'd be that way if they were accountants. You're using the number seven? I wanted to use it—take it off your books! Hey, he stole my seven!"

Many established comics supported Brenner in his career and so he feels that it's his obligation to return the favors to the next generation: "Buddy Hackett saw me the first time on TV and called the entertainment director of the Sahara and said, 'Did you see this kid? Get him in there—get him on the stage.' And I got in there and worked with Frankie Avalon and Sonny and Cher. He'd never even met me. Jerry Lewis, on my first appearance, was in the hotel, called up and said, 'Don't let that kid out of the room,' and he ran over. I'll never forget—I was always a big fan of Jerry Lewis—and the door opened and in a camel hair coat is Jerry Lewis. He said to me, 'You're good, you're almost so good I could hate you.' Shecky Greene helped me . . . Redd Foxx was the first man who ever introduced me in the audience—I was watching him in Vegas and he said, 'It's about time we got some new, young blood in this town.' Very supportive. Joan Rivers said in an interview in the L.A. *Times,* before I met her, there are two comedians who are going to make it, 'David Brenner and Albert Brooks'—I'd never even met her." But he also says that there were several other well-established comics who were supportive until he started to make it—then they stopped abruptly. He remembers, "Once someone asked me about one of them, 'What happened to you two?' and I said, 'My success went to his head.' But generally the stars were very nice."

The most basic, grass roots support one comic can give to another is that of the more established stand-up "donating" stage time to his less fortunate colleague. Judy Tenuta remembers, several years ago, during a very important point in her career, Richard Belzer came through for her in this way: "I was supposed to audition at the Improv for Letterman and Silver [Friedman] wouldn't let me on. Caroline Hirsch [owner of Caroline's in New York] was there and brought me to her place, where Richard had just gotten offstage. She told him what happened and he said, 'Tomorrow night, come here and do fifteen minutes in front of me,' which allowed me to be seen . . . and he didn't even know me." While this didn't necessarily take any stage time away from Belzer, since he was the headliner and therefore the last performer, it could have negatively affected him in another way—to follow an untested act is something few comics relish, and so to put oneself in that position, voluntarily, is a truly unselfish gesture.

Many times a comic's generosity comes back to him. Marc Weiner remembers auditioning for "Saturday Night Live" at the New York Improv when his career was "beginning to really happen." A friend of his, John DeBellis, was not on the list to be auditioned. Since Marc was the last name on the list, he told John, "'Go on before me' and he got hired—and when he got there, he got Joe [Piscopo] hired. Later on in the year, I was at the club doing Rocko [his finger puppet act] and DeBellis said, 'Joe's got to see this.' So he brought him in, Joe told the producer about me—and I got on the show. That's how I ended up on 'Saturday Night Live.'"

Robert Wuhl, who began his career by selling jokes on a piecemeal basis to Rodney Dangerfield, says that, while this support does exist among comics, it is conditional: "I just went to San Francisco and saw how they all watch each other, so there's that support, but on the other hand, they'd all cut each other's throats if it came down to 'me' or 'you'—there's only so many spots. It's like being in the minor leagues and you need a chance to be seen in the hometown." He also feels that the support is greater among comics in the early part of their careers: "It's tougher to get spots, yet at the same time there's more support because you're all in it together. After a certain level you aren't waiting around watching everyone else anymore—so you really can't support them."

Les Sinclair, associate producer of the "Merv Griffin Show," feels that comics are more supportive of one another than actors; what they're doing is so highly specialized that they share a greater sense of camaraderie. He cites Jay Leno and Tom Dreesen as two of the greatest examples of comics who are supportive of their peers: "What I like about Tom is that, not only is he a brilliant comedian, with a wonderful mind, but he's really a supportive man. He helps other comics, he's there for them, and he's a terrific guy. Jay Leno is the same way. He'll tell me, 'Hey, I just saw a terrific comic—you really should see him.' Actors don't do that—in my experience, they're very competitive. Of course we all are, but I find more camaraderie among comics than anybody else. That's why I really do like them."

Alan Havey says that, like Leno, he has gotten many jobs from other comics who have recommended him, but adds that while loyalty and friendships among stand-ups are very powerful on one level, these qualities are strangely fragile on another because often comics find themselves competing against each other. One recent example of this is the television show "Star Search" in which a comic is given two minutes to perform against his competitor. In many cases, the comics are friends and while the competition isn't based upon one belittling the other, Havey still feels that "it's bad for the soul," which is why he declined to appear when asked.

Tommy Blaze believes little camaraderie exists among comics; in fact, he says, the competition among them is acute and omnipresent, and can be traced down to the structure of the comedy clubs, which are based upon competition and comparison. "A rock-and-roll band is the only one in the club; but a comic is with at least two other guys, so the audience compares you—always." He points out that not only the audience but comics compare themselves to one another constantly—every night, every show, and this creates an atmosphere of paranoid aggression among stand-ups. "They'll stab you in the back the first chance they get. If an agent says, 'What about this guy, Tommy Blaze?' another comic will say, 'Yeah, he's funny—if you like dick jokes,' because they want the booking that you were going to give Tommy Blaze."

Bob Goldthwait has several friends who happen to be comics, but generally finds that he doesn't much like other stand-ups. In spite of his distaste for most of his colleagues, he enjoys a very strong kinship with the few he does like, including their use of a common comic language: "It's funny, when me and Tom and Danny [two comic pals] get together and talk, we get this language... we use terms like, if someone's middle of the road, he's a dead skunk. If someone goes up onstage and does all old material, it's called Nanny's Housecoat—cause it's made out of old material—if someone uses stock lines, he's Dow Jones. It's all these comedy slang terms. A lot of people don't even know what a take five is—it's like, 'Get off the fucking stage!'"

Staying onstage longer than their allotted time is, along with joke stealing, one of the most grievous offenses a stand-up can commit. Goldthwait says this is the ultimate act of selfishness on a comic's part—and it's often a good indication of a stand-up's sense of competition with his peers: "It's the rudest thing you can do—the only comics I really hate are guys who go over time. One night recently, when I was waiting for my turn, she [he names a rather famous woman] did about a year... absolute overindulgence. Another comic, last week at the Comedy Store, did a longer set with the flashing light on than off—so I went up and said, 'What do you need, a fucking laser beam to burn your retinas off to get you off the stage?'"

Abby Stein believes competition is not so much a case of the nature of the business as the nature of the person. She discusses various stand-ups' reactions to the PCA: "Some comics are very sensitive, compassionate people who truly want to help one another, but there are many others who aren't, and who are competitive enough with their brethren that they don't want to be in any organization. There was a big outcry when this organization first got together—there were certain comedians who wanted there to be an earnings requirement before you could join the PCA, like a minimum of twenty thousand dollars or something. So when the organization became what it is, which is if you're a comic you can join, those people did not join, and they still haven't. There is a group of comics who have a very elitist attitude about the business."

Excessive competition among stand-ups can also dull their appreciation for the craft itself. Of course nightly exposure to comedy takes its toll on the funny bone as well, but just as crucial in the dulling process is the self-preserving impulse that leads comics to laugh reluctantly at others' jokes—and then, only after careful scrutiny. George Calfa remembers, after passing auditions at the Comic Strip, which gave him "hanging out" privileges, thinking, "'I'm so lucky—this is what I used to pay to see, now I get it for free,' and I'd be laughing along with the audience . . . then one day I wasn't laughing along with the audience anymore and it dawned on me—I'll never be able to go back to that— really enjoying comedy clubs." Now, like many comics, he only enjoys a certain type of comedy that is "so sick or weird you can't do it on-stage. It has to be beyond the normal stuff, it's crazy, sick, filthy stuff." This nonchalant reaction to comedy is common among stand-ups. Its most obvious example is the standard, "comic laugh," which Calfa explains as "no reaction at all, then you laugh a second before or after the punch line, a real short, 'hah!' laugh, and that's it."

For Carol Siskind, thinking of stand-up in competitive terms is not only counter-productive, but unrealistic: "There's room for everyone; you have to remember that." She has found among most stand-ups there is a great sense of camaraderie based on each one's essential solitude: "We all do this separately, we all empathize with each other because we know what it's like—we understand what it's like to kill and to bomb. . . ." But strong comic to comic identification within a highly inbred community makes each comic feel that they are directly influenced by the good and bad fortunes of all others: "When someone gets something you may say 'This has nothing to do with me or my career, or my life,' but there is a lot of angst and a lot of upset. I remember a while ago, Paul Provenza and I were talking about other comics and he said to me, 'What the fuck happened to my career?' Two weeks later he gets the movie of the week . . . so you just never know."

Bob Goldthwait avoids talking with other comics in the clubs because these kinds of comparisons are unavoidable. "Once I was at the Comedy Store—I was in the middle of doing my Cinemax special, I'd just gotten the movie, *Burglar*, with Whoopi, real good stuff going on—and I talked to some guy and said, 'How are you doing,' and he said, 'I'm doing blah, blah . . .' and rattled off a million things, and I suddenly felt unemployed!" The camaraderie stand-ups talk about is often a cover for veiled hostility: "Everybody is everybody's friend in the comedy world, but we're not really." He feels that "mutual occupation" is not a synonym for "friendship," and that he is disliked because he sees through this hypocrisy: "I know what real friends are, I have some who have picked me up out of gutters and shit, and said, 'I love you, stop killing yourself.' In L.A., I didn't make a lot of friends, I didn't pretend to like people I didn't really know or like—I'd be polite, that was it. I didn't spend the night out partying with the boys. That's why I think I'm pretty misunderstood in the comedy world—why another comic went on Letterman and bad-mouthed me."

In most occupations, money is often a central issue in the competition between rival factions. The situation in stand-up today, with regard to this issue, is not unlike that in the computer industry; because the business is so new and its growth has been so rapid, there are very few precedents with regard to payment. Also, because the current demand for comics is so great and the outlets in which they can work so many, novices' incomes are often immediately greater than those that their predecessors earned over many years. A comic who began in 1976 may have worked four years before earning enough money to quit his day job (and even then, only because clubs had begun to open—if they began in 1974, it may still have taken five or six years), whereas a comic who began in 1985, like Tommy Blaze, was earning enough money to live on the road in a matter of months. Lois Bromfield, who entered the business before the current "boom," says that "the money is always the issue—you say you don't feel competitive, but then someone goes out and makes a thousand dollars more than you and they've been out a year and you've been out for seven. But I've learned to say, 'So what, I've done real well for seven years.' I'm as happy as I could possibly be—I have everything I need, why be jealous? Karen Haber is someone who's new. She's been in it for about two years, and a lot of people resented her because she was moving up in the ranks real fast, getting the kind of work it took everyone else a long time to get. But one night she came up to me and said, 'You're Lois Bromfield? I love you—I think you're great.' She was really sincere and sweet—at that point I learned a lot about how to just be a person, not an asshole."

Mitzi Shore believes that the recent glut of comics, regardless of how many new clubs open, creates a keener sense of competition. The need to stand-out from the crowd is what drives them to become unique: "In one night you'll see fifty different comics here—all different and original and doing their own material. They used to steal each other's material. Henny Youngman? Milton Berle? Who are they kidding? They were doing the same acts for years!" She says that, aside from those comics who began the trend of writing their own material, like Bob Newhart, Woody Allen and Shelley Berman, the most important catalyst to uniqueness in the business has been competition: "It has made people be more original and innovative—the quality standard is so much higher now."

"Development people," such as agents, managers and club owners, also compare comics. Stand-ups with similar acts, personas, or even looks are judged and "the best" is chosen while the other(s) are advised to seek guidance and support elsewhere. Mitzi Shore says, "I'll tell you something I have to do that isn't pleasant. If there are two comics that work almost alike, I have to pick the one who I think is going to happen. Judy Tenuta came to me when she and Roseann Barr started —I made the choice, and I made it with Roseann. Same with Yakov —there was another Russian comedian that wanted to work out, but I had to pick the one I thought had the most potential."

Sometimes this process is not quite so up-front, according to David Brenner, who believes that a manager purposely gave him bad career advice, "because he could see I was going to muscle out his boy, which I eventually did. He said, 'I'm going to give you two tips: one, don't do first-person material; two, stop doing the stand-up, move to Chicago, get into Second City, stay there and work five years, then come back and do television,' but within three months of his 'great' advice, I went on 'The Tonight Show' and became a star doing first-person material. I like to think his judgment was off, rather than his character."

Rita Rudner believes that the competition between comics with similar styles is more acute than that among comics in general. It is this aspect particularly which makes friendships among stand-ups uniquely close and conflicting at the same time: "I'm friendly with all the comedians; it's like a club you belong to that's wonderful. Friendships among comics are conflicting—they're close, but competitive. For instance, Margaret Smith and I are sort of similar, so I feel inwardly competitive with her, like, 'She's written that joke and I haven't written anything. Why haven't I?' That makes it hard to be around them all the time."

In order to rise above competition, a comic must have blind faith in himself—or at least enough confidence to ignore others' work and continue his own. This, too, brings dangers, however; a careful balance must be struck between believing enough and believing too much. A. Whitney Brown says that too much ego and too *little* attention to other stand-ups' acts can freeze a comic in the position of his last triumph: "So many people are killed in this business because they can't learn. The only reason I've had any success, this sounds awful, is because it's more important for me to learn from someone than to act like I'm better than they are. If you're not willing to learn, you end up getting to a certain point and not going any farther. Ego is the biggest killer in this business. No matter what job you have, there will always be somebody who can do it better than you—you've got to remember that."

The very act of performing stand-up requires a great deal of ego with regard to the audience—regardless of how humble one tries to be vis-à-vis his peers. According to Jerry Seinfeld, "The ego statement of stepping up onstage by yourself for the first time is unbelievable. I'll never forget that. The first time I got up onstage—that statement of, 'Okay, so you're a hundred fifty people sitting there, and I want you all to listen to me now, I'm going to be your entertainment all by myself. You can talk with your friends, but you'd be better off listening to me.

You can enjoy what I have to say more than any of the people you know and that you're with right now, because I'm so much brighter and more aware of what's going on in the world. Plus I can point out observations you never would have thought of; you'll just barely be able to comprehend them until the point where you'll explode with laughter when you discover the accuracy of my thinking.' That's what you're saying, essentially. They're paying money to hear you talk." A comic must constantly deny this to himself, though, or fall into a state of stagnation: "I still don't feel like I deserve all this, which is why it works for me—because I'm constantly trying to earn it still."

Jay Leno believes that he is dependent only upon himself and therefore has only himself to blame, or congratulate, depending on the situation: "I don't feel jealousy over someone like Letterman who passed me by like a shot—or Robin—and I started long before these people; I've always worked at my own pace—and I work alone, so it's all up to me." Larry Miller agrees that the only real competition in stand-up is with oneself, which is also true of life: "Being a whole person is realizing that in many areas the responsibility is your own." With regard to other comics, he is not above envy, but explains that this isn't necessarily negative: "There's a difference between envy and jealousy. Envy is healthy; it's saying, 'I'd like a car like that, I'd like a part in that movie . . .' Jealousy is dark, it's where you go: 'Look at that guy with the car; somehow he's preventing me from getting the car.' That's not sane."

In the case of television where the writing is more collaborative, ego can become a problem. As Jay Leno says: "Maybe you know your joke is funnier, and you don't get the chance to do it." Working as an opening act can also create ego problems for stand-ups, in that they are forced to submerge their egos in deference to the headliner and his audience, which ultimately helps neither the comic nor his act. Leno says that, for this reason, he decided to stop opening for other acts in the past—he didn't want to compete with the headliner or have to alter his act to suit the headliner's audience: "I enjoyed working with Tom Jones and John Denver and those people, they were very nice, but I always had to change my act to suit the people I was playing for—their audiences. I'd rather play in front of eighty people at the

Knights of Columbus with my name up there—at least I know those people are there to see me and I can do what I want to do. This is why I'm in no hurry. I'd rather have them come at their own pace, rather than having me round them up with a stick to see 'The Greatest Comedy Show That's Ever Been.'"

This is not an uncommon career decision and it is more than a matter of ego; many stand-ups feel that opening for other acts (usually singers) casts not only themselves but comedy in an unflattering light —that of the perennial, poor entertainment relative, the warm-up act. Paul Reiser explains: "It's like opening for a band—I don't need the gig that badly. I've been to concerts where comics open and it's tough, like, 'Before we hear Mr. Buddy Rich, here's another Jew with thoughts.' And there's a big, 'Oy!' I cringe, and think, 'Imagine how someone feels with no orientation toward comedy.' It's like, before your cake and cookies, do some push-ups."

Paul Provenza remembers touring with Diana Ross, where his contract with her stipulated that he get no billing, "so the crowd didn't expect to see me until I appeared onstage. I'd go out to two thousand people moaning, 'Oh no-o-o!'" After several nights of this, he solved the problem somewhat by yelling back, "Let's get one thing straight, I don't know who the hell any of you are either... I know how you feel, the lights go down, you're expecting to see Diana, and I show up. Let me explain it to you—you know how you go into a deli, and they give you the pickle with the sandwich? You don't ask for the pickle, they don't tell you they're giving it to you—they just give it to you. Well, I'm the pickle." Having solved this problem, however, he was still faced with the legacy of the opening act, which is that "you have to answer to the headliner... whereas if I'm in a club, headlining, I don't have to worry about alienating the audience and bringing them back —or leaving them there if that's what my particular self-destructive/ creative bent tells me to do that night. I'm the one who pays the price and I don't have to worry about fucking up the audience for a woman who's a legend in her own time."

Comics must also engage in the battle against their own inertia— the insidious competition between themselves... and themselves. In order to perform stand-up successfully, a comic must find the proper balance of energy, both mental and physical—too much will make the act seem forced, too little will send it limping across the stage toward its inevitable death. According to Carol Leifer, "To make people laugh for an hour and fifteen minutes is a concerted effort even though it may not look like it. It's a constant, 'Where should I go from here? That joke didn't work too well—how can I save it?'" But while this constant evaluation is going on, it must never be betrayed to the audience; the moment to moment process of creation works only when hidden completely in the inner recesses of a comic mind.

Richard Lewis says that this process of constant creation and analysis onstage results in "physical manicness" in his case, but that shouldn't be confused with actual nervousness: "I don't feel out of control; in fact, I feel very much in control and centered—it's just that I have a lot of information, creatively, that if I don't channel it I look manic." Offstage, due to years of training, his mind works the same way— which can be taxing. It is difficult, however, because he does not create material sitting down at a typewriter; instead, he is constantly writing notes on an ever-present pad or whispering possible bits into a tiny tape recorder.

The stress of having to be constantly creative is only part of what saps a comic's energy; another burden is the need to be "up" when required—to be physically and mentally healthy, regardless of what's going on offstage. A. Whitney Brown says that this is the most important ingredient for success: "I've found that in show business, there are so many traps to getting where you want to go that it's not enough to have a sense of humor, be able to apply yourself and have talent. You also have to have stamina. A lot of how well you do depends on how long you can stay awake, or how good your work habits are, or how well you can avoid wasting your time on personal relationships, or how well you can avoid drugs—and if you can't, how strong your constitution is, how well you can avoid being sick or losing your temper."

For some, a regimented routine is the solution. Paul Reiser used a system in the beginning in which he had to follow a certain rhythm to get "up" for the show. After working all day in an office, he'd take a shower and go to the club. He says, "The movement of work-to-shower-to-stage was the momentum I needed. I knew I'd done my work." A comic must also protect himself from being shot down before he walks onstage, because regardless of how much preparation has been put into the act, those final seconds before he grabs the mike can make or break a performance: "We have this homework mentality embedded when we're kids, but it doesn't apply here. It's like with acting, you can prepare, do intellectual exercises or whatever, but it's the ten seconds before they say, 'Action,' that are your primary concern. If somebody says, 'P.S., your parents just both blew up,' that's it—you're through." He remembers recently, "I saw someone I knew thirty seconds before I went onstage, standing at the door, who said, 'Hi, the last time I saw your parents was at a funeral,' then walked away. The last thing I heard was, 'parents—funeral—goodbye.' I laughed, because I couldn't believe how she zinged me. I work so deliberately to avoid any contact with people, and she totally motherfucked me, so to speak."

Emo Philips keeps to a schedule not only to insure his sanity on the road, but because "habit is a good thing—otherwise, every time you had to wash your hair, it would take three hours to learn the whole thing over again. Now it only takes me two hours, because I underline the instructions in the diagram." He describes being on the road (which is, for him, the majority of his life) as living like a caveman: "You have to go out and forage for food—and that's not easy. I don't like sugar and white bread and I cut down on meat because it's expensive. I don't like to eat too much health food though because it makes you lose your immunity to junk food. A lot of people who eat health food all their lives have one potato chip and they die." After finding food, he walks around the town between local interviews, but because of their frequency and the amount of travel from one gig to the next, there is often little time for any real relaxation.

In hearing an average example of Emo's schedule for one week, one gets an idea of how important physical stamina is to a comic: "I'm at Lake Forest College, then I'm in Burlington, Vermont, then in Montreal, then the next week I'm in Kalamazoo. So I'll do the newspaper interviews in every town, usually one or two. I had a one-nighter in Albany and for that, four newspaper interviews and four radio interviews over the phone." While this lack of privacy is a sacrifice, he says that granting countless interviews is part of the business—free advertising that a comic would be foolish to turn down.

Larry Miller's routine is a regimented one: "Exercise in the morning, jump in the shower, pray, eat breakfast every day at the same place, make calls, then write. Jerry Seinfeld and I always kid around—you have a great routine, and every time your agents get you a meeting for something, it screws everything up... like, 'What about my routine?' You get what you've always wanted, but it louses everything up. I try to be creative every day, even for a little time—not just onstage, but off, too." He tries to work out onstage regularly when in New York and Los Angeles, alternating his periods in these cities, where he pursues media opportunities, with road gigs, which support his city lifestyle. Unlike many comics who find it difficult to maintain a balance between the road and "the coasts," Miller's amazing sense of planning and control seem to work as efficiently in his long-range planning as in his daily schedule. In response to the question, "What's happening after this?" he rattles off: "After New York I go back to L.A., where I'm pitching a TV show idea to a production company I've worked with before, then I have a little more road work planned, a college, then the new Punch Line in Jacksonville, and my plan for the next year is to keep doing good road work, alternately doing good work in L.A., writing, pitching, acting, talk shows—my next shot will be a Letterman, around June, then Griffin, around July or August, then another 'Tonight Show,' if all goes as planned."

His schedule of road work is by no means light; his average amount of travel is one to two weeks a month. He also stands in direct opposition to most comics in his feeling about the road, saying, "I enjoy it very much. The road is a very creative place for me—very unencumbered. For me the road is utter freedom: I have my show at night, and during the day I have all the time in the world. I can check in with my manager by phone, exercise, write an hour or two during the day—it's my club and my show. On the road days go by like that! I don't even have time to see a movie during a whole week in a given town usually." With regard to the sharp contrasts of the road—the supreme high of being onstage versus the abysmal lows of empty days—he says, "I don't feel that way at all. You shower, shave, dress, go to the club, do your show, go to the magical place, and come home. I don't have low points in my day, so there can be no real high point that rises above the abyss. It's a nice thing, very nice, perhaps the focal point or goal of the day, but so is my writing, exercise, and praying—they're all growth."

While Jerry Seinfeld depends upon a fairly regimented schedule, including yoga, to keep him afloat on the road, he seems to depend just as much on a philosophy of his work as a sort of crusade: "I try to think of myself as a master of the road—it's like I'm on this mission. I think everyone wishes their life was a little more dramatic, and I kind of see mine that way. There's a lot of drama to it. I'm in a town all by myself and I'm going to face these people . . . it's Friday night, it's late, the room is hot and it's smoky, the audience isn't coming around—maybe I can pull this out . . . It becomes this super hero kind of exis-tence. The crusade is to survive, to see how good I can get, not to prove anything about comedy. It's like rock climbing—you nail that sucker in and pull yourself up a quarter of an inch, and it may take you a year, but you get there."

Other comics find the day to day grind of road work unbearable, regardless of what tricks they employ to camouflage their misery. Abby Stein used to travel forty weeks out of the year and now says simply, "I hated it." Combined with her job as president of the PCA, she was "getting up at nine, working for the PCA all day, getting on a plane and going away, doing my PCA work on the plane, doing the shows, then calling my husband at four and having him say, 'Do you want me to move out so I won't bother you when you get back?' It was too crazy." So she gave it up and hardly travels at all today.

Alan Havey agrees that the price of road work, late-night hours and constant worry is high, but he says, "The pay-off is great. I don't know many people who love their work the way I do, including other come-dians—I love what I do." Comics constantly worry about not working hard enough, which adds up to their high level of stress: "We suffer from that white-collar guilt, even though we have a lot of free time—you worry you're not doing enough. Even if you do one twenty-minute set a night there's a lot of head work involved: going there, preparing, doing it, hanging out picking up information—who's paying what, who's fucking who—but it's all part of the business...loosely defined."

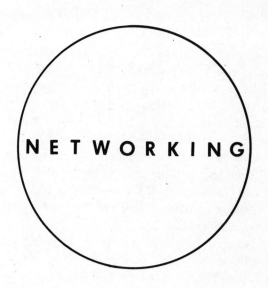

NETWORKING

"I need a Carson . . ." "I'm waiting for a Letterman . . ." "My agent's talking to the Rivers people . . ." Listen. The rhyme of the not-so-ancient comic floats through clubs across the country, as it's sung by countless yearning stand-ups trying to liberate themselves from the albatross that is "no TV exposure yet, but I may get a Letterman or Carson soon . . ." Compared to this ordeal of infinity, waiting for Godot is like a day at the races. But still they wait and wait, until they can wait no longer; then they do another set, write a new bit, work on their "stage attitude," do another set . . . and wait some more. Why? Because TV spots are a stand-up comic's ticket to visibility, credibility, higher club fees and, though individual strategies vary, everybody's got to have one. Its far-reaching power is perhaps exemplified best by Steven Wright's analogy: "Appearing on television is like going to a party with nine million people—and you're blindfolded. The next day you walk down the street and they go, 'What a great party!' and you think, 'Oh! Were you there?'"

In order to qualify as network TV material, a stand-up must be two things primarily—funny and clean. In spite of this, many comics continue to work dirty in clubs, assuming they will make minor changes in their acts for television. Jay Leno sees performers attempt this all the time, and it doesn't work: "I tell comedians who work dirty, 'It's real easy to take a clean joke and make it spicy or racy for a nightclub audience, but it's almost impossible to take a dirty joke and clean it up for "The Tonight Show."'" He says that dirty comedy is like a drug; it produces big laughs with relatively little effort—and that's hard to give up. "When you do the clean version of the same joke, the laugh may be more sophisticated and more subtle, but it's never as big." When they audition for television, he says, "instead of 'shit' they'll say 'garbage,' instead of 'asshole' they'll say 'butthead' or some stupid derivative." They become nervous and frustrated because the jokes—and the laughs—are not the same.

Because audiences have been conditioned by seeing acts that play for easy laughs, in many clubs they expect—and demand—that the comic work dirty. "They've been whipped into a frenzy by some guy who says, '. . . it's a fucking dick!' so when you come out saying, 'Did you ever notice? . . .' they look at you like you're nuts," says Joe Bolster, "but you can't stop and give them a comedy lesson . . . you have to trust what you're doing is the high road." Tom Dreesen takes a less philosophical approach to working clean but, in teaching aspiring comics how to succeed in the biz, he tells them this is the only way to work: "I'm a business man, and the name of my corporation is Tom Dreesen. As a comic, you're a commodity, like Right Guard or Seven Up, and you're trying to sell yourself from Boston to L.A. What's the first rule of sales? Create a need. How do you create a need? Advertise. How do we advertise? Television. How do we get on television? Work clean. I'm not a prude—I grew up on the streets and I know every dirty joke there is, but I also know what sells and what doesn't."

A comic primed for television needs more than a clean, funny act. His material must not be based on audience interaction. An act based heavily on this may kill in the clubs but in a TV studio, where the audience isn't miked and the camera can't find the interactee, the viewer is treated to what sounds like half of a telephone conversation. Like blue material, this style of stand-up is often used in clubs to deliver an easy laugh and has come to be expected as part of the club experience. While there are some comics who have elevated the practice to an art, others use it in a more antagonistic way, simply to provoke a few members of the audience in order to elicit nervous, shocked and to some extent sadistic laughter from the rest of the room. Les Sinclair of "The Merv Griffin Show" doesn't appreciate this style on or off television; he says that many of the "new breed" of comics say things like, "Hey, nice shirt. What, did you get it at K-Mart?" to make somebody the butt of the joke, and he feels that a good comedian laughs with—not at—the audience. Budd Friedman says that, with the exception of one or two comics who do it well, talking to the audience is the "height of amateurism . . . and is used as a crutch by all the rest, including myself [in addition to owning the Improv, he is also its emcee] and a good comic doesn't have to do that." Whether or not one agrees with this opinion, comic/audience interaction has managed to become a fixture in the clubs, despite its continuing absence from television.

In addition to the above, there are other considerations for the comic who plans to audition for television. While Joan Rivers could get away with "Elizabeth Taylor is so fat . . ." lines, most talk shows do not consider jokes by unknown, unproven comics worth the risk of a lawsuit. Therefore, comics trying to get a TV spot should cut all libelous material. In some cases, the use of product brand names is also frowned upon, rendering such humor staples as McDonald's ("What part of the chicken is the McNugget *from*, anyway?" etc.) out of bounds—although, according to Laurie Zaks, who has run the talent departments for NBC's "Saturday Night Live" and Motown/Kingworld's syndicated "Nightlife with David Brenner," this can vary from one show to the next; brand names were censored by the network on the former program, and not on the latter. She says also that NBC censors were most concerned with foul language and gestures, violence (comic/magician Harry Anderson was barely able to perform a trick in which he pulled a needle through his arm and drew fake blood) and "positive" drug messages. In fact, the latter issue has become so important that a portion of comic Sam Kinison's set was censored from the West Coast broadcast of "Saturday Night Live" (the East Coast show is live, making editing-out impossible) in October of 1986 because of his drug references.

According to Kip Adotta, television shows, above all, edit out controversy: "Censorship has nothing to do with fuck or shit; anyone with half a brain can say whatever they want without using four-letter words. The censorship comes in here: you can't mention Ford Motor Company, AT&T . . . you can't say that until you're big enough that the public will say, 'Kip said it,' rather than, 'Some guy on "The Tonight Show" said it.' They don't want you to voice your opinion, or do anything that doesn't have precedents—when you put those shackles on a person, they have to go on TV and say, 'You know in New York, you don't go in the park, and those cabbies . . . and in L.A. they're so laid-back . . .' They force you into mediocrity. When I was doing the show, I submitted material over the phone. Once I had something about Pintos exploding, and they said, 'You can't say that on "The Tonight Show," because it's not public knowledge.' I said, 'Have you read the paper today?' On the front page, there it was—it had been going on for two weeks. Well that pissed them off." He feels that this type of restriction destroys one of the nobler aspects of comedy—its ability to tell the truth. "When historians go back to find out what really happened somewhere, they don't only look at the chroniclers of the time, they look at the satirists. Henry VIII was always referred to by his chroniclers as 'a simple man, a man of service'—but if you listen to the satirists of the time, they'll tell you about the nine-year-old boys strapped to the walls in his bedroom. Today the same thing is going on."

Comics must also abandon stock jokes like, "Hey, did you know I signed a contract with HBO? [audience applause] Yeah—I just got cable!" These may slip easily by drunk audiences on road gigs, but they're quickly spotted by talent coordinators who have heard them—and all their regional variations—before. Stolen material should also be given up for obvious reasons, because if it isn't spotted before the show, it certainly will be afterwards. Adrianne Tolsch points out that "this business is so involuted, that kind of thing will get you eventually, and with word of mouth among comics it won't take very long." While joke stealing is considered despicable in any context, it becomes a cardinal sin on television because, as Tolsch says, "The closest you can come to copyrighting your material is having it on TV." If both parties continue to do the same joke, the system generally works according to the caste system of stardom. As Emo Philips says: "If you're more famous than someone below you, people will think that they stole from you, even if they wrote the joke. But I don't worry about it—if you're good, you can always rise above the two-bit chiselers... if someone had stolen a sonata idea from Beethoven, would he not have gotten famous?"

Comics hear a familiar audience refrain around the country: "You're so funny, you ought to be on television." This makes sense—until one hears the comic's set after all the above factors have been edited out, in which case the act might sound something like this: "Hi. Thanks for coming. Goodnight!" In addition to those comics who are eliminated in this way, dozens of others meet all the criteria for television, but according to the powers-that-be, just aren't "ready." Les Sinclair defines being "ready" as the point at which the comic *knows* he is: "When there's a comfortableness about them onstage, when they're just receiving all that energy from the audience, when they really get off on that energy, when they're riding on it... it's breaking through the boundaries of your limitations—that's when it becomes exciting. Believe me, when you're ready you know it."

Bob Morton of "Late Night with David Letterman" is constantly monitoring the progress of comics in the clubs to see who is and who isn't ready. "You could probably name any comedian and I'd know what stage they're at—even if *they* don't realize it," he says. "They think I come in and make the judgment and forget about them; they don't understand that this is my business and I have to know what's out there on the market. I'm just like a buyer from Macy's or Bloomingdale's—they know each kind of fashion that's coming out. They know sweaters—and I know comics." He assumes that "any sane person taking the time, effort and guts to call a network show and say, 'Come and see me,' is ready to be seen." And though "there's nothing more annoying than a person who calls and is a million years away from doing the show... because they started two weeks ago," he says that anyone who calls is given a shot at being seen. After they've been seen, he continues to watch their act and when they call (which he says many comics do over and over) he tells them, "I don't have to see you again because you know something? I know exactly what you're doing and I know exactly how you're doing it based on what I know about the business and the fact that I keep up."

Rita Rudner, who had been performing for three years before she sent a videotape to the Letterman show, gives an example of Morton's ability to look past an off-night and see a comic's potential. "When he came to watch me," she says, "it was a bad night and I was awful, but he liked my material and said he'd come back on another night." He did, and she was good. After that, he brought the producer, Barry Sand, who also liked it, and she was on.

Alan Havey worked in New York clubs for five years before his shot on Letterman. He says, "I was aching to get on that show—dying to get on it. A couple years ago I told Morton, 'I'm not going anywhere —I'm going to be doing comedy for a long time—and I know the show will be here . . . I can wait.' I had to cut myself some slack and keep thinking, 'Just work on your act and the rest will come.'" Finally he got his shot and says one of the most rewarding aspects of that was "some of my material got out on the air—it's mine—and no one can take that away from me now." But most satisfying of all was the feeling of having attained a dream. He recalls the night: "I was on fire the whole time; I was surprised my hands didn't shake. When Letterman introduced me, it was what I'd imagined for years, what I'd visualized so many times, dealing with any situation that might arise. And it did! They told me I had to cut it short right before I went on and I'd already envisioned that happening, so I was prepared. Also, a couple nights before, I was at Catch and Jerry Seinfeld said, 'If you think you're going too slow, on the show, slow down even more—take your time,' and that helped, too."

Still another consideration in the comic's talk-show quest is style. As is the case with set design, wardrobe and music, each program has a very definite idea of what works for it, what's "right" for it. This decision is not arbitrary; it's based upon the show's audience, its host, the time at which it airs and what has worked in the past. A comic who is in perfect sync with Letterman viewers may send the Carson audience running to their joke thesauruses, and vice versa, though this isn't always the case. "Latenight"'s executive producer, Barry Sand, says, "We look for a breakthrough; a comedian who people are going to talk about. Sam Kinison is an example. I know my parents wouldn't want to watch him; they wouldn't have the stomach. Bob Goldthwait's another one, or Emo, or Steve Wright. We want a guy that makes people say, 'My God, what did he do!?' We're not looking for the traditional comedian who gets up and talks about their wife and kids. It's not that these people aren't terrific, but they're not something people will talk about and say, 'I didn't get this guy,' then in three years they go, 'This guy is the greatest.'" More conventional comics, like Jerry Seinfeld, are also right for the show because they "are uniquely bright, sharp and funny."

These "more conventional" comics, like Seinfeld, Larry Miller, Paul Reiser and Jay Leno can appear on any number of shows not because their jokes appeal to the broadest possible base of people, but because they have structured their character/stand-up persona and material in such a way that they can be slightly altered according to each audience's particular frame of reference. Provenza describes them as "speaking the Esperanto of comedy. They talk to human beings, not any one sector of the population. It's not selling out, but being able to speak to every one." Larry Miller offers an example: "There are various considerations. I might do something on the Letterman show that I think is more subtle, like the joke about car phones... how really obnoxious people will have answering machines on their car phones, and people who call can say, 'I know you're there, I'm right behind you.' Then I talk about how women don't get honked at enough on the highways; now guys will be able to call over a couple of lanes, like, 'Oh, hi—I see you're from Illinois... yup... Land of Lincoln'— some corny remark... Now saying 'Land of Lincoln' is a very small, subtle thing, but even if you don't know that's the license plate slogan of Illinois, a certain given mind-set will respond to the fact that that sounds like a license plate—that by saying 'Land of Lincoln' it's an attempt at conversation. So I did that on the Letterman show and got a wonderful response, and I specifically excluded it from 'The Tonight Show.'"

Other comics with a more defined point of view, particularly those who work in character (like Emo and Goldthwait), may have broader appeal with certain types of audiences, but find it harder to move

between shows with different sets of demographics, like Carson's, with
its middle of the road bent, and Letterman's, with its young, urban-
oriented audience. Goldthwait, whose "Bobcat" character, a cross between Winnie the Pooh and a rabid dog, was a hit on Letterman,
barely got on "The Tonight Show": "The way I got on there was that
Joan Rivers said, 'I don't want a birthday present, I want Bob Goldthwait on my show,' and the director, who was really opposed to me, was
on vacation—so they let me go on." He adds, "'The Tonight Show'
and Disney are the two most paranoid places in the world about taking
chances." Emo has not done Carson either. "Probably I wasn't exciting
enough for the show," he says, laughing, but "I've done several Lettermans, and they tell me I'll be on again and again . . . whenever those
shows are repeated." Laurie Zaks agrees that different shows demand
different styles. For "Saturday Night Live" she preferred to use comics
with a "twist," which at various times included props (Joel Hodgson's
machine in which he sawed himself in half), juggling (Michael Davis
spitting and catching ping-pong balls in his mouth) and magic (Harry
Anderson piercing himself with a needle). For "Nightlife," on the
other hand, she says that because of the program's format, audience
and Brenner's personal preference, straight monologists work the best.
Les Sinclair looks for a comic whose "humor touches everybody; if
they're so way out and removed from somebody's personal experience,
to me they're not funny. Basically, if somebody makes me laugh, I
know they'll work out."

The syndicated series "Comedy Tonight" is less particular about its
requirements than the national talk shows—and it has to be. Its talent
executive Rick Messina explains: "From the beginning its schedule was
ambitious—five nights a week, four to five comics a night, sixty-five
weeks of production, that's almost two hundred comic slots to be filled.
Anyone in the business would say it's madness to think there are two
hundred, or even one hundred comics that could do TV who weren't
already doing it." He says that, watching the show week after week,
people have been shocked at how many talented, unknown comics are
out there, but "the thing they're most amazed about is the lack of
terrible acts." Though this show provides easier television access than
some others, it is not necessarily the first step in a comic's progression

up the TV ladder. Depending on whom you ask, doing less selective shows can "only help," "only hurt" or "completely destroy your chances of doing the talk shows." Because of this advice, some comics choose to hold out for the Big Two (Carson and Letterman), and turn down the offers of less selective shows like "Comedy Tonight." Rick Messina says that this is an unwise decision: "I advise comics, as far as TV, do anything that's offered to you; don't be paranoid about it. A lot of them are afraid if they do show A they might offend show B—but the bottom line is that if you do any show and you're unusual, different, clever, it's going to help you and chances are it will lead to something else. When you're nobody, to say 'I'm going to wait for them to call,' you may wait a long time." He gives an example of one comic who cancelled three times because he thought he was going to do the Letterman show and he didn't want to make any waves. He never ended up doing the Letterman show and, because of all his prior cancellations, Messina says, "We don't even want to work with him. So what does he end up with? He ends up staying home."

Les Sinclair, however, says that while he doesn't place such exclusivity requirements on comics, "there is one show that doesn't like anybody to be on our show before theirs, which I think is ridiculous— 'The Tonight Show' . . . you didn't hear it from me. Well, actually, you did hear it from me, I don't care." Laurie Zaks has been told by some comics that they could not do "Nightlife" because "they were waiting for a spot on Letterman," while others say that it may hurt their chances, but they'll do Brenner's show anyway because they simply refuse to play politics.

"The Tonight Show" and "Latenight"'s preference for TV virginity is "understood" in the comic community, according to Abby Stein, but people are reticent about speaking out for fear of being blacklisted by the shows: "Rumor has been if you do 'Comedy Tonight' you don't do Letterman and if you do Letterman you don't do Carson and vice versa, and I'd love to get to the bottom of it," she says, because "it is a restraint of trade matter if it really exists." On the other hand, she points out that the shows have a legitimate complaint, which is, "If we give you four spots and make your price go up considerably, don't you owe it to us not to run away and do another show?" In this case, she says, like in that of rival comedy clubs in a given town, "I'd like there to be a more official line." Messina respects the shows if these are their grounds: "It's very similar to club bookings, when there are two in one city. We don't want to see Jay Leno working two clubs in one town a week apart. Some markets are absolutely clear about it, like, 'Don't ever work the crosstown club no matter what,' and others aren't. But if their motive there is to block comics from doing 'Comedy Tonight,' then I'm flattered because then they're obviously afraid we're going to hurt their ratings.

"Those shows used to be the only place for comics to perform and maybe they don't want to give up their territory. The Letterman or 'Tonight Show' used to be able to offer a stand-up comic the only six minutes this comic would get to hit a national TV audience. Now there are a lot of ways, and they don't like it." Shows like "Comedy Tonight" have opened the door for comics who may have been denied access to TV several years ago: "Kids used to spend their lives trying to get a 'Tonight Show' spot and if they didn't, where would their career go? There are a lot of unusual comics who would never get a chance to do TV, but now they're going to."

Messina points out another problem: "On other talk shows you're usually subject to the viewpoints of that show or to the ideas of that host. While you may do the show, if you're not funny for that particular host, you might not do the show again—even if you're very funny for the rest of the country. I've seen some very strong comics go on 'The Tonight Show' and the Letterman show and just kill, do terrific sets, then sit on the panel and be hysterical—and they're never seen on the show again. We're an alternative." Barry Sand seems to agree: "When I book 'Latenight' I know there are guests who would be perfect anywhere else, but would be inappropriate on our show because the chemistry would be wrong. When we book the show—and we're wrong sometimes, too—we consider: would this person make Dave funny; would this bring out something in Dave?"

Regardless of personal preferences and pet peeves, all bookers eventually meet on common ground—in the clubs. Contrary to popular folklore, the chances of them walking into a club cold, seeing a brilliant new comic and "discovering" them are virtually zero, although this has happened on occasion. A case in point is Steven Wright who, at the age of twenty-six, had been working as a stand-up for three years in the New England area exclusively. He recalls, "What happened one night was that Peter LaSalle, co-producer of 'The Tonight Show,' was in Boston because his son was looking at universities in the area. While they were in Boston they went into the Ding Ho [a Chinese restaurant/comedy club] and he saw me perform. Three weeks later I was on 'The Tonight Show.'" Usually, however, bookers have either seen, heard from, or heard about a comic. Then they set up a time, with the comic or his representative, to see them work in a club. Auditions, set up by the showcase clubs on the coasts, are another way of seeing "new" talent. According to Alan Havey, "The management picks certain comics they think should be on, based on whether the show is looking for a certain type, or maybe they just want to see five different comics, or twenty. It's all political, who's getting on, when, who's following who, who's the emcee going to be."

Budd Friedman avoids the latter problem by appointing himself as emcee: "I do it partly because I'm a ham—because it's my basketball, so if I don't play, no one's going to. But that's one thing that's so great about this club; when we do a showcase, all the industry knows they're going to get a tight show, because there's no emcee auditioning for a job. Casting people say they go to other places, and they're there all night because the emcee kept doing joke after joke. What I do is get them on and off. Like last night, for the Disney audition, there was a comedienne who went on too long. She said, 'I didn't see the light...' Well, I got her right off." "The light" signals a comic that his or her allotted time has elapsed, but occasionally, with all of the pressure, fame and money involved in these auditions, some choose to ignore it.

Richard Fields, owner of New York's Catch A Rising Star, feels that a club owner should actively pursue television opportunities for the regular comics, though, he says, few do: "We're different at Catch— we're much more involved in people's lives. We provide, aggressively, opportunities for our people to get exposure. We went to CBS TV and said, 'You're missing the greatest talent pool right under your noses— come in and cast shows that you're developing in New York from the people who are right here.' We set up an audition for them—so they don't have to go to L.A. to see what's right here already. We found out there was an opening at NBC radio for a deejay, so we're all over them to come see the 'Catch' people, and we bring our people up there." Of course the owners do not only do this out of their love for the performers; every comic who is discovered hammers a deep notch into a club's publicity belt. And so the auditioning system in showcase clubs works, in differing degrees, to everyone's benefit—bookers have shows set up for them, comics are exposed to bookers, and owners help their club to become "home of" the newest (with a little luck) comic star.

Once a comic has been selected, a date is set, their (roughly) six-minute routine is de-bugged and approved by censors and segment producers, they rehearse, and finally perform.

The emotions one feels in the early stages of a stand-up comedy career are those more closely associated with the diagnosis of terminal illness—shock, anger, denial and, finally, acceptance. In the case of terminal illness, one "accepts" and then dies; in the case of stand-up comedy, however, acceptance is often followed by a monomaniacal obsession with being seen by Johnny Carson—passing, if you will, "From He-e-e-e-ere to Eternity." For many comics, "getting Carson" is what they have dreamed about since childhood.

Tom Dreesen explains that Carson is the only measure, for most people, of what a "real" comedian is: "You see, wherever you go in America today, if someone asks what you do for a living and you say, 'I'm a comedian,' they say, 'Oh, yeah? Have you ever been on "The Tonight Show?"' Until you can say yes, you're not really a comedian in the eyes of this country—and all of us know this." He remembers, after moving to Los Angeles, "When I was sleeping in an abandoned car and hitchhiking to the Comedy Store, begging to work for free, I would envision in my mind, every night, Johnny Carson talking to me, saying, 'You're quite a guy Tom Dreesen... you're a funny guy Tom Dreesen,' laughing at me, what I'm saying, because I think that what the mind can see and believe, it can also achieve, and if I was sitting next to Johnny, it meant I had already succeeded over in the stand-up spot."

Finally, in the fall of 1975, he was auditioned at the Comedy Store (along with Billy Crystal, who was also selected) and got a "Tonight

Show" spot. He remembers: "They rehearsed me, okayed my material
—and then bumped me four consecutive times. I'd go there, they'd
run overtime... then they'd say, 'Come back, please.' Meanwhile not
only is the whole country watching the show, but my mother has all
the neighbors in the house, so if I fail I can't even go home.

"On the fifth time [December 2, 1975], I was in make-up and Fred
DeCordova [the show's executive producer] walks in and says, 'I've got
some bad news for you...' I said 'What?' and he said, 'You're going on
tonight.' Okay. So the time came. The talent coordinator came to get
me, he took me from the green room, and we took that long walk
around the back. He stood me behind that curtain, and said, 'They're
going to open the curtain when it's time, and you will walk out to the
little green "t"'; then he left me alone. Doc Severinsen was playing,
and now I'm talking to God one on one, saying, 'Please go on with
me... I can't do it alone...' Then all of a sudden the music stopped,
and so did my heart. Johnny Carson said, as he always does when he
introduces a new comic, 'Well, we're back, and I'm glad you're in such
a good mood tonight because our next guest is making his first appearance on "The Tonight Show."' He always gets the same message
across—let's give this kid a break now, you're in a good mood, you
hear me?

"I got big laughs and applause, like eleven applause breaks, and my
last joke was, 'Thank you, very much, it's my first appearance on "The
Tonight Show." Show business is a tough life and I need all the help I
can get, so if you're Catholic light a candle for me, if you're Protestant
say a prayer, and if you're Jewish, someone in your family owns a
nightclub; tell them about me, will you?' And I walked off. Big laughs.
They kept applauding and applauding until Johnny had to call me
back. I came back out, took a second bow, and they applauded; Johnny
gave me the high sign, and the next day CBS signed me to a contract
for one year, where I got twenty-five thousand dollars—just for signing
with them. I didn't even do anything. It was a development deal,
which they did in those days. For the first time in my life I could say to
my wife, 'Rent and groceries are paid for one year.' We never had that
in our whole lives, and I was in my thirties at the time. [He pulls out a
picture of himself and Johnny laughing.] He's saying, 'You're a funny

guy Tom Dreesen'—it's the same picture I envisioned in my mind while I was sleeping in that abandoned car."

Many comics, waiting for their shot, tend to speak of "The Tonight Show" in almost reverent terms. Carrie Snow says, "Careerwise, for me, Letterman's better, but for my heart and for when I was a kid and didn't know why I was going to be famous, but knew I was . . . Carson is definitely the one." Steve Mittleman says, "I've done a Letterman, I've done Griffin . . . but I want to do Carson. I'm not ready yet they tell me. That bothers me when I think about it, so I just don't. When I'm ready, it will happen." Even those who have had their spot, like Dreesen, continue to be in awe of its power. But perhaps its impact is greatest on those who have prayed the most for it to happen.

"I'll never forget the night he did Carson," says Paul Provenza's mother. "He flew us out to California and we went to the show. We're waiting and waiting, and the show continues and continues—then finally he came on. Let me tell you, that was a thrill. He was so well received; Johnny Carson loved him—he fell off his chair laughing. I have a tape of it—I have a tape of everything he's done on TV. But it doesn't do justice to what it was live. I have a picture of him shaking hands with him. For Johnny to stand up and shake hands with him—that's the real test. Most of the time he'll say, 'Oh, that was very good.' But he got up and shook his hand, then Ed McMahon and the producer were telling him how wonderful he was." (Mr. Bass, Paul's stepfather, says, "You can't see him shaking Paul's hand on TV . . .," but Bea quickly interrupts with, "But you see him extending—that's what counts!")

Paul believes: "I think it meant more to them than it did to me. That's the final proof. People say, 'Oh, your son's a comedian? Has he been on the Johnny Carson show?' Now they could say, 'Yes—we flew out, we saw him . . .'" But they were not the sole beneficiaries. "All the things that used to happen from a phenomenal first shot on 'The Tonight Show,' that supposedly don't happen anymore, happened to me. I got a pilot as a direct result—I did the show on a Friday, the following Monday I was testing for CBS and that Wednesday I was on a hot set doing another pilot. I got on the national tour with Diana Ross, dates with Sheena Easton, Air Supply—my price in the clubs went sky high." "This doesn't happen anymore" refers to the days when "The Tonight Show" was virtually the only national showcase for a stand-up comic, and because of the relatively small number of comics in the country, a spot on it often translated into huge, immediate success.

In 1971 David Brenner appeared on "The Tonight Show" and "after that, the whole world opened up for me . . . I got ten thousand dollars worth of job offers in twenty-four hours, and that's something." But today, with a few exceptions, most notably Steven Wright, "The Tonight Show" can no longer make careers. In Wright's case, Carson was so impressed after seeing his set that he asked him to sit down at the panel on the first night. Wright recalls: "I was in shock. It happened so fast—like a car accident—and the next thing I knew, the show was over. Originally, they told me, 'Do the set, put the microphone back in the stand, and when he says, "we'll be back right after this," you go back through the curtain.' But when I finished the set, I looked over and they were all waving me over to him. I had no idea what to say—the audience was hysterical because they knew it was my first time. On the panel, I looked like someone they had taken out of the studio audience and made sit up there—he asked me questions and I was going, 'Uh-uh . . .' and there were these huge pauses. He said something about how they let me out for the evening, like I was crazy —but in a nice way—he liked me."

And there was more. Wright recalls, "The next Wednesday I was still in Los Angeles and 'The Tonight Show' people called me up and asked me to go on again the next day. I thought they were referring to the one I just did and said, 'What do you mean—I just went on!' But they said, 'We want you to go on again tomorrow.' I was going back to Boston on Saturday, so I said sure—and I went over the next day and did it again. After that, everything changed. I started working the road clubs [as a headliner] for two years, until the HBO special aired, then I moved to two thousand and three thousand-seat auditoriums." But Wright's is not a common case. "Today, if you do Carson several times, it'll mean more money on the road," says Alan Havey, "but it doesn't mean the same thing as when Brenner and Rivers did the show. Maybe that's good in a way; it means you can't just rely on one show to make you a household word." Rita Rudner remembers: "Being on Letterman didn't change my life, but it was a new place to build from. I had a tape of myself that I could show to different people and say, 'This is what I do and I have a national TV credit.' Audiences also paid a lot more attention to me in clubs after I did TV. Before I had no credibility—I had to compete with the drunk guy trying to pick up the girl, ordering the drink, but now they're giving me more courtesy." Larry Miller says, "Between 'The Tonight Show,' the Letterman show and the Griffin show, I've done about twenty-six TV spots. I'm happy and proud about that, but you must remember, whatever you do in this business is a job. If you get 'The Tonight Show,' that's a great job, but it's a job. So it's all just a series of better jobs—not really a matter of 'big breaks' unless the owner of Caesar's Palace is in the audience one night or something . . ."

What national TV spots, particularly on Carson and Letterman, *can* do, and do well, is raise a comic's club status and, because of that, the fee he can charge. For this reason, says Joe Bolster, "a comic must ultimately go to a media center and expose himself to the networks and people who cast the talk shows, because to make the jump from middle to headliner, you need some TV exposure."

While there is not a specific quotient for club fee pricing—like one Letterman equals $1,500 a week—there is a fairly uniform procedure for price negotiation based upon a comic's TV credits and name recognition, and the clubs keep tabs on each other to make sure their prices are all in line. For example, Joe Bolster, who has done "The Tonight Show," "Latenight with David Letterman," the "Merv Griffin Show," "Star Search," "PM Magazine," "Entertainment Tonight" and was Showtime's National Laugh-Off Champion, earns about $2,500 a week on the club circuit. He says that this is probably the high end of the scale for a headliner who's "not completely a draw" (meaning that people come more because of his credits or to see "a professional comedy show" rather than to see him specifically). The low end for a headliner is about $1,100 he says, and the highest end would be for a "name" act (someone who has achieved household word or significant cult status, like Leno, Emo, Steve Wright, or Howie Mandel); their price can range anywhere from $10,000–$25,000 a week, depending on the size of the room, the number of performances, and the price of admission.

Without TV spots, a comic will either remain a middle act or, if lucky, work the low end of the headliner scale, but the decision to break into TV doesn't come without a price. In order to be considered by casting agents for a national show, a comic must spend a significant portion of his time in either New York or Los Angeles, working out nightly on the chance that he'll be seen or talked about by the right (TV) people. This means that, instead of the thousands of dollars to be made on the road, they will have to settle for the obscene hours and bare subsistence wages to be earned in the showcase clubs.

After getting a TV spot, the goal for a comic is to achieve cult or name recognition status. This has been achieved recently by two comics on "Latenight," whose rapport and personas worked in perfect synchrony with Letterman's, allowing them to attain "regular" status on the show and build national recognition. Interestingly, neither was an overnight sensation; Richard Lewis and Jay Leno had both been actively working and struggling in the business for over ten years before their big breaks.

Richard Lewis's first taste of success came in 1976 when, he says, "I moved to Los Angeles after touring as the opening act for Sonny and Cher. Frightening gigs, ten thousand people—me down by like an ice rink in Montreal, trying to be intimate; I was in a coma for most of the trip. I even played a state fair." He had moved to California to be on "The Sonny and Cher Show," but quit in eight days because he was embarrassed by it: "I had to dress like a banana at one point—and I think I played a rutabaga in a chef salad sketch. When I quit, some executive caught me by my lapels, which weren't really lapels, since I was a vegetable, and said, 'If you quit it's the biggest mistake of your life.' I looked at myself, dressed up like a rutabaga, and I went, 'Oh, really? You think I came three thousand miles to let a schmuck like you tell me this?' but I couldn't help thinking, 'Am I being destructive? Or am I doing the right thing?' What happened was, I had a friend there who was watching the taping and I saw the whole audience was laughing, except for him. I looked at his eyes and he looked at me like,

'You've got to get out of this,' and I knew—so I quit. I went to the L.A. Improv that night, and got signed by William Morris. It was like a reward from the comedy gods."

He had done "The Tonight Show" in 1974, but was not quite the right type: "I was too frenetic and Johnny wanted me to calm down and work slower—so I did. On the next shot with Johnny I went way over on the time without realizing it, but the spot was good. My agent said, 'Hey, you just did two shots in one night,' and I said, 'Yeah? Great. I'm dead.' Later that night, I saw Carson with his lawyer and I still had my make-up from the show on—I looked like an assassin or something— and I apologized profusely and he said don't worry about it. That was quite a relief."

His friendship with Letterman began at the Comedy Store, in L.A., then continued when Letterman moved on to the Improv. "We were fans of one another," Lewis says, "and I knew his girlfriend, Meryl Markoe, who had gone to my elementary school. One day I was doing a club date in Malibu, where they were living; there was a storm watch—hurricanes—and they were the only two people who came. It was a good sign, a harbinger of things to come. Soon after that, he got his show and said, 'Whatever you want to do, fine...' We really respect each other. It's like that fantasy I used to have of 'being with Carson,' like him and his cronies, the affinity he has with Don Adams —that's what I have with Letterman. It's incredible—he's my peer."

For Richard Lewis, this show was the only way to come across effectively on TV: "Doing six minutes, with my style, isn't great. But Letterman was perfect for me. As David said, 'sitting down and wailing' for ten minutes is far more effective for me than doing five minutes. I don't really do jokes, per se, and Letterman knew that. So now, for the last four years, I've been on so often, I have a following of fans—like Brenner and Landesberg got from Carson. They were equipped for that, I wasn't. When Letterman got his show, he called me in his office and said, 'You come on as often as you want; I want you to just sit down and wail—that's your energy.' To have a guy like that in his position is too good to be true. I mean I have jokes, too, I'm not Bergman... what I do is like a Jewish oil painting. It's not that I'm a late bloomer, I just had to find the right forum. If Letterman was doing this eight years ago, I would have been more well known then."

Jay Leno also knew David from his Comedy Store days when according to Mitzi Shore, Letterman "came here wearing a lumber jacket and a beard—he looked like one of those Mormons from Utah." (Leno gives the same description, but likens him instead to Dinty Moore.) During this time, David was working as emcee, which he did for three straight years. Shore says, "Every night he was on that floor working. Then, the emcees handled half the evening—we open at seven and go till two, so David was on the stage about four hours every night, continually. That's why he's the top host of the country." While she says that "when he started working there was a wit to him, a very clever wit—but he couldn't perform yet," Leno remembers differently: "I saw Dave audition at the Comedy Store—he was great, excellent from the first day, excellent material. There weren't the Chicken McNuggets and Dolly Parton stupid jokes; he just had straight material. I walked up and introduced myself and told him he was great, and we just became friends that way. Now, because we're friends, I try extra hard to have good material when I go on there; I try not to depend on just straight stand-up."

Leno works best on the show playing a sort of cat and mouse game with Letterman, with each trying to circumvent the direction of the other's planned path, each trying to find the biggest laugh in uncharted water. Jay says, "I meet with Bob Morton and I'll say, 'Here's the kind of stuff I want to talk about,' and we go over it for the censor, but he never tells Letterman any of it. . . . When we get out there, generally, Letterman will sense a thing coming and he'll try to throw me a curve by asking me the opposite question. That's where we have fun on the show. I'll start to laugh and go the other way, and if I say something funny, then Letterman will laugh, because he'll know the real joke was the other way around. For example I know Dave tries to be noncommittal—the other day I asked him if he sang in the elevator or shower and he said, 'No, I never do that.' So I said, 'What are you, Robitron man?' and I started insulting him that way. He started to laugh because it was so stupid. We have a thing between us, whenever I go to ask him anything, he'll deny it—he doesn't get involved at all, it's so funny. Like, 'Dave have you ever been to this place?' and he says, 'No,' no matter what. Did you see the show where I came out with the street urchin [before his Carnegie Hall show]? Now Letterman had no idea I was going to do that . . . it just makes it funnier; that's what I like about the show, I can take a chance."

Barry Sand says that not only are Leno and Lewis ideal because of their rapport with David, but because they can be counted on to appear again and again: "It's important to have someone we think can sustain it—who isn't going to come on and do one shot and you'll never hear from them again; we'd like to have someone who you can count on five or six times a year to come back. It's very hard to find those people." The reason for this is that TV eats material like a famished Pac Man, and many comics cannot continually refill their joke coffers. Rita Rudner says that "for the first show I did five minutes of material I'd been working for three years on, so I knew it was good. The second time I did the show was harrowing, because I had to do newer stuff. They called me, five months after the first spot, to be there that night to do the show and my manager felt I shouldn't turn them down because I'm not that 'in' with them that I could say no. So I went in and did it that night and it wasn't as good. It was fine but it wasn't slam-bang."

Steve Wright remembers the alternate exhilaration and depression of having his material appear on television . . . but knowing that it was "eaten up" for good: "During my three years as a stand-up, I had developed about thirty minutes of material. When I went on 'The Tonight Show' I did two sets in one week, then one two months later—so that was seventeen out of my thirty minutes right there . . . solid stuff that was gone. Then when I did another spot, just about all the stuff I'd built up over the past three years was gone. At first that was like, 'Oh my God, my career is over!' I said to Jim McCaulley [the talent coordinator], 'If I do two spots, that's over ten minutes—half of what I've worked on for three years. I'm supposed to do that in one week?' He said, 'It's such a boost and such a unique thing to do, it's worth it. You're going to have to write new material sometime anyway—you might as well do it now.' And he was right, so I did. It's still the same; now, every time the show is over, I have no more new material."

Chris Albrecht, former manager of the New York Improv (now senior vice president in charge of comedy development at HBO), says that in the past the problem of comics not having enough material to do second, third and fourth spots didn't exist because "the process of development was different then. It used to be you auditioned at one of the showcase clubs and it may have taken months to get on. Once you got on, you'd come in and wait, and maybe you'd get on twice a month. You'd hang out till four every night and not get on—but you'd watch everyone. You worked until you got on at prime time, then you stayed and honed your act and only when you were really ready did you let 'The Tonight Show' people see you. Not because you had one shot but because you had seven! Now, the business uses up these people and spits them out because they don't have any more material—and there's someone else with five minutes waiting right behind them."

Herein lies a catch; television appearances help a career, temporarily, but unless the comic can continue to deliver the goods and keep himself on the air long enough to become a regular, like Leno or Lewis, the effects of TV spots fade quickly. Unlike clubs, where jokes can play for years to different audiences, material used once on television has been effectively "eaten up," and if the comic wants another shot, he's got to write—or buy—some more.

But then there is another catch, says Tom Dreesen, which is that a comic will not become a "name" if he hangs around too long without getting into a series or sit-com: "The talk shows have diminishing effects, and I'm speaking from personal experience. I've done dozens of Mike Douglas shows, dozens of Mervs, over fifty Carsons and dozens of Dinah Shore shows. I've done 'Rock Concert,' 'Midnight Special,' 'Soul Train,' 'American Bandstand'—everything, but the name of the game is to become an 'asses in the seats' act. When your name on the marquee puts asses in the seats, that's when you're a star; that's when your price really goes up. I make fifteen thousand dollars a week in Las Vegas and believe me, that's not a lot. I make five thousand dollars for a one-nighter—my price is they'll fly me in first class round-trip, give me five thousand dollars and pay for my hotel. That sounds like a lot, but I'll tell you, tomorrow if I get a sit-com, the same act I'm doing now will get me two hundred thousand dollars a week in Las Vegas—with the same act . . . but to get that you have to be a star. When your name on the marquee—nothing else—fills the room, you're a star. If your name doesn't fill the room, you may have been a star, you might gonna be a star, but you ain't one now."

Comic manager Bernie Brillstein says television has such power that even commercials (as long as the performer is identified by name) can make a star: "In my humble opinion—which is not very humble—every year you stay in network television, you have another five years of acceptance with the public. There is nothing like the power of television commercials; people still think today, four years later, that Norm Crosby, another client of mine, is still doing the Anheuser-Busch commercials, and he hasn't done them in four years. They sure helped Rodney—they helped make him a star. It kept Bill Cosby alive for years. He made this tremendous transition because the white Protestant buyer said, 'My God, a black man selling Jell-O? And kids like Jell-O and they're white? My God!' This was amazing!"

Becoming a star via television is a delicate process; the right vehicle can make an overnight sensation, like Robin Williams, but the wrong vehicle can cripple a career with equal speed and force. "For a long time I didn't go out for sit-coms and I turned down TV shows," says Dreesen: "They wanted me to host 'Real People.' I turned down game shows because whatever I do on TV has to lend itself to my long-term career. Here's why: TV will chew you up and spit you out. They'll get rid of you like that, and you're history pal—they don't give a shit about you. So you have to be very careful about what you take. I'll always be a stand-up, that's how I'll always make my living, so I have to protect that completely, when I do TV." Richard Lewis says that, though he's done five pilots (and starred in four of them) none of them became shows, "With any kind of luck I might have been a series star, but on the other hand, maybe that's good. Now I'm getting really known as a comic with my personality—whereas if I got known as some guy who played a Martian ping-pong player..."

David Brenner agrees that it's rare for a comic to hit big, like a Jimmy Walker, Freddie Prinze or Robin Williams, without benefit of a sit-com but, he says, he was one of the rare exceptions. "In 1976 I did seven programs named 'Snip' for NBC—a sit-com with Lesley Ann Warren, who was the co-star. The weekend before the premiere, the first time in the history of TV, they cancelled it. Had they not, I think I would have really exploded then. But what happened was that when I went back on the road, after the show was cancelled, *that's* when I became a star. I think I'm the only person who became a star with a TV series that never aired." He says that his stardom resulted from a steady compilation of TV spots as opposed to the weekly exposure of a series: "I did one hundred and two appearances on talk shows in '74 and one hundred and one in '75, and in '76, when I was still doing all of them, that momentum caught up to me. When I walked out in the fall of '76 and went onto the stage, they were screaming and jumping up and down... that's when 'Brenner Mania' started."

For a comic to achieve stardom without benefit of a series or "regular" status on a given show, but through sheer quantity of appearances across the board on all shows, is particularly difficult; he must have a constant supply of material that's not only fresh, but that fits in with the styles of all different shows and that meets the standards of all censors. One week on TV, during his height, Brenner says, "my father called it 'David Brenner Week'; I was the host of 'The Tonight Show' five nights, I was the co-host of Douglas five days, I was on five Hollywood Squares, I did a Dinah and a Merv Griffin—and if anybody was stupid enough to watch me on every show, they would not have heard one joke repeated. And if, after that week, they'd gone to see me in a nightclub, they wouldn't have heard one of the jokes they heard on all those programs. That's how I kept my head above water." Brenner says that the problem of TV eating up material is a nuisance for all comics, but it can be avoided by the constant generation of new material: "I've always changed my act, and if I did something on TV, I didn't do it onstage for at least a year and a half. In my appearances on 'The Tonight Show,' I did over twenty-three hours of original material, but once I did jokes on TV, I put them away, and forgot about them for a while."

Quite apart from what a television spot can do for the stand-up comic is the issue of what a stand-up comic can do for that television show. Their most obvious contribution is comic relief, as Les Sinclair says: "If you're talking heavy stuff you need variety, and comedy is always a welcome addition." Another of their assets is that they come as a complete, finished entertainment package that works for scale ($618). Occasionally, this fee is higher when a comic is "bumped"—another result of being the last talent in the night's line-up—because they're paid for every night they show up.

Sinclair says that while this usually happens only once, if at all, there are times when it seems to approach infinity: "The one who has the record for being bumped on our show is, I think, Ritch Shydner [ex-husband of Carol Leifer]—five times. What happens when you get bumped is that your energy goes from being so up, for doing it, to falling dramatically, when you find out you're not on. After five times, when Ritch finally did get on, the set just went boom! It was awful. But I brought him back, because I knew he had it in him." And, of course, he had the consolation of earning $618 for every appearance he didn't make.

As opposed to other guests, comics are a bargain. While most people only talk, the comic brings an act which, as Tom Dreesen says, "they will write, direct, act in and produce themselves... the show figures, 'We've got a segment to fill, let's get a comic to do it for us!'"

Panel discussions are generally made up of pre-arranged set-ups for the comics' jokes. Jay Leno says that, like most people, he didn't realize these exchanges were planned in advance: "I'd watch Carson and he'd say to a guest, 'Now I read somewhere you had an incident at a party at Steve Lawrence's house...' or 'Someone mentioned to me that something happened...' and I'd always think, 'Ooh, I wonder where he heard that—it must have been in a restaurant when he was talking to his friends.' It never occurred to me that someone would sit down with a guest and plan the questions. The audience is still wonderfully naive—there are people who get mad because they went back to see Liza Minnelli the second night and she cried a single tear again at the same place. Carson does it incredibly well: 'I heard of an incident where your pants fell down...' and you think gee, how did he hear about that?"

Many comics prefer to steer clear of these set-ups, particularly when they're over-zealous because they tend to take away the comic's humanity by reducing him to a human joke. Leno says that this is often a problem with radio shows (which comics do frequently to publicize local appearances): "I say let's just talk—I know what you want, I'll talk in sound bites, it'll be funny. So they say okay, then the first question is, 'Jay, have you been to a McDonald's lately?' It seems like whenever I go to a town, they say, 'We've got a guy live in the studio—he is the wackiest, zaniest, off-the-wall guy...' and I say, 'I'm not zany, I'm not off the wall—I'm not a young comic!' I'm just a guy who hopefully has some funny observations—I don't drink or smoke or fool around, I have a normal life—I'm not wacky or zany! There's always a pretext of, 'Jay, you're not normal.' The other day I told what I thought was a reasonably intelligent joke and the deejay said 'Man you're wacky, you're off the wall.' And I said, 'I'm not crazy, madcap or zany.' Another guy would say, after every joke I told, 'That's fantasmagorical.' I spent half the time saying, 'No, it's not.'" Kip Adotta agrees: "I love television—I don't know about the talk shows though... it just gets my hair up when someone says, 'How do I set you up?' Read the bio man, how about that! Today, I'm going to do the 'Soupy Sales' radio show, and he's going to say, 'How do I set you up?' and I'm going to want to say, 'Show some interest and I'll be set up.'"

For most comics, the years of worry and hard labor leading up to the sacred six minutes are forgotten in the twinkling of an eye—provided that eye is Johnny or David's. But as soon as that ecstasy passes, the true purpose behind the "spot" comes into view, and new priorities rush quickly into place. Living in Los Angeles, Carol Siskind has come to realize: "These talk shows need comedians badly, and they'll use you up if you're not careful." For this reason she divides her time between the showcase clubs and acting classes—so when the right opportunity comes to parlay a TV spot into "the big vehicle," she'll be ready: "You get only so many chances... and when I get mine, I don't want to fucking blow it."

PRATFALLS AND PITFALLS ... THE SWEET HELL OF SUCCESS

"The big break" can be hidden in any TV spot; the trick lies in capturing the prize before it gets away. And that's only the beginning. In comedy, as in life, to the victor go the spoils. In stand-up, however, the spoils are not simply a decadent stew of money and power; they include a volatile third ingredient—the harsh, overpowering taste of fame. Steven Wright's view of this rarified state is that "no one's really famous, a lot of people just think you are." In striving for success, most comics have only a vague idea of what will face them when they reach their destiny, and maybe this isn't such a bad idea. Yakov Smirnoff says that after years of struggle, when the phone finally begins ringing there is a temptation never to put it down: "When you're hot, everybody wants you and nobody wants to take no for an answer; that makes it very hard to say no. I'm like a kid in a candy store: 'Forget that there's diabetes, let's just have as much as we can.' But after a while you have to say no. Physically, my body can't take anymore; it will shut down. I travel about twenty days a month, but next year I'm cutting down to ten, because if I don't take care of myself there will be nobody doing Russian comedy anymore—including me."

Steven Wright spent 1985-86 promoting his album, "I Have a Pony," by performing one-nighters in auditoriums in eighty different cities, and while he was grateful for people's interest in him, he found the demands of that kind of traveling overwhelming: "For me, with my pace, it was unbelievable... I don't know how Jay Leno does it; it's insane. The show is over at ten thirty and you're all wound up, so you go to sleep at one or two A.M. Then you get up at ten A.M., go to the airport, fly to the next city, get to the hotel at four or five, lie down for an hour, go to the show at eight and then the same thing... I never saw any of the cities. I saw the airport and the road from the airport to the hotel, from the hotel to the concert, and back. One of the sections ended in Albuquerque, New Mexico, on a Monday, I flew to New York on Tuesday, then on Wednesday I flew to England and performed on TV in their version of 'Saturday Night Live' in London—I was the guest host. I was a zombie—but they didn't know; they thought it was my act."

Emo Philips says that success speeds life up to a greater degree than he had anticipated: "It's like playing Ms. Pac Man... when you reach thirty thousand dollars, the ghosts are moving five times as fast... that's what it's like now—little things are eating me left and right. I'm really just a four-walls-and-carpet type of guy; I don't like a lot of objects or sensory stimulation." He says, also, that while there is less time to perform certain business duties, there is much more to be lost by failing to perform them: "There are a lot of people pulling at me. I can't return calls as often as I'd like—I'd like never to return them, but you can't afford to do that. You never know who might be famous. As the saying goes, 'Be nice to people on the way up, because you meet the same people on the way down.' People want a piece of my time, not me. That's what I mean. Being famous is nothing more than having millions of people, each wanting to talk to you for a few minutes. It's like you have to wear disguises. And I do. In the winter it's okay, because I have a big hat and scarf. But in the summer at the beach it's harder; I often wear a Benjamin Disraeli beard and a stovepipe hat. It's mainly a question of time." And certain institutions must take priority: "I always have time for the media, because the press giveth and the press taketh away."

For Steven Wright, one of the more difficult aspects of fame has been people's inability to differentiate between his onstage and offstage personas: "It's strange because if I laugh, people say, 'Oh, you really laugh?' They have this image that I'm always like the way I am on-stage, which isn't true; onstage, I'm me—but magnified ten times. My voice is a monotone in real life, but not that much, and all those thoughts I talk about—the jokes—are all my regular thoughts concentrated into one hour. It's like in a movie, if some guy's shooting someone do they think the actor walks around with a gun?"

Even the most self-assured, talented comics are somewhat shocked by success when it hits. Rick Messina has learned through his years in the business that "you can't tell who's going to break. Just when you think you know who's hot and who's not, someone you never would have thought of in a million years pops up with his own TV show." He gives as an example Paul Rodriguez who in 1980 was working in Los Angeles at the Comedy Store, "doing late night spots at one thirty to two in the morning, never traveling and not showcasing much. He was probably in the lower third of the comics at the Store and then boom! He was cast by Norman Lear as 'a.k.a. Pablo'—and he's a star." Although the show was cancelled after five episodes, Paul was able to launch a successful club and film career from it, and while Messina says he deserves it, "That's something no one would have guessed."

Even if a comic is ready to hit, as far as the maturity of his performing and material, and he is emotionally stable, the shock of instant fame can still be disorienting, at the very least, but with time he will grow into his success. If, on the other hand, a comic is picked before he's ripe, his meteoric rise can be quickly followed by an even swifter fall from grace to the sea of despair. About his own overnight success, Rodriguez says, "It turned me upside down. It exposed me to too many people before I was ready, and put me under pressure to be better than I really was at that time." The result of this, he says, was that fame "came fast but it went even faster." He feels that "unlike a seasoned comedian—like Jay Leno who worked the road years before anyone knew who he was—I had the opposite thing happen. I got famous before I could refine my act. When I became popular, lots of clubs began requesting me. I turned a lot of it down simply because I wasn't ready. I had fifteen minutes of material when I did my first 'Tonight Show.' What happened was that the series made me neglect what got me the TV series . . . which was the stand-up. So after a while it caught up with me. Like, I'd get a booking in Tahoe or Vegas—the dream bookings you pray for—and I had to turn them down because deep down in my heart I knew I wasn't ready. And I didn't want to admit it to the press—or anybody—that I wasn't, so what I did was say, 'I'm busy, I'm doing another project.' And I did; I'd find another schlock project, another B-movie to do—anything to keep me from doing an hour of stand-up."

Having not worked adequately on his stand-up before becoming successful, he found it virtually impossible to correct the problem afterward: "It became harder and harder to work on. If you're obscure you can get onstage and bomb because nobody gives a shit—nobody knows you. But if you're known, people actually call up the club and ask if you'll be appearing. So if you go up there and bomb they're going to be tremendously disappointed . . . and they'll discover it's just hype." Finally, out of desperation, he hired a professional writer: "It was dreadful. He didn't know my point of view—and the words he would put in my mouth didn't fit at all. I'd go up onstage and do stupid jokes that I didn't care about . . . it was miserable. It must be how a woman feels when she sleeps with an ugly, older man simply because he's rich— that kind of filthy feeling. I felt like a comedy prostitute after a while."

Paul blames himself, ultimately, for his rapid rise and fall from stardom. But he, and many performers like him, are also victims of the media hype which instantly uplifts nobodies, destroys somebodies, and raises the dead to positions of immortality. About the latter power he is particularly outraged, perhaps because his career is often wrongly associated with that of Freddie Prinze: "If I were to die tomorrow—especially under tragic circumstances—there would be a shit load of people who never helped me in life who would sit back and say, 'I remember meeting him once and boy, he really had a great comedy perspective . . .' Well you know what? I don't want it. I want to be mediocre and alive. I think longevity is more important in the long run—that's why I admire George Burns far more than Lenny Bruce."

In retrospect, he says, the price of fame really isn't worth the trouble: "I don't see myself as ever becoming a superstar or big celebrity—I'm not immortal or anything like that. What I am is practical. My parents were very poor. I'm grateful to be doing this, and I'm grateful that I don't have to kiss as much ass as other people do. Of course I'm making light of it, but if your goal is to become a big star and you never do—my God it must be awful to live with yourself—and if your goal isn't to be a star at all, you're a fool, because who wants to be in this business just to be obscure? But there is a gray area, and that's where I want to fit in. I've been famous for three months and I've been obscure. Then I do a project and get a little more fame, then I go back to being obscure—and that's fine with me. I don't get up in the morning and beat myself. I don't hurt Paul Rodriguez."

Coming from a background of poverty, in which his parents were migrant farm workers trying to support twelve children (he's the youngest), Rodriguez says that he's damn happy to be where he is right now—not only for selfish reasons, but because it allows him to help his parents: "They were very against me going into this business . . . but it's amazing how my buying them a home can change their minds . . . To quote my father, 'Son, you're a Mexican—Mexicans don't become stars in America unless they're part Irish like Anthony Quinn. You're a Mexican and you always will be. Come to your senses. Get a job with the city—work with the water and power department, have a steady job there. I see the lines of kids around the studios waiting for their break . . . and you think you're going to succeed where they've all failed?' And I said, 'Basically, yes. Yes, Dad.' So I left home. My father said, 'If you're going to quit college and pursue this nightclub baloney, go ahead, but you won't have the shelter of this roof.' It sounds like *The Jazz Singer*—like I ended up singing 'My Yiddishe Momma,' but I ended up being able to help them . . . and that's nice."

Just as the reasons for someone's becoming an overnight sensation are often mysterious, so they are for those who never become one. Rick Messina says, "A lot of guys just never get discovered—and you never know why . . ." But, he adds, other factors affect a comic's career besides his work onstage: "Personal management has a lot to do with it, and how the comic reacts to the business—his personality. People become poisoned very quickly in this business if a guy is hard to work with or unreliable. Jackie Mason recently did 'The Tonight Show' for the first time in twenty years. He's one of the most brilliantly funny comics in the country, always has been, but he turned off a lot of people when he did the 'Ed Sullivan Show' that time; he went over on time, made a certain gesture—and got a very negative result. The industry stayed away from him for many years because of that."

Rodriguez, like Messina, believes that a comic's ability to "do business" is a factor critical to success; in fact, without doing it in the proper way, success is impossible: "There is no such thing as not kissing ass to make it in this business, I want you to know that. There isn't one artist, major or minor, who can tell you, 'I did it my way,' except for Frank—and even he had a Godfather to go to. It's not a question of 'Will you have to kiss ass?' as much as 'How many butts will you have to kiss—what's the magic number?' So what I did was get it all done in one day. I lined up all the important butts and kissed them. And it's fair, because eventually someone will have to kiss your butt—your ass becomes one of the kissable ones."

The very fact of success can pull down a comic because he loses his hunger. Jerry Seinfeld points out that this is why he admires people like John McEnroe: "Where does he get the drive to try that hard with that much money? That problem has nullified more comedy careers than any other element—success is the enemy of comedy. You see these comedians when they're coming up—there was nobody funnier than them when they used to go out with the guns blazing—but then they settle into indulgence and complacency. I guess that's true of any artist, but a comedian really needs that edge where he's not really sure of himself and he's got to prove something—tonight! It's got to be 'I've got to prove it tonight—again—to myself and to everyone that I can really do this.' Once you feel you've proved it, that show has lost a lot of sparkle."

Bob Goldthwait agrees that too much success too fast often destroys a comic's edge, but adds that after years of struggling, the pressure to accept the trappings of success is intense: "The other day my friend asked me if I was going to do 'Police Lobotomy [Academy] IV'—cause the magic continues, you know . . . they just keep pounding them out. Well, I said I wouldn't do 'II,' then I said I really wouldn't do 'III'— and I was in both of those—but finally I stopped resisting. I said, 'Let's put it this way—if a truck of money pulls up in front of your house,

are you going to say, "You want my neighbor, that's not my money."
No way, you fucker, you'd be in there with a shovel, going, "Hooray!
The money's here!"'" Some comics, Goldthwait believes, never
achieve success because they have a career death wish: "They cut their
own dicks—I know so many guys who could get TV parts. They came
real close to getting on, after a million auditions, and it's such high
pressure, on the sixth or seventh audition, they say, 'Fuck your show, I
don't need you!' when the producer's there. I know a lot of guys who
have done that.

"Or else, the people say, 'We like you, but could you steer away
from that material?' and the comic says, 'Man, that's what I do!' It's
like, well, why don't you do the *other* forty-five minutes of your act,
and then just slip one of those Reagan jokes in . . . These guys are just
afraid of doing well—it's easier to say, 'It's hard being me,' than it is to
do well, I guess. They're all tragic, you know." Of his own success he
says, "I'm powerless over my career, it's just that I work hard—and, if
anything, what I have is the common sense not to cut my throat on a
regular basis."

A successful comedian's fall from grace usually comes from two
places, both of which are out of the comic's control: public demand or
the comedian himself. The latter almost always results from "too
many"—too many drinks, too many drugs, too many "yes men" or too
many neuroses. Managers and agents are fond of saying that a comic's
creativity runs in inverse proportion to his number of vices and sycophants. Bernie Brillstein, a personal manager specializing in comedy,
whose roster runs from Norm Crosby to Garry Shandling, believes that
the self-destructive behavior of comedians is often the result of what
makes the person a comic in the first place—an unhappy childhood
—and the sycophants, as people who prey on an increasingly helpless
person, are the result, not the cause of the problem.

As manager of the late John Belushi, Bernie spent a great deal of
time trying to separate a client from his vice(s). Ultimately, however,
Brillstein's efforts resulted in a confrontation, with Belushi telling him,
"Don't be my father, Bernie, don't tell me how to live. I won't tell you
not to go home at five thirty and see your kids, so don't tell me what to
do." After that, Brillstein retreated, and he still insists, "John was right.

It was his life. He chose to die . . . I really miss him, but that was his decision."

Brillstein says that whether or not that confrontation had taken place, he would have backed down eventually, as he is not "that kind" of manager. He explains "that kind" as the type he was trained to be at William Morris, where he began, in which the agent's goal was to service the client in every possible way—in essence, to be present and available all the time. While not deriding this approach for certain clients, those people he chooses to represent are not the types who want or need that kind of constant attention. "Imagine coming home at the end of a day's work and there's your agent saying, 'Come on, I'm here for dinner—I'm servicing you!' That's what it's like; I operate under the assumption that you'd probably rather be left alone!"

This approach did not work in the case of Belushi, but it was in spite of Brillstein. Generally, the spoiled child syndrome applies: for almost every overindulging client, there is an overindulgent, smothering manager. The reason for this, Brillstein explains, is fear: "Some managers are just scared of their clients—desperately scared. Look, if you handle one client, as a friend of mine does, who pays him a great deal of money you're not going to say, 'Hold it you son of a bitch—don't yell at me, listen to me'; you're going to say, 'Okay, I'll take care of that.'" In his case, he alleviates the problem by having a roster of clients: "Say you have ten clients and each pays you fifty thousand dollars—if you lose one of them, your day's not over."

Whether or not Brillstein's hands-off approach to handling clients is better than other methods is debatable; perhaps it's just a case of different methods of management working best for different types of performers. David Brenner says, "Some managers act as father figures—some have actually made their whole careers by managing comedians who really needed fathers—so they become the father and they can *manage* them, it doesn't matter if they're making good decisions or not . . . I don't need that; my agent and manager are my friends. I don't have a slew of agents, I have one—and one manager. I have a lawyer, an accountant—and that's it."

While proper management is an important factor in the making and maintaining of a career, Brillstein asserts that "it's not the deciding factor . . . and I say that even though that's what I do for a living—the staying power, especially, always depends on the performers. Managers and agents can help—a lot—but I don't think people's careers have died because of bad management. They might have been slowed or sent left, but I don't think you can kill something that's good. You can only hamper it. The trouble with money and power and success is that you buy a house in the hills and you have sycophants telling you what you want to hear, or bringing you the drugs you want to get . . . You can have anything you want—studios, managers, agents, women, men—whatever. What you need around is a voice to argue with you. You may fire them, you may argue and hate them, your wife or husband may want you to get rid of them, but, boy, you should listen to someone—other than the crap you're fed in this business."

Goldthwait sees similar patterns in his life: "It's strange, what really drives me crazy now is people agreeing with me all the time—not disagreeing with me. I'm so tired of saying things and people just accepting them; you don't get honest feedback. I have the same ideas I had when I wasn't famous, but now the same people who hated me agree with me. So that's pretty bizarre—I don't listen to them. People who call me a 'genius' are the same people who used to say I sucked and who were never there when I was blowing it—when I was clearing a club, when I bummed everyone out and they complained to the manager for hiring me."

Paul Rodriguez remembers, during the "a.k.a. Pablo" period, he was surrounded not only by a new host of sycophants but by old friends and family who seemed to have been transformed overnight into extras from a Hollywood horror movie, "It was horrible—my family changed. Not my parents, but my brothers. One of my brothers came over every day, and where before that he was very loving, suddenly he came only to say, 'I need one thousand dollars . . .' And I always gave —until I stopped one day, and then I was shit. All this happened within one particular month. I went from making one hundred ten dollars a week at the Comedy Store to thirty thousand dollars a week —where do you go from there? You go to parties and realize everyone's having a good time on your money, but at the time it's the thing to do. I never had a drug problem—and I grew up among junkies, winos and

GILBERT
GOTTFRIED
IN A
PENSIVE
MOMENT

Ⓜ️ARC WEINER IN HIS STREET-PERFORMING DAYS (IMPROVISING
WITH ROBIN WILLIAMS).

The Weinerettes

Ⓐ LAN HAVEY ON THE BEACH

Ⓟ AUL

REISER

Credit:

Broūn

Credit: Karen Kuehn

TOMMY BLAZE ON STAGE

JOE BOLSTER

WITH HOST ON

SET OF "ROBERT

KLEIN TIME "

Credit: David Jasse

LARRY MILLER WITH PAUL REISER

GEORGE
CALFA
ON THE
ROAD

LOIS BROMFIELD

GARY LAZER

JAY LENO

Credit: Gary Bernstein

GEORGE
CARLIN

Credit: Aaron Rappaport

Ⓨ AKOV SMIRNOFF WITH A FAN

Credit: Bob Knudsen

Ⓡ OBERT WUHL

Ⓡ OBIN TYLER

hard core people—but during that one month, I blew ten to fifteen thousand dollars on every kind of drug, and I wasn't even using them! Everyone around me was having a great time, telling me what a great guy I was, and I said, 'If it makes you happy, fine.'" The end came with as much speed and fury as the beginning: "The night that the party was over—the party was *over*. It's like all of the sudden, you're in Argentina or something . . . your friends have disappeared. The thing about 'The phone stops ringing' is true—it really happens."

Brillstein gives an example of a comedy team, each of whom was his client and friend at one point, who refused to listen to his advice, and ultimately paid the price: "Fifteen years ago Marty Allen and Steve Rossi were making thirty-five thousand dollars a week in Las Vegas, and believe me, they were very good. But Marty had a group of people around him who told him he was Charlie Chaplin—and Marty wanted to hear he was Charlie Chaplin. He wanted to be Charlie Chaplin. Not a bad wish . . . but someone had to say, 'Hold it! Become Charlie Chaplin over here, but still do this . . . just be slow about it.' He didn't listen and that hurt him a lot. Now, fifteen years later, they're back together again, making nowhere near thirty-five thousand dollars a week; I don't mean to pick on Marty, but I'm saying people choose to listen to what they want to hear."

But Paul Rodriguez says comics must know when to ignore managers and agents: "I needed to do the road—travel, work around the country—and it's very hard to do that when your managers and agents are constantly offering you movie scripts and roles. I've turned down more films than I've done, simply because I don't need to do them that bad. I'd rather wait for that good role now. Now I have managers look at me and say, 'Are you crazy? This is a movie!' But it comes down to who's in control . . . and I am. I'm the one. They say, 'But kid, you're never going to make it big!' I think they're more afraid of that than I am . . . and that's all right!"

A quality that seems to flower with success among comics is an enlarged appetite for booze and drugs—such is the general consensus, anyway. Many comedians, however, insist that the problem of substance abuse among their ranks is far smaller today than it was fifteen years ago—and where it does exist, it doesn't necessarily have to do with success or failure; it's a result of the same things everyone else takes substances to avoid—boredom, inadequacy, fear, and a whole catalog of other "Me Generation" catch words. Of the "drug routines" (inspired by and used to celebrate drug use), so popular in stand-up in the 60s and 70s, comic Richard Belzer says they were "just a stage we went through, like folk music. Drugs now, at least in my circle, are taboo. If people are doing them, they're discreet about it. It's not looked upon as cool anymore." Belzer adds that he still makes occasional drug references in his act, not to celebrate their use but to point out the extremes to which they can be comedic.

Jerry Diner explains that "the comics who are really serious about doing comedy find that no matter what drug you attempt to do, doesn't work—for comedy. You'll find a lot of guys who might get high before they go on, but they're not only cheating the audience, they're cheating themselves, and they find that out eventually." But, according to Paul Rodriguez, some members of the audience find nothing more appealing than a comic headed for a fall: "There are so many women who look at guys like this and are attracted to them—they want to help and nurse them, so it encourages comics to do that."

Diner explains why a comic must remain more alert than the audience: "A lot of times the audience is drinking, so you have to be above where they are to get your jokes across. I haven't found a drug yet that doesn't get in the way of that ... I've tried. It would be nice to do a couple lines of something and be crazy and real funny, but what happens is you have no idea what you did, you say dumb things ... I don't drink and I don't perform on drugs; anything that I imbibe gets in the way. A lot of comics are a lot straighter than people think."

If this is so, why do people insist on viewing comics as portable dens of iniquity? Perhaps it's the lingering image of Lenny—the comic who goes onstage to "let it all hang out," mumbling irony and truth incoherently into a lonely microphone, foreshadowing his own despair and death with every misunderstood one liner. Perhaps it's an unspoken need, inherent in every audience, to project their own lack of reckless abandon onto the comic, attributing his daring onstage to liquor and drugs, instead of to inspiration and chutzpa. Perhaps it's because people aren't used to seeing sober people acting silly. Or perhaps people are right.

Alan Havey doesn't think so: "I know some comics who are ex-alcoholics, but I'd say your average midtown businessman is a heavier drinker than a stand-up." But this is not because there aren't ample opportunities for abuse: "As a comic, you're certainly exposed to booze a lot—you work in a bar and drink for free. Then, when you get offstage after a stressful night—and the bar's right there—it's real hard not to slug down a couple. And drugs are offered to you; not by some guy with shades in the corner, but by the refrigerator repairman in Cincinnati—those types. You do drugs with them and they tell you about the belt drive on a refrigerator, 'So anyway, it's broken, right? You know, I'm a pretty funny guy myself—hey, do you know Eddie Murphy? . . .' That kind of thing. But most of us get beyond that."

George Carlin, himself a recovered drug abuser, feels that the problem is not necessarily greater among comics; it's just made to seem greater because of comedians' high visibility—and because drugs stories make good copy: "I think it's like athletes—they're a more visible class so they get all the attention and all their warts show up much larger." As for the tormented artist theory of drug abuse, he feels it's based more on media hype than on reality: "There's always been a certain percentage of people in the creative world who have psyches that are more open to the self-destructive path. One of the ways to do that is with alcohol and drugs, but there are also people who just don't eat properly or have too many lovers and get the syph. You died from the syph in the 1800s and nobody said, 'Isn't that dramatic and glorious? He's got tertiary syphilis and can't control his feet—how romantic.' That kind of thing never gets on the cover of *People*—they want people who are snorting something."

Paul Provenza has observed that comics' constant proximity to these substances makes them straighter than people expect. "I find most comics don't really drink a lot—on the road it's lonely so some do, but most spend so much time in bars, around liquor, that it loses its fascination. Most of the real artists have a clear perspective about it—they don't want to be the next Freddie Prinze or John Belushi." But he adds that the effect of famous comic drug casualties upon other comics is overplayed and verging on the ridiculous. "Journalists ask questions like, 'How did John Belushi's death affect you?' I say, 'Look, the bottom line is that some people like to do a lot of drugs—some are lawyers, some are comics, some are air traffic controllers, but it has nothing to do with me personally!'"

David Brenner agrees that drinking and drugs do exist in comedy, but no more than everywhere else: "I think there's a big correlation between drinking, drugs, smoking—and life. Because whatever you're doing, you go to any field, you find it. Advertising—coked out of their minds; uptown, same thing—it's part of life. A lot of people had unhappy childhoods. Some are funny about it though, some are successful because of it, some sleep in the streets today because of it—and others are causing more unhappy family lives because of it. There are a thousand tentacles coming out of the ugly head of being unhappy—it's which one you choose. Or chooses you, in some cases."

Bob Goldthwait, a former alcoholic and drug abuser, claims his abuse didn't result from fame and success but the combination of his desperate terror of—and his equally desperate need to—perform. For Goldthwait, the experience of standing onstage and trying to be funny was so terrifying that he did bizarre things, like gutting a herring, reading a Dear John letter—and getting bombed: "I didn't expect to be twenty, especially at the time when I was drinking and taking any drugs I could get my hands on. When I lived past twenty, I was really surprised. Once I was on mescaline onstage, and I'd been drinking for two days, and someone said, 'How do you act so weird?' I said, 'Jesus lady, how do I talk? How do I fucking cross the street?' I'd see people in the front row who looked to me like they had fur coming out of their faces, and I'd be thinking, 'Oh my God, I don't want to be high anymore . . .'"

Tom Dreesen (who in addition to his many television talk-show appearances, opens across the country for Frank Sinatra) is something of a philosopher comic. In his spare time, he lectures students on the subject of stand-up comedy and positive mental outlook. Comics' abuse of alcohol and drugs, he believes, is related to their inability to accept success; it has nothing to do with the act of performing stand-up. He believes, also, that the most powerful aspect of comedy is its healing quality, which he discusses in his lectures. Citing Norman Cousins' *Anatomy of an Illness*, he talks about how, in addition to the psychological uplift of comedy, which comes from forgetting one's problems, there is a positive physical change that takes place. "When the body laughs, endorphins (the same enzymes, released by the brain, that cause runner's high) are released into the bloodstream so the sense of well-being you have after a good laugh is actually due to a chemical change in your body—it actually has a healing effect."

Whatever the healing powers of stand-up comedy for the audience, they are sometimes lost on its practitioners who seek the comforts of drugs and drink. Sometimes, the lost weekend is complete; in the cases of Lenny Bruce, Freddie Prinze and John Belushi, lives were lost along with careers. In many other cases, such as Richard Pryor (and many other well known comics such as Robin Williams and George Carlin, whose brushes with drugs and alcohol were publicized only after the fact), their problems were corrected and careers and lives restored. Still other cases of lesser-known comics abound in which they never corrected their substance abuse or corrected it too late—and lost their careers before the stories became grist for the scandal mills. These cases are, by far, the most frequent.

Twenty-four-year-old Goldthwait says that AA meetings are held for comics at both the Improv and Comedy Store in L.A., and they're well attended. His own experience with alcohol and drugs began when he was a teenager in Syracuse, New York. He describes himself as being "a total Catholic guilt boy . . . who thought it rained because I jerked off—everything I liked was wrong . . . beyond guilt is how I felt all the time, you're instilled with that." As an Irish Catholic he was raised with conflicting messages that were difficult to resolve: "You're supposed to love black people but you're not supposed to marry them." Catholic school drove these unwelcome lessons home, and the fact that he had to work at his school as a janitor to pay the tuition made the experience still more unpleasant.

He feels that the children of his generation were weaned too early on the unsolvable problems of a complex adult world. "The generation ahead of me was told, 'When the world blows up, you go in the base-

ment and put a cardboard box over your head—stay there for a week
and you'll be okay.' My generation was raised knowing that was bullshit—that we could all go, and the Bible is telling us we're all going to
die, and Nostradamus . . . I wasn't brought up with, 'I'm going to have
a wonderful family, my sons will be proud of me, my sons will have
children . . .'"

Goldthwait was the kind of kid who "knew everything—I knew why
everyone did everything—I was the coolest guy in the world, and by
the time I was twenty I was completely hopeless. I was always a real
charmer—I could always call my buddy and weasel a ride . . . 'Hey,
guess who's moving to Boston? Me! Guess who's driving him? You!
Come on, let's go!' I wasn't a guy who just wanted vengeance on the
world—I was real well liked in high school, but I could care less about
it. I was a wild guy—like 'Let's make him Homecoming King,
wouldn't that be funny?' I wasn't charming, I wasn't handsome. I was
just the wild man. I knew even then that a lot of people liked to live
vicariously through my actions."

He describes himself as being popular in a uniquely outrageous way,
saying, "I was Elvis!" This was primarily because Bob had other things
to worry about, like his act: "Everyone else was worrying about prom
dates, and I was worrying about a tight fifteen minutes for my set."
Always precocious, he began performing at age fourteen, and drinking
not long after. "Out of control," he said he was a romantic figure to
read about, "but if you had to hang out with me and live with me
during that period, it wasn't fun. People who hung out with Keith
Moon did not think he was a riot, they thought he was a dick, like,
'Jesus, could you just show up sober for once?' When I was drinking, I
was a bore, I burned out all my friends and myself. Alcoholism is a
disease, you know—plumbers get it, only if you're in show business it's
much more glamorous."

On a whim, he moved to Boston at the age of seventeen, expecting
to find a bunch of "pithy intellectuals smoking pipes," but instead
found "a bunch of racist lunatics." He began performing in the small
clubs there, where he encountered a "bunch of hardcore Irish Catholic
drinking comics . . . everybody was loaded—maybe three or four guys
weren't drinking, but everybody else was into power drinking—and

cocaine. It's always the same conversation when you're drinking—how we're best friends and we all love each other." He says that in the clubs, that was a way of comics bonding with each other and when he stopped drinking, he was worried that he'd lose all his friends. But quickly he realized, "The people who really loved and cared about me would be there. When I was in my disease—a full-blown drug lunatic —I didn't have it in me to love other people, to show it. And so I realized it was the same with my buddies; they couldn't love when they were in the depths of disease. I couldn't anyway. Now I hang out with people who care about me, and who are glad that I'm sober."

Bob adds that just as success and substance abuse don't go hand in hand, neither does being self-destructive make a comic any more creative: "Boy, I don't miss those days—that tragic artist horse shit." He remembers, "The most creative periods at that time, when I was drinking and drugging, would be those three months when I'd be in control —when I'd be clean. I never got any ideas that were worth a damn when I was fucked up."

As for the consensus, among many comic observers, that success is inextricably linked to deviance of some kind, or self-destruction, he disagrees, saying that fate can take care of everything without any help from the individual stand-up: "When I first got sober, I was so happy ... but all of a sudden I thought, How can I do comedy? I'm too happy. And then a friend of mine said, 'Don't worry, God will put enough pain in your life—you'll still be able to do it,' and lo and behold, he was right!"

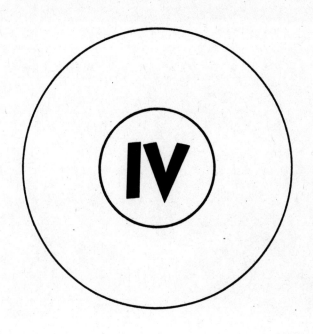

W R I T I N G

Creation is a delicate, time-consuming process. Admittedly, the earth was created in six days . . . but that was God. Jokes, on the other hand, are the product of mortal comic minds—overworked, overextended bundles of gray matter that struggle tirelessly to identify and then mold idiosyncratic truths of humanity into catalysts for laughter. While a successful joke must sound as effortless as an offhand "What time is it?" its creation is fraught with more blood, sweat and tears than the average Egyptian pyramid. Carefully placed between opening, hook and punch line are perfectly sculpted layers of words, chosen, discarded and re-chosen night after night, according to the whims of the paying jury, until they have been polished to the final sentence, phrase and syllable. Larry Miller says, "I analyze down to commas—and I love it. Comics are like poets. No one would ever think to say to a poet, 'Gee, why did you have to add that extra syllable to a line?' That's what poetry is about—a thousand different considerations—balance, rhythm, texture. And so is comedy."

He gives as an example the progression of a single joke from birth to its delivery on "The Tonight Show." "It's a joke about moms using tricks to get you to eat. She'll say, 'Eat the lima beans,' and you say 'I don't like lima beans,' and she says, 'But I made them a different way.'

The joke becomes, how different are they gonna be? I used to say, 'Are they peanuts now, Mom?' Then I thought no, there has to be a really vast difference, then one of my friends pointed that out and I changed 'peanuts' to 'M&Ms.' That was the first step. Then, in a discussion of the bit, another friend suggested I drop the 'Mom' at the end; it weighs the sentence down and stops people from laughing. So it was, 'Are they M&Ms now?' Then the last step happened on my way to 'The Tonight Show.' During the ride over, I was talking with a friend of mine, Jimmy Brogan, who suggested putting, 'What,' in front of it so it became, 'What, are they M&Ms, now?'—and it's a dramatic difference from, 'Are they peanuts now, Mom?' It makes all the difference in the world." The primary difference, he says, is that the new words changed the age of the questioner from a child to an adult, and it was "that additional piece of oddity within the bit that makes it funny. It's an all-important change—and it's all important to be concerned with it."

Joe Bolster says that, because "the difference between a laugh and no laugh is often a single syllable," doing stand-up, and particularly doing it well, is more difficult than it appears. As in advertising, the small, easily overlooked detail can sometimes make or break an entire line: "You remember the 'Where's the Beef?' campaign? Initially it was, 'Where's all the beef?' But the director took out 'all' and without that, it probably wouldn't have been as effective." He also points out that "the difference between a laugh and no laugh has been, not just a line or word, but the way I twist my head on the punch line." While, to some extent, a lot of comedy is instinctive, there are no hard and fast guarantees as to what will and won't get laughs, so one must keep experimenting, rejecting and honing new bits, and take consolation in the fact that "hitting with twenty percent of your new material is probably a high batting average. You've got to remember what you're trying to do here. You have an audience of strangers, made up of various social, economic and educational backgrounds, and on every line you're trying to say something that's funny enough to get enough of those people to laugh—and to make that laughing sound loud enough so everyone thinks it's funny. To consistently have material that accomplishes that is a very hard thing."

While a comic may refine the punch line to its most flawless form, it will mean nothing with a sloppy delivery. A punch line, or "payoff," is the payload—the precious cargo that must be guided gently through a crowded room, insinuated into every corner table, nurtured to maturation, then delivered at the right instant, of which there is only one. Regardless of what happens to the bearer, it is the punch line that must take precedence; if it's not delivered intact, there's no purpose for the delivery. Knowing this, a comic will protect the punch line from its natural enemies (who double as its most ardent admirers), the audience, making sure that it isn't suffocated on the way up, or stepped on on the way out.

Jerry Seinfeld is frequently pointed to by other comedians as one of the most disciplined, prolific writers in the business. For him, the process of creation does not involve desperate, impotent hours spent courting the muse in a lonely urban garret. Instead it is a job, like any other, that demands dedication, introspection, and hard, consistent work. Rita Rudner quotes him as saying, "People don't want to get up and drive a truck every day either, but they do—that's their job and this is my job." He believes that whether or not the comic engages in creative angst during off hours is irrelevant; the job of being a comic is to present funny, polished, unique humor in a professional manner—to entertain. Period.

If he glosses over the more artistic aspects of writing and performing comedy, it's because he, and most comics, have been conditioned to do so in public. Because of its less than Brahmin origins, comedy is not thought of as an art form meriting much, if any, analysis: "People don't want to hear about its pretensions to art, because it's a street form. It comes from people who are supposedly unsophisticated, who are reckless for doing it. It's not a thoughtful person's medium in general . . . it's like, 'If you were really thoughtful you'd be a writer. If you really had a head on your shoulders you wouldn't have to get up there and do *that.*'" And so, like most comics, he keeps the "art talk" to a minimum around civilians, indulging his comic intellect only among those of the stand-up inner circle.

But the writing process is no joke, particularly since comics began writing for themselves in the mid 50s. "Before then," says Carrie Snow, "everyone bought their stuff; now you have to do everything. Well, everyone except [she names a female comic], who hasn't written a joke in her whole life. That's where I got the line, 'If you could blow your way to the top, I'd already be there.'" In the old days there was no real-life, situational or observational comedy—the stand-up comic worked in characters and caricatures like "My wife is so fat that . . ." or "My brother is so poor that . . ." Human feelings, relationships, common memories—subjects that are the backbone of today's comic repertoires—were not addressed. Lenny Bruce is viewed by most comics as the driving force behind the shift from schpritz to reality.

Seinfeld explains the misconception behind the common characterization of Lenny as "that dirty comic": "The big thing he did wasn't to change the language, but the style. He talked about life the way it is. He was talking about the comedy of the life we're all really leading. He was talking about how people really felt when they had sex, which is a tremendous jump from 'My wife is so fat . . .' He fathered all of the greats—Alan King and Robert Klein, George Carlin and Jay Leno. It's all been handed down." Today's comics work from real life and, in doing this, preserve the sense of personality that was lost inside the purposely generic "mother-in-law" humor of the old days.

Just as audiences have some die-hard notions about *why* comics perform (these concepts can range anywhere from oedipally induced psychosis to penis envy), they also have opinions about *how* they perform. One notion is that, almost as a matter of course, comics steal material from one another. Like many mistaken beliefs, this one has some remote basis in fact. In the days of vaudeville, line-lifting was as much a fixture of the comedy circuit as baggy trousers and rim shots, and while stealing was nothing to brag about, neither was it a cause for great shame. As Mitzi Shore says, "In those days, they all used to steal each other's material."

This practice continued to a lesser degree during the nightclub era. Until the time in the late 50s and early 60s, when stand-ups like Shelley Berman, Nichols and May, Mort Sahl, Lenny Bruce, Bob Newhart and Woody Allen began writing material which expressed their individual viewpoints and opinions, jokes were valued for their quality—as in "killer material" or "feh"; there was little if any thought about innovation, or breaking new ground. Because comics could get away with it, they did, and it made them lazy. They used hired writers who were paid a piecemeal wage for each laugh, and there was little incentive for them to experiment with new techniques. The fact that their name wasn't on the finished product didn't help much either. "Latenight"'s producer, Barry Sand, began his career as a joke writer for Joan Rivers, then moved on to writing stints with many other comics. He explains that the process is a difficult one because the material can kill one night, then bomb the next . . . and it makes a writer "very unsure of [him]self and schizophrenic because you don't know whether it's good or it's not—whether it's the comic's fault or yours." In those days, when every comic bought material, they used to have a trick for holding out on paying the writers: "They'd say, 'If the stuff works, I'll pay you,' and then they'd wait years to see if it worked . . . using the material every night of course."

He says the going rate at that time was, "For guys starting out, you wrote a three- or five-minute hunk for five hundred dollars, and you'd have an agent who would set it up. I wrote for Lonny Shore, Jimmy Dean . . . Comics need material badly, especially once they get to be in demand—they've got to keep coming up with the stuff." Today, while jokes are still bought and sold, stand-up has changed in the same way as the music business: "The old-time singers like Tony Bennett and Sinatra had people who wrote songs for them . . . now it's more that the real artists write their own music. They may fill in with stuff that other people wrote, but by and large they have their own identity and write their own stuff. It's the same thing with comedy; the real breakthrough comics are great writers. The only time they resort to having people write is when they've already established the form and style and somebody can write to it. It used to be in the old days guys would be saying, 'Get me an act, get me an act . . .' or 'Get me a hook . . . get me something that'll make me famous.' It doesn't work that way anymore; there's far more put into it by the performer."

When stand-ups started writing for themselves, there was a much stronger bond between comic and joke, both in terms of the audience's and comic's perception; material became more individualized, more custom fitting. This made stealing more difficult, less acceptable and, ultimately, an increasingly infrequent happening. But there is still a yuks-for-bucks network in operation. Often, once a comic becomes successful, his requirements for material begin to exceed his ability to create it—particularly in the case of TV spots, which "eat" it instantly. Rodney Dangerfield is a case in point. While he is acknowledged by many comics as a prolific and talented writer in his own right, Rodney is also known as one of the most prolific buyers—a fact he makes no attempt to hide. Robert Wuhl (in addition to countless other comics) began his career in stand-up by selling jokes to Rodney: "In 1977 I just came back from college in Houston and saw Rodney doing his act. Afterwards, I knocked on his dressing room door, approached him for a job, and started writing and editing jokes for him . . . back then it was about fifty dollars a joke. He's real good to young writers, and he's one of the best joke writers in the world—he's up there with Woody Allen and Neil Simon as far as gag joke writers."

Although stealing hasn't disappeared altogether, it does exist on a much smaller level than people believe, according to Rita Rudner. She says: "People who aren't in the business think stealing goes on all the time, like, 'So, whose material did you take tonight?' They just think that's the way it is. So when you work so hard to get each original idea, that kind of thinking is really frustrating." She adds that comics are often preoccupied with the fear that their material is being stolen: "I've had people accuse me. It's happened twice in six years—one time I didn't even know the person had that joke, and the other time, the guy was just paranoid and the jokes weren't even similar."

Generally there is a unilaterally respected code of ethics: "Good comics never steal from each other. Period." But there are those who breach this code knowingly—and in some cases, unknowingly. Rudner was faced with the latter situation at Caroline's comedy club in New York: "A guy was opening for my friend Ronnie Shakes and he did one of my jokes verbatim—one I had done on Letterman . . . the exact set-up and exact punch line. When he got off, I went to the dressing room and said, 'I just have to tell you, that joke you do about swimming is mine—verbatim. I used it on Letterman two years ago, and I want you to know that if you say that joke in New York, all anyone is gonna think is that you're doing Rita's material.' He said,

'But I bought that joke from somebody in Tampa.' I found out that's another thing people do—write down jokes they see on TV, then sell them to other comics who don't realize what they're doing."

She tells of a similar situation involving Rodney Dangerfield: "A friend of mine, John DeBellis, wrote some jokes and sold them to Rodney, who buys a lot of material. Then, a while later, John hears Rodney doing some of the jokes from *his* act and confronted him about it. Rodney called the guy who sold them to him and asked where he got the jokes, and the guy said, 'I was at the Improv the other night and I got a lot of them there.'"

Adrianne Tolsch, too, has heard about this practice. As an emcee at Catch A Rising Star, "If I hear someone doing someone else's material, I go up to them afterwards and say something. We had a case of that last week with a comic, who we all knew, who had been away for a while. He came to Catch, did a set, and my mouth dropped open— you could ibid. or op. cit. every line in his act. I've known this man for a long time, but when he came offstage I said, 'You did one of Gilbert Gottfried's bits . . . If you want to go on here again, you call the office or you call me and tell me you've got ten minutes of your own material. But you can't get away with that stuff here—go play around town, but not here.' It's like Rodney says: 'When someone takes your material, it's like they're hitting your kids.'"

Abby Stein says that many comics don't actually steal but are very derivative: "They don't take the joke, but they take the premise and switch it around. I don't even know how you'd avoid or stop that. It's happened for so long—Milton Berle made his fortune doing it." As president of the PCA, she intervened in several cases, making phone calls for the complaining parties when the offenses were blatant enough to warrant that. Ultimately, there's little anyone can do about stealing, particularly on the road: "You can't follow people around the country . . . you can copyright the material, but that's only as strong as how much money you have to sue the person."

On the road, "there are some comics who get by solely on stealing people's material. There was a classic story like this. A comic went up to a club in Canada—a deal where you had to do an hour-and-a-half show. And he completely did another comic's act—for two weeks.

Then the other comic was booked into the club a month later. He goes up and does his act and the owner came over and wanted to fire him for stealing the other guy's material—for stealing his own act. So comic number 2 tracked down comic number 1 and confronted him with the story. The comic said, 'Look man, I needed the money and I didn't have the time. Sue me.'"

But there are also cases of simple coincidence and, often in the case of observational material, parallel thinking. According to Stein, comics must take these things into consideration when accusing others of stealing material: "Comics sometimes forget about those possibilities; they'll say something like, 'Wait! I do a joke about a relationship!' Like they invented the topic. I had a comic say to me, years ago, in Florida, 'You can't do that—I invented talking to the audience.' Comics get crazy because jokes are like children. I heard one comic who accused another one of stealing his personality—that stuff happens all the time."

Alan Havey agrees that "people can get paranoid of having their material stolen . . . they get bitter after awhile. A comic came up to me recently and said, 'You're stealing my attitude.' If there's any similarity in anyone's act, they worry. Jay Leno has the best philosophy about that: 'You have to write faster than they can steal.'"

Emo Philips shares this belief and explains its necessity by quoting Oscar Wilde, who said, "'To lose one parent is a tragedy, to lose both is sloppiness' . . . I think that's how it is with jokes; if you have hundreds of them and one is stolen, that's part of the price you pay. But if you have like five jokes and one is stolen, well who are you to try to make it with just five jokes?" He adds, "I've had jokes of mine sold to others, and I got worried about it. Then, maybe two years later I realized that all the jokes that had been stolen, I didn't ever care about anymore. I wouldn't do them anyway; I'd written more. Judy [Tenuta] just had a line stolen. It was by [he names a comic]—that line about breast feeding pigeons in the park . . . it doesn't seem like a man would do that . . . she was really upset about that. Of course someone else could have said it to him—or he could have thought of it spontaneously. With all these comics' minds working feverishly to think of jokes, it's not inconceivable . . . I used to call my lawyer, who always went to fancy restaurants, an 'ambience chaser.' Then, about a year later, I saw it as a caption in *The New Yorker*. That happens. People come up with things spontaneously. You just have to keep doing it."

When a comic's jokes are stolen, he's not only having his material taken, but years of experience, according to Jerry Diner: "You take somebody who's worked in New York and traveled around the country for years, like Joe Bolster—perfecting his act, spending night after night working at three o'clock in the morning to five people who are already drunk, in order to get the lines so that they work consistently ninety percent of the time. And then somebody says, 'Wow, I relate to that so much, that's really funny, I can do that,' and takes those lines and starts doing them. Well those lines are already perfected; therein lies the art." Like Stein, he says that parallel thinking is inescapable, but usually that affects subject matter more than punch lines: "Everyone talks about cats and dogs, but when it's the hook, and I came up working with the person, and watched them write it, and watched them work on it every night, changing the line so it gets better and better, and refining it to where it works the best, then plateau with it, and switch it around again to make it even more intense . . . then someone else comes up with an identical line, that's stealing." While Joe Bolster finds stealing detestable, it is difficult to fight because, unlike songs, jokes are rarely associated with their originator in the minds of audiences: "If I went onstage and sang, 'Born in the USA,' they'd know whose it was. But if I went onstage and did a routine by Jerry Seinfeld—comics might know, but no one else would . . . they'd just laugh."

According to Bob Goldthwait everybody steals to some extent: "That's one reason I don't like to hang out at the Comedy Store; I don't want to be influenced by anyone else's act . . . But I don't know who I've ripped off; I'm sure I've been influenced by a lot of people. Steve Martin said that hiding your influences is what you try to do. I can't tell you how many times I've said, 'Hey, I'm gonna go onstage and do this or that . . .' and someone says, 'Sorry, Bob, Kaufman already did it.' So much has already been done."

Today's stand-up is more likely to move toward the punch line by way of a carefully constructed "story" than a one-line premise. This new, looser style allows comics to improvise more onstage and test the audience reaction in a way that would be unthinkable if they were armed with a bag of one-liners. Comics today are actually able to do their writing onstage. They can concentrate more on details, like word combinations, inflection and placement by hearing an audience's initial reaction to a joke, studying it and repeating the process night after night until it gets its maximum reaction. In this respect, the portable cassette recorder has done more for stand-up than any single technical innovation. In showcase clubs, where comics go to try out new material between road gigs, anywhere you hear a laugh, you'll often hear the steady "whirr" of the performer's machine.

Paul Reiser says that, while he can write "nuggets"—funny lines—alone, he needs to be in front of an audience to embroider them into full-fledged comic "bits." Unfortunately, the audience doesn't always comply: "I'll take them through my mental processes if they're good, but when I feel they're not with me, I'll shrivel it up and just give them the nuggets. For me, embroidery is the first thing to go when the audience isn't buying. On a bad night, like in Atlantic City, I think, 'Wait a minute; I just did my entire act and it only took me fifteen minutes. According to subject headings, there's nothing I left out . . .' but it was all the abbreviated version. On a great night, I'll think, 'An hour has passed, and I hardly did any material,' because it was growing organically." Even Seinfeld, who keeps to a rigorous schedule of daytime writing, says, "I like to work out onstage, too—to go on late at Catch, like at one A.M. to screw around—and I'll ask people, 'Has this ever happened to you?' or 'Is this funny?'" Jerry Diner says that some comics, like John Mendoza, have discovered exactly who their stage personality is and how to write for it, so they can "actually sit down and think in that character," which gives them a better picture of how the audience will react to a bit. For himself, he says, "I get out there with so many different characters that it's sometimes hard to write beforehand—but onstage it just flows."

Steve Wright, on the other hand, never writes onstage: "I'm naturally such an introvert that I have to know exactly what I'm doing when I go out there. But I never sit down and just think about jokes either . . . I write when things come into my head." Asked for an example he provides one quickly, "When I was walking to lunch today, I was thinking I wanted to have soup—and wondering what the soup of the day would be. Then I thought of a guy who could look into the future but that's the only thing he could ever predict—the soup of the day." Unlike other comics, he seems to feel none of the looseness and freedom that comes from years of working in front of an audience: "To me, being out in front of those people is fun, but mainly it's intense. And when you're in a situation that intense, it's serious work—it's like I'm at a blackboard trying to figure out this equation, except that I'm presenting jokes. To me, my act takes so much thought that there's no room for me to laugh or write new stuff—maybe it's easier for other people than for me, and that's why they can do it. But it's so intense and precise for me; I have so many jokes to say and if I say them even a little bit differently they won't work as well—or if they're too fast or slow—how is the joke going that I'm saying, what should I do next . . . there's no room for anything else."

For most comics, however, the process of creation lies somewhere between the typewriter and the stage—without one, the other is all but useless. For Robert Wuhl the process is often "conversational . . . I like sitting in a room and jamming together. My friends and I come up with funny stuff. I rarely just sit in a room and come up with material for my stand-up; it's mostly a collaboration. In that way, it's a more immediate art form than others—it's an art form you can try out on people as it's being created." Tom Dreesen used to have a daily writing routine in front of the typewriter, but now his most effective method is note taking, carrying a tape recorder throughout the day and then working this material into bits onstage at night. "Just yesterday," he says, this happened: "I saw a woman who's a Radcliffe graduate and her husband went to Harvard. She came into a room and her child proceeded to leap over the desk, knock things over, pull stuff off the walls . . . and she pretended not to even see that. Finally she said, 'Look at that—even at this age, he's able to express himself.' I thought about the poor people I grew up with—the difference between a poor and rich person is that the poor person would have said, 'You wanna walk with a limp the rest of your life? Keep it up!' That's the difference between the affluent and the poor." Afterwards, he wrote a note to remind himself of what had happened and said, "This weekend I'll probably go onstage and start goofing with that idea until I have a whole bit."

Dreesen believes that the art of joke writing does not lie in a comic's being able to come up with brilliantly funny bits consistently. Rather, it comes from writing down everything with possibility and having the guts to try that material out onstage: "Of the geniuses I've met in my life, I've noticed the one thing they've had in common—everything they say isn't a gem, a lot of it is bullshit, but they are willing to go in there, on that stage, and let everything spew out. You're going, 'That's not great, that's not great . . .' and all the sudden, boom! Holy shit— where did that come from? They're not afraid to take the lid off of that creativity. Richard Pryor onstage, when he's breaking in new material, not what you hear on the albums, isn't afraid to let his head go, then . . . all the sudden, that gem will flow out of there! Ask any comic. He'll tell you he writes twenty jokes and two of them work, eighteen suck, but two of them are really solid babies."

Using personal observation and experience involves finding not just what's funny to the comic, but hitting the intersection between what's funny to him/her *and* the audience. Sometimes this means discovering that a "surefire" bit is useless; other times it's finding that a personal observation is actually appreciated by thousands. Paul Reiser says that Seinfeld does this in a way that leads the audience to think they're getting ahead of the comic, then he sneaks up behind them and delivers the punch line like a mean left hook: "The way Jerry writes is like, 'Here's what I think and here are all the tools. Okay, you got something in mind? That's nice—now here's what *I* thought of.' It's like he gives them all the tools, they're laughing, thinking of something, and then he goes, 'Aha! But here's what I thought of, and that's why I get paid.' It's always a step further than what they would have thought." Of his own writing, Seinfeld says, "It's just a process of getting a feeling and trying it out, again and again to see if it works or not. I do this joke about how I didn't touch a thermostat until I was twenty-eight years old—because my parents made such a big deal over this thing, I had to stay away from it, not touch it . . . I was in this hotel room when I finally got the guts to make it warmer and all night I thought my father was going to come in and say, 'Who touched the thermostat in here?' It's funny, when people laugh at that, they realize, 'We all had that experience,' and it's a real sense of community." Like many premises, he had no idea whether or not it was a universal feeling until he tried it out onstage.

A joke may work for an audience in one part of the country, but not in another. In the case of the thermostat joke, Seinfeld says that while it works everywhere, "I just did that joke in Winnipeg, where it's real cold, and they were howling. Thermostats are obviously a real big part of their lives." He gives another example of jokes that are funny, but only to New York audiences, "Like cab drivers—what do they need to get a license? A face. And I talk about how their names have those strange letters, like the 'O' with the line through it. I'd need a chart of the elements if I wanted to report this guy... 'Yeah, his name was Amal, and then the symbol for boron.' That's a big laugh in New York—just getting to say 'boron' onstage is a big thrill."

Comics tag the ability to distinguish between what works and what doesn't as "laugh ears." Without them, Jay Leno says, you see the following situation: "A comedian goes onstage and doesn't do particularly well. He comes offstage and says, 'I killed.' You say, 'Bob, they didn't like you,' but he refuses to hear. It's very sad, you need the ability to edit and grow—you have to hear yourself." Listening is, for the comic, one half of creation; the other half is writing. The two are not mutually exclusive; to listen without writing is to be an audience, to write without listening is to be a bore, neither of which make one a comedian.

Laugh ears are grown, not inherited. In the beginning, all stand-ups struggle with the primordial comic question, "What is a joke?" Enlightenment occurs at various stages in life, but is usually remembered by the comic as a moment of distinct clarity, when years of class clowning and random silliness are crystallized in a single punch line, from which its speaker emerges with new knowledge. Jonathan Solomon explains, "One day I was sitting at the dining room with my whole family and I said something funny: 'I'm suspicious about this whole Apollo moon landing thing. The first thing they did on the moon was put a flag down, then they got out a ball and played golf. The next moon landing they planted another flag, the third landing another ... I think what's happening is in fifteen more moon landings, we'll have a golf course.' Suddenly I realized that, if it was taken out of context, what I'd said would still be funny. It struck me, 'This is a joke.' That night, I went to my parents' bedroom with another joke I'd thought of, and they laughed. That's when it all started." Carol Siskind's first realization that she was creating a joke came in early childhood: "I know when it was—exactly. I remember being four years old and sitting at the table—it's one of the earliest memories I have—and saying something that I knew was funny. Everyone laughed, thinking, 'She doesn't even know how funny she is!' But I did. I knew I was funny—I knew I made them laugh—and I felt enormous satisfaction knowing that."

Many comics, however, begin stand-up only to discover that jokes aren't necessarily someone saying something funny; they're intricate devices, built according to rigid specifications, and set to explode in a precise manner at an exact time. During Rita Rudner's first performance, she noticed that people laughed *between* the jokes. She remembers thinking, "There's something funny, but it's not the material." So she began listening to Woody Allen's albums, studying and analyzing them: "This is a joke, you go da-dum-da-dum ..." and applying it to herself. "Now," she says, "I know exactly why people are laughing at every joke; you learn that after awhile." Paul Reiser agrees that "in the beginning you don't know anything. You may get a laugh and you don't know why. Maybe it was topical that week, or maybe it fit in with something you did before—a lot of times you chase the wrong thing ... and you work on a bit that's not going to go anywhere, but eventually, you learn why bits work and why they don't."

A "bit," Reiser explains, "is a group of words used to incorporate a premise and all variations thereof." Words, the components of bits, are the basis of the comic's life; they are the rope by which lesser talents hang themselves and the stuff of which comic genius is made. Molded against the immovable truth of reality, bits circumvent the dictates of logic by mimicking them to perfection ... until the final moment, when they're turned 180 degrees and left standing—if people laugh— as monuments to the malleability of human nature. Jerry Seinfeld's Halloween bit (where he complains about being Superman as a kid but "having to wear a light jacket over the cape... like, 'I've got to leap a tall building in a single bound, but I've got this sore throat, and I don't want to catch a chill—because then we've got the speeding bullet races tomorrow... and I want to feel good for that...'") was built entirely around his desire to use the words "trick or treat" onstage, because they are inherently funny together. But "bit composition" isn't just analyzed down to words; letters, also, have various laugh-getting powers. "For example," Seinfeld adds, "any 'k' sound is good—it's a very strong letter that impinges on people."

David Brenner has found that "certain numbers are funny for me; maybe it's the accent. Four's always been funny for me—I don't know why, maybe the 'f' sound. They say 'k' is funnier than 'c'—I don't know, but I'm sure it's true. I always used to use 'Guam' as my country—it always cracked people up, then other people started using it. I also use the word 'suck' and people laugh, like when I say I'm afraid of sitting on the toilet of a plane because I don't want to get sucked out over Oklahoma—now that's funnier than 'fall through' to Oklahoma. George Schultz, from Pip's, used to say, 'What kind of suck joke do you have this week?' and I'd have my Guam joke... I should just go out and say, 'Four, Guam, Suck,' and I'd be a superstar."

The goal of every bit is to impinge on people, to stop all competing talk and scream, "Listen to me—marvel at my cleverness—laugh!" When the bit is just right, this happens. And no one knows what hit them. Larry Miller compares the execution to "a batting stroke in baseball; the sound is there, but it's a function of the swing rather than the actual thing itself. You know when you're on a hot streak with certain bits, when they're hitting just right. You know the right breath, the right pause, the right take, the right everything." But like a hitter on a hot streak, he says, you know that at some point it's going to fall out of focus: "It happens when they realize they've encumbered themselves with too many things—wrist turns, head cocks, and everything—and what they do is take it back to ground zero: just hold the bat and meet the ball. Once they feel they're hitting it solidly again, and evenly, then they swing for power, they start bringing the other stuff back, lifting the leg and really swinging into it. That's very similar to comedy I think. If you feel you've lost a line, you don't even see it happening because it's so slow and subtle—little pauses you hardly notice. And when you know, finally, you take it back to square one and just say the words—not like a robot, but set it up and say it clearly to the audience. Let the joke carry its own weight, then you start to put the attitude more on it, perform it more, and get it back."

Paul Reiser gives an example of the rise and fall of a bit: "There's a bit I do where I say, 'I appreciate the little things in life—like this and that—or after you go swimming, about two hours later, there's a little leak of hot water from your ear, and suddenly you feel better than you did a minute ago. It's great. You didn't know you were hearing badly, or that anything was wrong—and all of a sudden, you feel even better.' Then it's my job to make it funny and put it into context."

Each bit must be constantly manipulated, sculpted and refit because, if left alone, "bits have a life of their own." He describes the ear bit, in its early days, as "a little puppy running out of the gate." So he started highlighting it in the set, then moved it into the spotlight at the end of the act, "and suddenly, its legs weren't strong enough to hold that kind of weight and it died. For a month it was just a shit joke." But he realized that, if it worked for a month, there must be something to it, so he "started hitting it with confidence again, just doing it," but still it didn't work. Finally, he says, "I was working on the road one night and a comic said, 'You know why that didn't work this time and it did the last time? Because you did it softly.' He was right; I realized I stood onstage and said it softly, like a grown person, saying, very child-like, 'You know—I love that.' The other time, I said, real loudly, 'Boy, I love that!' and the audience was thinking, 'It wasn't that important, relax!' They weren't laughing because it was so true, they were laughing because of the *way* I said it."

Just as the raw material for a bit must be created from random thoughts, so must its presentation onstage be whittled down from an infinite number of possible deliveries. Steve Mittleman has only performed about a fourth of the material he's written. "I just haven't allowed myself to find out what I'm made of as much . . . because I set a standard to do well and it's hard to maintain that while introducing new stuff." Germinating bits need time and patience from the audience; the performer must create a safe atmosphere for them by lulling the audience into a state of well-being, while piquing their sense of adventure about the uncertain things to come. As Reiser says, "At the Improv, where they know me or see I'm confident, I try to get a couple laughs in the first few minutes, then I've bought some time to work out. I've learned you don't start out with the abstract stuff—you have to let them get used to you, to the sound of your voice, your sentence structures, then you go for a ride."

For Rita Rudner, like Mittleman, the hardest part of introducing new material is putting aside her personal standards of perfection, of feeling that every joke must kill, and every set must be impenetrably tight: "Last night I didn't want to try new material. My rhythm was so good and they were going with me on every joke, I just couldn't stand it if I said something new and they thought, 'But she was so funny a minute ago.'" To solve this, she works out new bits in smaller showcase clubs on Sundays and Tuesdays, slower nights, when she can relax even further.

Joe Bolster explains that the pressure against introducing new material is much greater on the road because, not only does the comic have to worry about disappointing the audience (who is paying a lot more money than in the showcases) but he also has to contend with the club owner, who has paid for a "professional, perfected act": "Once you're on the road, getting paid X number of dollars a week to work, based on your act, and yet you want to work out new material—it's sort of like working on your left hand in a basketball game, during the actual game. The coach wants you to score with your right because it's your better hand, and you want to work on your left. But there's no practice anymore—everything's a real game. That's like the road—every time you're onstage, it counts. They're paying you and they want your best show. I don't think they'd know if you threw in a line or two but that's a matter of seconds. To work out two to three minutes can really slow a show down if it doesn't work. And the difference between new stuff and stuff that's been honed and edited can be great. You get caught up with killing all the time and it's hard to take risks."

This is an important issue for Bolster and other comics: when and how to take the risks necessary for working in new material. While it's difficult to experiment with an unenthusiastic crowd, it can be even more so with an enthusiastic one. Bolster explains: "I have a problem trying new stuff out in front of those three hundred people who just laughed uproariously for ten minutes because now they have certain expectations—like that every word out of my mouth will be funny. And then you have to try a brand-new bit—you don't know where the laugh is going to be, yet you have to deliver it with the same confidence as everything that's preceded it. When you feel confident, you try more, but it's a constant struggle."

The ability to make good bits work and great bits kill—the ability to sell material to an audience—is what comics mean when they talk about "technique." Abby Stein says that there are some basic rules for writing bits that will click: "In order to work, material usually has to ring a note with everyone in the audience—whether it's your sex life, or sex life in general." But she adds that certain comics are able to work around this rule by virtue of their "salesmanship": "Steve Wright's act doesn't really ring personal notes, but he, and his material, are so funny and unique that it doesn't matter. There are a lot of different opinions about what the most important factor for success is, but I believe personality is far more important than material. I think you can take lousy material and in the hands of a good enough salesman, it will make the salesman a star."

Seinfeld agrees: "Most of the comics I spend time with seem funnier to me than I am, and I don't think I'm wrong most of the time. But the thing is, a lot of them aren't as good a comedian as I am, because that involves something different. I'm good at picking up details of performance—I'm good at the craft." Part of this craft lies in not just selling bits, but directing the audience to buy bits from themselves. He explains how this works in the case of his "nightclub of clothes" bit: "I say the washing machine is the nightclub of clothes. It's dark, there's bubbles, they're all dancing with the agitator going around . . . then you come by and open up the lid, and they all freeze, like, 'We were just soaping.' I'm dancing around like the clothes onstage, and when I do that 'freeze' that's one of the biggest laughs. It's just so incredibly silly . . . when they go with you on that: okay clothes have minds, they have dances and nightclubs . . . and when you go one step further—that when you open the door they're all embarrassed—it's funny, and it's even funnier that they're even laughing at it. The audience itself becomes part of the punch line."

Paul Reiser explains that now, after years of trial and error, "I have enough confidence in my ability to make people laugh, so I can throw a premise in, and if there's a flicker of identification, if they're not mocking me, I know it's worth going with and working on—it isn't something that only tickles me. In the beginning you don't have that security or confidence to take the chance of something missing. You may throw out something great, and maybe the only reason they're not laughing is that they don't know who you are."

But what about writing without the constant pressure of selling? After working as a writer for "Saturday Night Live," Carol Leifer realized that writing did not satisfy the same needs, creatively, as selling the material herself: "The job made me realize that I enjoy writing, but if I'm not performing, it's not really fulfilling. I'm not good at being behind the scenes. I'm sure I have performer blood in me now—when I hit the studio at eleven thirty I was really charged; then I realized I wasn't going on. It's like getting all dolled up for a party you're not invited to. When the show started, I would think, 'God, I wish I was out there tonight.'" A. Whitney Brown, on the other hand (who works as a writer on "Saturday Night Live," and also performs), described the experience of sketch writing as "thrilling," because he was constantly working with new material, as opposed to working with the same bits over a long period of time, as in stand-up. He also found it satisfying to write something with a beginning, middle and end, that has "internal sense," as opposed to set-ups and punch lines. Richard Lewis decided early in his career that "opening for Sonny and Cher in front of fifteen thousand people was something that was going to kill me emotionally." Writing, in addition to his stand-up work, would give him more control over his destiny. Today, though he continues to perform, he has "gotten into the writing business," selling pilots, scripts and "going from deal to deal."

As each comic's usage of material varies (some say they use as few as two jokes a minute, other comics say they need a laugh every fifteen seconds or the act goes "in the toilet"), so does the manner in which they gain inspiration. After an initial act is established, comics can choose to vary their output of new bits according to personal desire, ability and professional need. The struggle to reach this point can take years, however, as Rita Rudner explains: "When I started, I wanted to be funny for five minutes. That was my goal for two years—and because I do three jokes a minute, on the average, that was fifteen jokes. I'd write about one joke a week, some funny, some not—so it took me two years to be consistently funny for five minutes." In writing, she gains inspiration by sitting down daily, leafing through magazines, newspapers, old notes until "something hits me." But like many comics, she places restrictions on what material she will include in her act: "I never do anything contemporary or topical because it really brings me out of my world into the real world and it's disturbing. Like I would never mention a proper name . . . 'Joan Collins' wouldn't work in my act. Recently I thought of a Rocky joke, but I know I'll do it a few times and get tired of it. I did it on a radio show yesterday though. I said, 'Well, another Rocky movie is coming out, but it's a little educational at least . . . all these Rocky movies are teaching young children Roman numerals . . .' but I just don't feel like I should say 'Rocky' in my act. I don't say brand names either, like 'McDonald's.' Also by the time I get topical material right, it's no longer topical."

Phyllis Diller has been disappointed by topical material in the past: "I mean, when it was Liz and Dick, oh my God, did I have Liz and Dick material, and when it was Jackie and Ari, oh my God, did I have Jackie and Ari material—fabulous stuff. It was on people's minds, they read about it every day—that's one way of staying with it. But with topical stuff like that you can lose huge lumps . . . when Rock Hudson died, I lost the biggest hunk of gay material—it was wonderful material, too." She says that, as in the latter case, topical material is not only subject to being dated, but also to the changing sympathies of both comic and audience: "I did the 'Rock' material once after he died, and I thought, 'Oh God, this isn't right at all.' I'm extremely sensitive to what is right and wrong in my work. I'm the first one who's offended, and the last thing you want to do is offend an audience."

Jonathan Solomon restricts his material in a number of ways: "Making fun of anything that someone doesn't have in their power to change—like physical stuff," except for specific situations when he must do it to protect himself. "If I'm up there doing my thing, and someone fucks with my space, I'll fuck with them unmercifully. But even then it's rare, and I won't ever gratuitously go after them." He explains that "there are different kinds of 'fuck yous.' I hate when someone's embarrassed. I won't mention herpes, because I think twenty-five percent of the audience probably has it, and I don't want anyone to be sitting there bummed out about it. I won't do a fag joke or any of that stuff, and that's thought out. Sometimes I'll get loose and go over the line, but it's my moral challenge not to. I've tried to write cheap, fun, angry, doesn't matter who you hurt material, and I can't do it. To be honest, there's a bit of tyranny in how moral I am. Sometimes I feel like, 'Who am I to be so moral?'"

Solomon focuses not on people, but themes. In the last two years, he's written solely about children, parents and his own childhood. He says this started because "my cousin has kids and they'd spend the weekend with me. After the weekend, I felt real loving and I had nothing else to say onstage...so I started writing about kids not by choice, but sheer need." Now, he says, that subject has exhausted itself and the next topic to which he's orienting himself is "illusion and America—in other words, why is it fucked up today as opposed to eighty years ago. That's on my mind all the time...I used to see kids, now I see that everything's fucked—and it's just starting to seem funny."

PITH AND VINEGAR
...
INSIDE THE COMIC MIND

The concept of a "comic psyche" has been discussed, diagrammed and theorized about ad nauseam but ultimately, the fact of its existence is no more certain than that of Santa Claus or L. Ron Hubbard. The question of whether there exists a mental common denominator that runs through all comic minds is a compelling if unprovable notion for both comics and their observers. Just when it seems that a psychological variable crops up over and over in countless comics, along comes that unexpected stand-up who says, "But I *didn't* have adolescent sexual fantasies involving Henny Youngman and seltzer bottles..." and it's back to the proverbial drawing board.

David Brenner, in speaking about the "comic mind," offers an interesting solution; he says that comics are not necessarily different from other people, psychologically, but what sets them apart is their "third eye" through which they view the world and synthesize their observations. He adds that this creative eye is not restricted to comics, but what makes theirs unique is its humorous filter: "A poet walks through the woods and those little spurs catch on his wool pants. He thinks of it aesthetically, 'How nature attaches itself to man, as the spur does to the wool of my pants as I walk through the greenery, blah, blah... running brook, cloud, blah, blah...' Now the scientist walks through and the same thing happens, so he spends eleven years in a laboratory and invents velcro, because he has a scientific mind. Then a comedian walks through and the spurs catch on his pants. That night, he gets onstage and says, 'What is it with these spurs? What's that, nature's way of getting even with us for stepping on the grass?' He thinks of it that way because he has a comic mind."

Robert Wuhl takes it one step further. He says, "There are two ways to look at it—one is from an artistic standpoint, the other is professional. A comic mind is someone who sees things funny, who has a twisted point of view, and a professional stand-up is someone who can make a workable joke out of that point of view. One is something anyone in the street can do, and the other is a professional craftsman's way of working."

Steven Wright agrees with this distinction: "Everyone knows people who are hysterical at parties or at work—but with stand-up, the catch is to convey that funny thought to an audience. That's the difference between funny people and comedians—that ability to convey humor, on purpose, at nine P.M. exactly... and have an audience react. I don't know how it works, but I feel really lucky I can do it. Really lucky."

Bernie Brillstein believes that comics share certain fundamentals: "I've found comics to be similar morally, mentally and emotionally. They're all very smart, and each one is an island." He describes them as "dinosaurs"—overwhelming in presence and sheer determination. He says, "The best example of this was the time I was backstage with the comedian Pat Cooper in Las Vegas and he was angry about something, screaming at the top of his lungs. His veins were popping out, and all of a sudden we heard onstage, 'And now, for your laughing pleasure, Pat Cooper...' Boom! In one second he was out on that stage and he was Pat Cooper, comedian." Unlike most people, comics are able to transcend their worldly troubles when it's time for work, not only because of professional dedication, but because their work acts as a salve for the pain: "I think nothing in the world compares with that ... one of the great highs they have is walking on the stage."

George Carlin agrees: "A stand-up comic wants to take risks, which are big in terms of immediate failure and in terms of never getting the rewards. So what he or she hopes to get from it must be pretty good stuff to risk the down side, because it's a very real rejection when they don't like you." More specifically, he defines a stand-up comic as "some combination of needing and wanting attention and approval. I've found that comedians are looking for a lot of things that begin with 'A': attention, approval, audiences, applause, approbation, affirmation and acceptance. For me, those are all the As I wasn't getting in school —I'm getting them in my real life. The comedian needs most or all those things and they want them on their own terms."

Robin Tyler is a feminist-activist comic who spends much of her time traveling around the country speaking on the history of stand-up comedy in America and producing women's music-comedy festivals. One of the points she brings up in her lecture is that there is a characteristic common to virtually all comics—manic-depressive personalities (not to be confused with chemical manic depression). She says that comics are very angry people, which is good—as opposed to hostile people who repress their anger, which is bad—and when they're on-stage they can let this anger out. When a comic leaves the stage, however, he or she must turn off this open flow of anger, and this produces manic-depressive symptoms. Because she is an activist, she says, she has an outlet for her anger offstage as well as on, and this has allowed her a personality consistency not afforded to most stand-ups: "If you have no outlet, only that twenty minutes onstage at night, what do you do the rest of the day?" She adds that another common characteristic in comics is the desire to be loved, by a group, which is what keeps them on the road, chasing acceptance and laughter from California to New York, although she remarks: "I got off the road for a while because I lost my need to be loved. Instead of wanting love, I wanted my rights." After losing this need, she describes the way she feels now in front of an audience as not a stand-up, but rather a teacher who is using comedy as her medium of expression.

Tom Dreesen feels that no comic really transcends the desire to be loved by an audience, but that, instead, each works according to his own level of need; he says that, with many variations, there are two basic types of comics, "those who want the love of an audience, and those who need the love of an audience. I consider myself one who wants it. Those who need it are driven... *driven*. They can't stop, they're only as good as their last performance. I know old-time comics who are neurotic wrecks—they'll drive you crazy. All the old-timers are like that. I used to do the Dean Martin Roast with those old-timers and they're not happy, not with anything in life, except the quality of their last show." Although he is a professional and has been making a living by telling jokes for quite a while, he notes, "When I don't do a good show I don't feel great—I feel bad." But, unlike those who are driven by need, he says, "a half hour later I bounce back and say, 'Hey, it's a show. It's not life and death. Children are starving in Ethiopia. Do I really matter?'"

Richard Fields, of Catch A Rising Star, says that the comic's vision of the world is slightly "skewed," and adds (laughing), "Yeah, and they either do this or they're up on a building with a rifle—'I'm either going to be a comic or I'm going to kill people.'" He feels that comics are, in general, much more sensitive than other people and more in need of protection: "They're closer to poets than musicians." He cites, specifically, stand-up Gilbert Gottfried, whom he calls "an endangered species," and says, "I'm watching him carefully. If anything happened to Gilbert it would be a crime, and nobody would know it."

Gilbert is, according to many comics in New York and Los Angeles, one of the greatest artists working in stand-up today; he is also perceived as an enigmatic, mysterious personality who is, with regard to his career, bent on personal sabotage and self-destruction. He is a living legend among stand-ups—a guaranteed killer act who is every comic's nightmare to follow and dream to be like—and he is also a striking exception to Dreesen's rule that all comics want an audience's love. In fact, many stand-ups feel that Gilbert actively avoids that, by never pandering to the crowd, but his talent is so great that he finds it impossible to alienate an audience no matter what he does. Paul Reiser says, "Gilly is the most brilliant, funny person I've ever met. He makes more comics laugh than anyone else can, but built into his comedy is the presumption that 'I don't want to be big—I don't want to appeal to outsiders.' I'm amazed when he takes a TV show or movie. It's like 'I can't be patted on the head.'"

Gilbert's personal history is sketchy, but the following is close to the truth: he began performing stand-up as a teenager in 1971 at a Village club, on a Hootenanny night. Since that time, he has been a cast member of "Saturday Night Live," in 1980–81, a cast member of "Thicke of the Night," in 1983, and, this year, a featured comic on MTV and the subject of his own comedy special on Cinemax. His comedic talent is so prodigious, unique and compelling that, in addition to killing regular audiences during virtually every performance, his act consistently awes other comics on a nightly basis. George Calfa describes him as "probably the funniest person in the world. At one point he was so hot in this city . . . I've never heard laughs like he got—screams, where people were moaning they couldn't take it. This is with audiences *and* comics."

Calfa says, however, that Gilbert is determined to sabotage his act: "He must have fifteen hours of material, but whenever it gets to where people request it, he refuses to do it anymore, like his 'Tony Del Vicho' character (an inane Brooklyn comic), who would say things like, 'Why did the moron throw the clock out the window? Because he was a fuckin' moron!' But when people screamed, 'Do Tony!' he stopped doing it." One of the many unique qualities about Gilbert's act is its almost complete independence from the audience; he performs with his eyes either shut or covered by his hands during the entire show—and yet, because of the overwhelming strength of his material and the sheer charisma of his character, the audience is virtually unaware of this. Calfa says that Gottfried has always performed this way, but in the past he made some effort to maintain a link with the audience by becoming a character called "Murray," who "put on glasses and said to the audience after a sick joke, 'You think that's funny? That's not a joke. A joke is, 'Two Jews walk into a bar . . . That's a real joke.' Then he'd take off the glasses and say, 'The pope loves rats—give the pope rats!' Then put the glasses on again and say, 'Stop laughing at that sickness!'" Calfa adds, "He's one of the only comics who refuses to give in, and yet he keeps getting offered TV shows and movies—people still want to use him, because he's so brilliant."

This "giving in" that Calfa speaks about is Gilbert's determination to do the opposite of what is expected of him. Paul Reiser says that before

Gilbert completely refused to do his "Tony" character, he would do it, but stop in the middle if people clapped, and do something else instead. He feels that Gilbert has "an inability to be contained, patronized or told what to do, because he's afraid of finding out that the antiestablishment thing [stand-up] he's doing has now become yet another confinement." Gilbert, on the other hand, says that he is not at all self-destructive and that he does not actively try to alienate the audience. He says, instead, that the reason he refuses to do characters like Tony in the showcase clubs is because he doesn't need to work on them anymore. He has established that they do well, so he uses his stage time to introduce new characters and bits. He says that those comics who continue to do the same pieces over and over, in order to get the guaranteed laughs, are actually the self-destructive ones, because they will never go beyond this. He adds, also, that in paying clubs he will do older characters like Tony, but in showcases, whose purpose is supposedly not to strictly entertain, but to work on new material and characters (which is why the comics are paid so little), he chooses to work out. About his general reputation for neurosis, he says: "It's part of the package—if I wasn't like this, maybe I wouldn't be this kind of a comic."

Gilbert seems to be one of the few stand-ups who are able to completely transcend their need for audience approval, or at least to submerge it enough to concentrate only on the work itself and not be tempted by getting, or not getting, the maximum amount of laughs. Most comics, however, fall somewhere within Dreesen's two categories—those who want laughs and those who need them. For comics who want approval, there is a constant temptation to go for the easy laugh and get the much-needed love fix, whether it involves telling a dick joke or pandering to a sexist, racist or ultra-nationalist audience. For those who need approval, who need to feel that supreme blanket of love that comes from the constant laughter of a crowded club, stand-up can begin to feel like a compulsion. Cathy Ladman says, "Sometimes I feel too attached to it. I wish I didn't. I do need it—it helps me validate myself." For her, comedy is not a job, it's "a part of me, and I can't separate it. I think after I'm dead I'll be looking down at this

saying, 'What a fucking jerk you were. None of that was important.'
But that's how I feel. It's as important to me as eating, breathing and
sleeping—and being regular."

Many stand-ups today, unlike comics of past generations who often
bought material, have the added pressure of not only proving themselves to the audience as performers, but also proving themselves as
writers. This becomes particularly touchy when, as happens with Ladman and many others, a comic writes jokes based on personal experience. This makes each performance a triptych of vulnerability,
composed of "Do you like my performing?—Do you like my material?
—Do you think my life is relevant?" For example, when Carol Siskind
talks about her past love affairs ("I used to be involved in a love/hate
relationship—we both loved him and hated me"), though the story is
obviously distorted for comic purposes, she is letting the audience in
on a private thought. Regardless of how far removed this joke is from
the actual experience, we can be fairly certain that she has had some
experience with this kind of relationship.

The drawbacks of this onstage vulnerability are obviously outweighed by the benefits, as is evidenced by the fact that (loosely) auto-
biographical comedy is the dominant form of stand-up today. Although
Cathy Ladman continues to feel a great deal of anxiety about performing because her act is rooted so firmly in reality, she maintains, "I want
my work to be as close to me and personal as it can possibly get—that's
what makes it work."

Perhaps the comic who makes the most use of his psychological
inner-life is Richard Lewis, to whom "sane" seems to be a four-letter
word. Lewis appears to be a walking "Who's Who of Emotional
Trauma," onstage and off. While a talk with both him and his mother
turned up no evidence as to what happened between birth and now to
make him the way he is, he nevertheless carries all the earmarks of a
recovering basket case. For him, stand-up has served as not only a
creative outlet, but an emotional outlet as well. He began performing
during a very painful time in his life and, apparently finding that it
helped, continued. Why it worked, however, he doesn't know, but not
for a lack of trying to find out.

He relates the following history: "After my father died, for about three to four years straight, my whole life was consumed with stand-up. I must have driven into New York from Jersey at least six nights a week for three years, and did five shows a night sometimes; I drove all over creation. I worked my ass off, but I had no idea what was going on—I was trying to figure it out with various and sundry doctors. I remember playing my act for my Freudian analyst—the simplest bit about going to Shea Stadium was about eight penises and a vagina. After that I stopped playing tapes for doctors." He thinks a moment. "Well, maybe a bat, and the glove is sort of like a vagina—maybe I'll go back to her. I should never have left!" But he did and, he emphasizes, there was more of where that came from: "I've been in and out of therapy for fifteen years—almost every type known to man. Nothing primal though—I was in groups, marathons, everything. 'Group,' in theory, is supposed to be a support group of people who don't judge you, but that's not always the case. Particularly when you're getting better. These are crazy people. They're not going to say, 'Hey, good luck, you're not crazy like us anymore, good-bye!' That takes a healthy person. I had to build a tunnel to get out of group—like Steve McQueen." (He says into his own tape recorder, "Steve McQueen tunnel out of group," then writes it down on a pad.)

What caused this compulsiveness, and what is its relationship to stand-up? His mother, Blanche Lewis, says that the answer almost came once when her son was a guest on the "Larry King Show": "Larry said, 'You're so successful, so handsome, why are you so neurotic?' But just then, the speakers fell out of Richard's ears and he couldn't hear, so I still don't know." She continues: "Sometimes I look at David Brenner, who's so calm on stage compared to Richie, and I want to say, 'Richie, can't you just stand still like that?' But I don't because then it just wouldn't be Richard. He's not that way in real life at all. I mean he's not the calmest person in the world, but when I see him and we walk in New York, he's just my baby, you know." Whatever she believes, her acceptance of his possible neurotic charade is undeniable. In a restaurant, she approached a busboy and proclaimed proudly, "You know Richard Lewis, the neurotic comedian? That's my son!"

Richard, however, is the extreme case. Most comics, when asked for a definition of the word "neurosis" would probably respond, "Richard

Lewis." While insecurity is prevalent among their peers, hard-core neurosis is no more common among stand-up comics than to members of other professions. Perhaps they just seem more neurotic as a group because, neurosis being a ripe subject for comedy, they talk about it a lot, and they continue to do that because, obviously, we enjoy hearing about it. Why is that? Because, while there is an undeniable social taboo against airing dirty laundry in public, there is no law that says we can't hire a launderer or laundress to do it for us.

Mitzi Shore feels that stand-up comics are by definition insecure people, but says the reasons for their insecurity vary from one person to the next: "If they look like they're secure, it's a front. If they were secure they wouldn't be doing this. Comedy, for them, is a way of life. Being onstage is 'coming'—it's having an orgasm—that's how they look at it. Everyone has their own reasons for needing that, though, and in that respect they're all different." Tom Dreesen agrees with her assessment, to some extent, though his figures vary slightly: "Eighty-five percent of all the stand-up comics I've met were neurotic, love-starved wrecks, and the other fifteen percent were gifted, confident people who knew this was the profession that was chosen for them." In his own case, he is unclear as to whether his motivation was insecurity or an innate drive, but in the following example, any distinction between the two means seems to fade away in the brilliant glare of the end. Dreesen says, "For the last two-and-a-half years, I've been touring as the opening act for Frank Sinatra. On certain nights, there are twenty thousand people out there. I did a forty-city tour with him, and it was like, 'Tom, there are twenty thousand people out there, and I want you to go out and, for the next forty-five minutes, hold their attention. And one more thing, I want you to make them laugh for forty-five minutes—not just laugh, but laugh when you want them to.' I had to pull the emotional strings of twenty thousand with no props, charts, tricks or band—just me and twenty thousand people. Now what neurotic, love-starved nut would even attempt that? Or what gifted, confident human being?"

Jonathan Solomon, on the other hand, believes that people like Dreesen and Shore have it all backwards. He says that comics are, as a rule, hyper-aware of whether everybody is happy—and if they're not, they tend to feel responsible for changing that. This, and seeing the absurdity in life from a young age, combine to form a comic mind, and if they don't feel this responsibility, they're not "real comics... you can see it in their acts and when you meet them—they're performers, not comics."

Jerry Seinfeld believes that the reasons for performing vary according to one's moods; stand-up can become either a way to further heighten happiness, or an escape hatch through which to avoid pain: "Comedy is identical to sex," he says. "You know how you can be feeling happy and you want to have sex, and you can be feeling bad and you want to have sex? It's because sex is another mental place completely. You're another person when you're doing that. You're in another sphere of thought and action and sensation—it's all different. You turn to that as an active step into another sphere of sensation, and performing is the same. You turn to it and relate to it different ways, depending on your moods." The transporting impact of performing is heightened in the case of stand-up because the success of the performance is up to one individual, and with regard to laughter, there is no middle ground: "Comedy has only two scores—a hundred and zero, you know? Ninety-nine just isn't funny. My friend said the other day, we're like fighter pilots—that baby could go down at any time. You live with that, that danger all the time, that the whole thing could dissolve any second."

Unlike most thrill seekers, comics choose to face danger on a daily basis. Under the sweltering heat of spotlights and public opinion, in the place where dragons are slain and drinks are sold, the stand-up comic comes alive. Tom Dreesen explains the thrill by way of analogy: "I'm a gambler, and have been one all my life, though I'm not proud of it.... When I went in the navy, I'd gamble my month's pay when I got it. Sometimes I'd win, sometimes I'd lose. When I came out, being married and having kids, after wheeling concrete all week long, I'd still gamble, which was stupid. Anyway, now my buddies say to me, 'Tommy, you don't gamble like you used to—you've calmed down.' But they're wrong; the truth is, I'm gambling now more than I ever have. I've just learned to channel it. Instead of gambling my rent money, I walk out in front of twenty million people on the Johnny

Carson show and gamble with myself. It's risking everything—the
highest high," and conversely, he says, "When you bomb, it's the lowest of lows."

Part of the risk of stand-up lies in trying to prove that the implicit
assumption of funniness, on the part of the comic, is valid. As Paul
Reiser says, "You're bracketing everything you say with, 'I'm a funny
person, and this will be funny,' to which the reaction is usually folded
hands and, 'Oh yeah? Show me.' That's why it's the only art form with
heckling—because organically, people want to go, 'Oh, you're funny?
I bet you're not.' The fear of failure is always present, of course, but is
balanced by an even greater fear—not performing." Reiser says that
before he made his leap into the business, he did all of his agonizing
about failure, "so now it's not a matter of 'If I have three bad months,
I'll leave the business.' I know now that there's nothing I'd rather do."
When he first started, "Seinfeld was the big guy at the club. He was
about a year ahead of me in the process, and I thought, I never want to
be a businessman, sitting home with a beer belly, saying, 'I knew him
. . . I could have been like that'—that would just kill me. But if I was a
comedian, I wouldn't say, 'I wish I'd done that,' about anything else.
So it was the only profession I could do safely, with no regrets." The
highs and lows of stand-up cannot be duplicated in the "other world,"
as Alan Havey calls it. He pities those comics who, after years of struggle, give up, saying they are bored with comedy: "What do you do
when you're bored with comedy? You sure as hell don't go back to an
insurance office."

For Larry Miller, performing stand-up is less of a challenge than a
be-in. He eschews Type-A motivations, like risk and need to control: "I
don't see it like some people who say, 'I have the power—I am the
head of this.' It's very sweet to be the person who's responsible for it,
but it's more of a shared thing. I kind of step out of it and say, 'Gee,
how have we come through civilization to be at a time where, in this
room, these people have cocktails and are sitting in a darkened room
facing one point, and they're all laughing, and they're all at a certain
mood level?'" Tommy Blaze, on the other hand, says that many road
comics are motivated by the basest of desires, and that they are encouraged to be this way every night onstage: "They live in a world that

is not real, and it makes their libido and their id urge go nuts . . . they get laughs by saying things like, 'If I hear another word from you, bitch, I'll staple your uterus to the wall.' That's the life of road comics —fucking and drinking. It's a fake world and it prolongs adolescence. You never have to grow up."

Bob Goldthwait says that the reason he performs is not to make everyone happy, it is to make *him* happy, and when he feels the balance shifting in favor of the audience, he straightens things out right away: "I was onstage the other night, in front of three thousand people, and I said, 'You come out here at night to see me, and some of you are here for freak appeal, but maybe I don't feel like having a nervous fucking breakdown tonight; maybe today was the best day of my life; maybe I just barbecued. I'm not going to come out here and have a breakdown for you fucking Yuppie dickheads . . . maybe today I want to talk to you about computers.' Then, for about five minutes, I just started describing computers, and bored the hell out of them."

While this approach goes against that of the traditional comic (he of the shiny suit and shinier attitude, who professes to live and breathe only to make the audience happy), it seems to work for the Bobcat onstage and off. And he's not the only stand-up who feels that venting, not suppressing, anger helps. Alan Havey says, "I have a lot of hostility coming out now, and my shrink tells me I should lose it. But I see it another way. Before I got in touch with my anger, I was telling dick jokes for a hundred twenty-five dollars a week. Now, I'm telling real jokes, angrier jokes, and doing a lot better. So I'm pissed off, but happy."

He says that, several years ago, when his father got cancer, he became much angrier onstage. After he died, Alan expressed his rage onstage until, gradually, it began to dissipate—but he was left with a much clearer channel between his emotions and his onstage work. Is the anger still there today? "It is," he says, "but it's more in check. It comes out at strange times still, like when someone gives me a hard time onstage, or when the audience becomes judgmental or if they moan at jokes. The other night I was talking to some guy in the audience and someone yelled, 'Don't be cruel . . .' so I just dug into him. The other night I asked a guy if that was his girlfriend, which is a pretty innocent question, and he said, 'Don't do this to me—I like you.' I thought, 'I don't care if you like me or not—I still want to know that about you.'"

Does he feel that comics are different, psychologically, from other people? Only, he says, in the sense of arrested development: "It's the nature of the business. You get to stay up late and sleep late. You can get by, once you get your material down, by using the same stuff. You get up, go to a movie, look over notes, go to a commercial audition, go to dinner, go to a ball game, do a set and go home. You set your own hours. There's no one to discipline you except yourself."

But he believes that stand-up is basically just another option for people trying to dish out their private helpings of angst: "I think everyone has the same basic fears and anxieties and joys to different degrees. We want the same things out of life—to feel joy in our lives, and keep from being frightened all the time—and we deal with that in certain ways. We drink, we take drugs, we work harder, we meditate, we run, we fuck or commit crimes; we deal with it, but the same emotional base is there. Some people flip out, some are great, some are pricks, some are goody-goodies . . . and some are funny."

Whatever the reason for an individual's desire, or need, to become a comic, it is safe to say that that "itch" is most satisfyingly scratched when they kill. "Killing" is, in stand-up terms, what happens when an audience is helpless in the face of a comic's performance; when they are devastated by it; when laughter is not a choice, but a mandate. Killing is the high that comics dream about; the ultimate act of love in a loveless world; the carrot that dangles before them as they race from show to show and town to town. Imagine your most cherished vice, then double it; that's how killing feels. "It's like being Moses and parting the Red Sea," says Paul Herzich, club owner and former stand-up comic. Abby Stein adds, "When it's working, there's no higher high. Every comic will tell you, when it's good, it's breathtaking; you own the world. You can't say or do anything wrong because they're in love with you." But can it be described in a sentence? "Oh, okay," Abby says, "just general hysteria throughout the United States."

George Calfa says that for him, killing justifies every hardship that comes with the profession: "At the end when they laugh and applaud, they love you! It replaces everything. For a few moments you feel this deep love, the love of the world. Killing is better than any drug there can ever be. If you're having a hard time for a month, and then you get that set where everything falls in place—you kill—the audience thinks you're brilliant and they love you. That's when you say, 'This is why I'm doing it—for that feeling.'"

"That feeling," often characterized by comics as one of absolute love—love that transcends everything else—is felt so intensely by the comic because it is given by an audience whose members are laughing and enjoying themselves with equal intensity. And it's an immediate thrill, according to Joe Bolster, which is part of its power: "There's no lag time between creation and the reaction; if it's funny, I know right away. Sometimes you feel like a surfer in the middle of a wave: the laughter's coming in at you and you feel like anything you say will work—your timing is right on. How could you get tired of that?" As Jerry Seinfeld describes it, "A really hard laugh is like sex—one of the ultimate diversions of existence. Laughing is that pure moment of pleasure, and it's free, and there's no waste product. It's a pure high, I guess." In giving this sublime gift of laughter to people, the comic renders them grateful and, to some extent, dependent; a good comic's set has all the makings of an intense, but necessarily short relationship. This feeling on the part of the audience is interpreted by the comic as love because, in fact, it has all the qualities of love.

And so bombing, conversely, has all the emotional reality of hatred; it contains all the resentment of an angry patron's "How dare you subject me to this bullshit?" All the condescension of two hundred people shouting, "Who the hell do you think you are?" And, finally, the unwholesome aftertaste of many spoiled evenings combined into a rancid bouillabaisse, thrown into the face of the unsuspecting comic. Sometimes bombing is quick, like a snapped neck—there's that moment of recognition and regret followed, with merciful speed, by sudden death. Sometimes bombing is evenly paced and constant, like unmitigated gall or bad breath. But perhaps the worst kind of bombing is the slow kind, which Alan Havey describes as "an endless hell... when you have twenty minutes up there, and after the first five you still don't have them. You have to stay up there alone and die. It's like jumping out of a plane and your chute doesn't open so you accept the fact that you're going to die, but you never hit the ground. It's this constant falling and falling. You try to switch and your voice cracks; you mess up a word, your eyebrow twitches . . . they know."

In the beginning of his career, like most comics, he reacted to bombing by getting flop sweat—a cold, clammy chill that usually starts in a dying stand-up's heart and fans out to evenly infect the rest of his body with fear and hopelessness. The result of this, he says, is that the audience turns on you—"like dogs, you show them fear, they smell it," and they will react accordingly.

Eight months after she began performing, Carol Siskind remembers "bombing so horribly, at a club called the Good Times, that when I walked home from there, I said to myself, 'You either go back there tomorrow night or you forget about this and never do it again.'"

She had learned this method at an earlier gig: "After I'd been doing it about three months, a singer asked me to open for her at a club on Fifty-seventh Street. My brother came and brought all of his friends who had known me in diapers, my shrink came . . . a girlfriend came and brought twelve people. I was never into inviting a lot of people anyway, and I bombed. It was a nightmare. I wouldn't let my brother go home. I said you have to come and see me do another set. I dragged him to Good Times at midnight and it wasn't that much better. I'd just passed at the Improv and so I took him there—it was one thirty, then two A.M. Finally there were six people in the audience and they let me on, and I made him stay until I did okay. . . ."

Bombing, like killing, is not just restricted to clubs; it can also happen on television, where the experience is similar . . . except that millions of people are watching. While Bob Morton agrees that bombing on TV is probably one of life's more horrible experiences, it can often be avoided if the comic listens to the advice of a person knowledgeable about that show—as he is in the case of "Latenight." He tells of one stand-up who didn't: "Part of my job is to work with the comics. I'll hear them do twenty minutes in a club and I'll say this or that is the best stuff for the show. They may say, 'This doesn't always work the best,' and I say, 'Trust me. I know my studio audience and I know my home audience. I've done seven hundred versions of this particular show and I know what works best.'

"Will Durst, a funny guy, came on the show. He did the set for me and I told him what would work best. He said, 'Okay, great.' Well, he came on the show and did the other jokes—every joke I told him to do, he skipped. He got out there and he bombed. It's a depressing feeling to bomb here. Let's put it this way: it's a tough spot to be in whether you win or lose. You're coming on at the end of the show and you're competing with forty-five to fifty minutes of David Letterman's comedy. The audience is coming to see David Letterman, not the comic. You have to go out there and win them over. You have to be able to establish a personality in one minute and you have to spend four minutes in scoring points, getting good solid jokes across. Will came out, the audience didn't know who he was, and he launched right into the political material. We don't like that. His whole set was political. After the show I asked him why he did that and he said, 'The political stuff always works best for me.' I said, 'That's fine, you're right . . . but you won't do this show again.'"

With the initial joke, the comic sets in motion a process that will either lead to bombing on the worst of nights, pleasing the majority on most nights, or killing on rare nights, which, in spite of their infrequency, obliterate all others. Bernie Brillstein says that the striking power of comedy is closest to that of death in its impact on people, which is why stand-up uses such gruesome imagery: "The words of comedy are death—'I killed them, I laid them in the aisle, I blew their head off, I murdered them . . .' It's all death—it's how far can you take a human being."

Jerry Seinfeld agrees that stand-up is the most instantaneous way to get that "fix." He says, "It's mainlining. It's like an injection: no plot, no character, no scenes, no sets—just get to the jokes. Get to the funny stuff." If this surge of love power is what stand-up is all about, for some comics, the logical question is *why*? What do they need so desperately that they are willing to undergo years of almost certain rejection to get it? Tom Dreesen remembers: "One night on 'The Tonight Show,' Ellen Burstyn said that insurance companies did a survey ten years ago about the ten biggest fears of man—death was fourth, pain was second, and getting up in front of an audience was number one." Why are comics, who see themselves as people driven by insecurity, able to overcome this greatest of human fears? Cathy Ladman suggests that "maybe stand-up wasn't so traumatic for me, because I was so used to rejection." Larry Miller, on the other hand, did not have that fear, even the first time. To the question, "Were you even a tiny, little bit scared the very first time?" he answers, calmly, "No, absolutely not." Was he scared onstage, or afterwards? "No," he says, even though he didn't get one laugh: "I remember walking off, thinking, 'Oh, ah-ha.' I didn't feel badly, like crawling under a carpet. It was like, 'Oh, I see—this is it.' It's that your natural mechanism of talent and performing ability starts to work already, and tells you what adjustments will be necessary to grow in this. If you keep hearing that voice, you keep saying, 'Oh, uh huh.' Your natural performing instincts start taking over and that machine turns on. I realized, 'You can either hit the ball or you can't—and if you can't, how do you get better?'" Unlike most "civilians," he was able to step outside of his ego and analyze himself purely in terms of his stand-up.

Kip Adotta relates a similar method of working onstage, one in which he is able to tune out everything but the inner voice that says "funny" or "not funny." Even in the beginning of his career, he says, "I saw myself onstage as a 'remote control comedian.' It was as if I was sitting backstage with these remote controls and I didn't care if the guy onstage bombed, because I was in the back of the room controlling what he said. I had programmed him to say such and such, and we didn't worry whether it went over or not; we were experimenting. The things that worked, we would keep and put away; we wouldn't do them again, we'd go on to something else. As soon as a piece started to work, I stopped doing it and went on to something else, and I stockpiled things. I'd put the newest things at the top of the set and I went on and I'd bomb every night because I'd always bring untried things out. I had that discipline." The comic's ability to willfully block pain in order to achieve his or her ultimate goal seems to be a common personality component. But for many, it only covers up their greatest fears, allowing them to go onstage, while never erasing the smaller terrors that occur nightly.

Alan Havey can't understand comics who don't need to be completely alone before they go onstage, who are immune to the feelings of fear and nervousness that he needs to overcome before almost every performance: "They'll go up onstage and be talking to you right before, 'Oh, those Mets...' and someone's introducing them onstage! It's like, 'Hey, man, don't fuck with me—aren't you nervous?' It's so arrogant, especially with their bullshit material. I'd be nervous as hell...and they sleep like babies." He, on the other hand, is unable—and unwilling—to do this: "The other night a booker came up to me right before my set and said, 'Are you going to cost me more now that you've been on Letterman?' I said, 'I'll tell you after I go on—he's introducing me now...' and she kept talking. Finally I had to say, 'Get the fuck away from me!' Before I go on, I pace a lot, I pee a lot, so people think I'm doing coke sometimes, I chew on straws, I smoke, stretch out, practice my diction..."

While he is not actually terrified before going onstage, he says, "I get butterflies every time—not 'gee, willikers, I can't do this,' but do I feel nervous? Yes I do. There are nights when I'm pointing my flashlight" —which he shines into the audience when speaking to people during his set—"and my hand is shaking." While this nervousness is part of the difficulty in being a stand-up, it is also an essential ingredient that can't and shouldn't be lost: "No matter how many times you've done it, or how many credits you have, it's a brand-new experience every time you go up, and if you lose that your audience will know."

He enjoys the nervousness as part of the kick: "I get that little twinge in my stomach, but that's part of the thrill. The kick is getting up there, then taking control—and that control is a turn-on... it's erotic, sensuous. It's like seducing your audience. I've got your attention, your laughs... it's having the audience in the palm of your hand." When an audience is not being controlled, and the comic cannot feel the constant emotional push and pull—the silently recurring contest of wills between himself and his observers—the experience of stand-up has gone flat, and control must be re-established by his inciting the audience in some way... any way. Havey gives an example: "The other night, onstage, I said, 'Can I have some water please?' and then said, 'Control—see that? All I do is ask "Water," "Lights up," "Lights down," "Cigarette please," "Anything else, Mr. Havey?" Control—that's why I love this job.' And the people knew I was serious, so they got into it."

Before Paul Rodriguez goes onstage his thoughts are dominated by performance anxiety: "The fear... the constant fear that 'they won't love me.' I feel it every night. I've tried to think logically what it is I'm afraid of... my material not going over, people not responding. But it's not those things; it's a fear that has no logic. It's not like jogging through Harlem—that fear is logical. What's the worst that can happen onstage? They could say, 'Boo—you suck, get off.' Would that kill me, destroy me?" He pauses for a moment, thinks about it, and then says, "Well, yes, actually—yes, it would destroy me... and probably for months. I did a show in Bakersfield recently and I killed—I got a standing ovation. But at the end of the show, this elderly Hispanic woman came up to me and said, 'I'm just ashamed of you. I used to love you, but I was so disappointed tonight; it was garbage.' And even though I'd just killed, that one lady wiped me out for a long, long time."

What is it, then, that makes it so worthwhile? Granted, bombing is not a common occurrence for most comics, but neither is killing—so even the in-between nights must have something pretty compelling to offer. One possibility is order—the feeling of being onstage, getting laughs at just the right second is a way for the comic to impose order on an otherwise anarchic universe. Paul Reiser says that, while it doesn't allow him to know all the answers in the world, stand-up lets him "spend all my time looking for them, and that's order—that's good. That's what I feel like I do onstage. When I'm sharp, I'm saying, 'Okay, what's the deal, what's going on here?' The things that work best for me are small observations that get big, like, 'This happened to me, and that's kind of the way it is in life.' You can't do that all the time, of course, but... you take something real, twist it, and that twist becomes you."

He feels that, while a comic can't actually define objective reality, he can define his own version of the real world, and by transmitting that onstage and having it accepted by the audience, he can come damn close to re-creating a new reality: "A comic may not be addressing the world at all, like Steve Martin. You don't know what he's doing or if that's really him, but you know it's really his own stage persona—and if you go with it, it's real."

The rush Richard Belzer gets from performing well involves his creating a new "space" around himself and the audience which is charged with energy in a way that it wasn't before: "There is a dynamic at work, but I can't say what it is. It has nothing to do with words. It's like when a great dancer is working. They create a space around themselves, and the greater the dancer, the greater the space. If the dancer's at Lincoln Center, it can take in thousands of people, so the dance is not just onstage, it encompasses the entire audience. And I think a true comic performance onstage must tap into, on some level, everyone in the audience, so that everyone in the audience knows that the guy onstage is in charge, and they feel a sense of relief that they don't have to be nervous for that person. So once they know the act is in charge, then they can go with the act and take leaps of faith and imagination with the person."

For Abby Stein, performance offers similar rewards to what she experienced in sales, but obviously with a few more volts of electricity thrown in: "Performing is like doing a tap dance on the customer's head. When I'm performing I'm selling myself, and I'm the vehicle through which I'm selling my material. There's a definite give and take between you and the audience, unlike other things where you do the spiel and you either win or don't win. In stand-up you're getting feedback every ten seconds, and it's all energy, good or bad. Sometimes you're brilliant, sometimes you're lousy, but it's always high energy."

She says, also, that there is a certain feeling comics strive for—a feeling of rightness, when nothing has gone wrong and nothing can go wrong, ". . . and it doesn't necessarily have to do with how loud they're laughing. We've all had the experience of getting onstage and killing, getting tremendous laughter and applause, but knowing it wasn't happening 'that' way. The audience may think it's happening, but you know you fooled them. And then there are nights you can be on and get fewer laughs, smaller laughs, but know you're right on the money —you said and did all the right things . . . and the ultimate is when both those things happen together." George Calfa agrees: "There are times when they're laughing big, but they don't really love you. You're killing, but when you leave, you don't have that love. Then other times, they're not laughing that big, but they really like you, and when you leave there's this tremendous applause. And then there are times when you have incredible laughter and incredible applause at the end, and when the emcee comes up at the end, you get an even bigger hand—it's indescribable."

Instead of feeling super-charged after a set like this, Alan Havey instead feels ". . . calm—the adrenaline's there, but it's with this feeling of incredible relaxation, and a sense of power. It's exciting to come offstage and have people like you, that's what we're there for, to get laughs." But he adds that there is a trade-off; because he feels the effects of his sets so intensely, both good and bad, it's that much more difficult for him to decompress afterwards. "I try to leave after I work out now—go home, read, go to my girlfriend's—but you want to be there. You just got offstage, your adrenaline's going, it's hard to go home and turn that off, especially after you've had a real exciting set. You have to give it time; there's no way to dissipate it. That's where alcohol and drugs come in. You have this incredible adrenaline rush, people are telling you you were great, women flirt with you—so you have all this attention and this rush, and you have to just go home and cool out. Showers help."

For some comics, the only way to remain sane is to protect themselves as carefully from the highs of killing as from the lows of bombing—to constantly inject themselves with emotional lithium, as it were. David Brenner reminds himself that "I'm funny. I may not always be popular with the public, but I will always be funny. I'm six foot two—as I get older I'll shrink, but I'm really six foot two—and I'm a male: these are things I'm going to take with me all my life. I'm Jewish, I was born and raised in Philadelphia . . . and I'm funny."

Joe Bolster takes a similar approach, displaying a delightful example of the comic mind in action. He says that, regardless of his performance, he always remembers two things: "I'm funny and I have an act, and no one can take that away from me. As long as people want to laugh, I have work in show business. Tomorrow I could get on a plane and go to Oklahoma City and work for a week in a club—and I love performing. Actors can always act, but they don't always have a place; at any given time, they're unemployed. I could literally work every night of the year if I wanted to." While some people use stand-up to showcase their acting talent, for him, "This is it, and the rest is gravy. I like that it's my show, that the clothes I'm wearing were bought with money people gave me for telling jokes that didn't exist in the world until I came along."

COMEDY
AS ART...
NO KIDDING

For most comics, comedy is more than a living; it's a part of life. It is the unbroken thread that connects their oldest memories to their current life, and races ahead of them into the future. Comedy is the stand-up's parent and child. It supports him, unconditionally, from cradle to grave, but is, at the same time, his dependent offspring in need of constant inspiration for growth, and protection, from those who, blind to its subtler shadings, might cast it in an unflatteringly harsh light. For many comics, the audience's perception of their craft as something less than "art" is both a personal and professional affront, and more frustrating to fight against than hecklers, bombing and even the writing process. Because, regardless of how pervasive it is, ultimately it's still an invisible enemy.

Some comics feel that the nightclub setting, upon which stand-up must depend for its nightly rebirth, often sets a tone that runs contrary to the creation of art. As Paul Provenza says, "What I would love is to see comedy become a form that's not necessarily regarded as only part of selling liquor. It would be great if the comedy itself was the sole motivation for people going to see a comic." He compares stand-up to jazz, which in its early years was considered saloon music—a background beat that accompanied the selling of booze—certainly not "the stuff real musicians played." But when it "pulled itself from the gutter," moving from basement bars to Carnegie Hall, it became a primary entertainment form; it was no longer a means to an end (pushing liquor), but an end in itself—and an art form.

But even if stand-up continues to be co-billed with booze, it's still come a long way since its days as "strictly a warm-up act."

Mitzi Shore traveled the nightclub circuit in the 1950s with her husband, comedian Sammy Shore: "Those were the only clubs I knew . . . the little variety joints in the Midwest, which usually had a stripper and a singer and a comic. If Sammy played in the Village, he'd work with Barbra Streisand or another comic. But there were no clubs with only comics—there weren't that many comics. Stand-up was something you did to warm a crowd up for a stripper or singer." The Catskills was one of the few places where comedy wasn't just used as an opening act. But even there stand-ups were treated as second-rate entertainers. Shore remembers: "The comic had his little hour by himself, for the late show. They never had any respectability—always at the end of the list. I hated that. Their sound was bad, their lights. No one gave a shit."

This "opener/second-rate act" view of comics no longer exists on a wide scale; today there are countless clubs and television shows that exist solely for the purpose of presenting comedians, so their headline status is obvious. But like old soldiers, old mentalities have a hard time dying, if not fading away, and the image of comics as something less than artists lingers, to their continual chagrin.

Comics are both the creators and disciples of their craft. They pay tribute to it with each new bit that dazzles their audience, and it, in turn, provides the format through which they (the comics) can channel random observations, ideas and memories. The comic alternates between worshipping stand-up and basking in the glory as it worships him. Because of this dual role, comics tend to feel strongly not only about slights to themselves, as performers, but to their craft in general. Paul Reiser was recently asked what, in life, he gets most passionate about: "They said, 'What is it—politics, Nazis, women . . . anything,' and the first thing I said was 'disrespect for comedians,' which even surprised me." In describing the casual attitude with which people view comics, he says that it is something that "cuts to my gut... I remember when my friend, Glenn Hirsch, opened for Barry Manilow, it was the first big gig for anyone in my group of friends. It was in Atlantic City, it was this big, big deal, very exciting. I was in the elevator of the hotel afterwards and these two girls were in there talking and one said she'd been to the show. She described it like this: 'First the light comes down, this guy comes out and talks, and then the real show started.' I thought, 'Whoa!' The thing you just dismissed was the highlight of this man's life... it's so easy to do that with comics."

Jay Leno believes people dismiss stand-up (and comics in general) because, like sex, comedy is something that almost everybody thinks they can do with some proficiency: "No one thinks they're a bad lay," he says. "Everyone figures, 'I may be fat and acne riddled or stupid, but I know, in the sack, I'm the greatest thing in the world'... and it's the same thing with comedy. Telling someone they have no sense of humor is like telling someone they're bad at sex. People look at musicians, and think, 'Now that's something not everyone can do,' but because everyone can talk and be funny (to some degree), a comic doesn't get the same respect as a guitar player or even a guy who's banging garbage lids on the street." Because of this, it is not only easy to dismiss comedy as being something less than art, but it's hard to prove it's something special at all. Leno is constantly amazed when he's introduced to "Bob, who is the funniest guy we know," after which Bob proceeds to tell the most sexist, racist, vulgar story Leno's ever heard, and then says, "You can use this in your act, Jay!"

In addition to proving that their craft is not as easily executed as the opening of a peanut butter jar, comics face another uphill battle in trying to define stand-up as an art—it is highly resistant to qualitative definitions because, as Jerry Seinfeld says, "Everyone is an expert on judging stand-up comedy... in *Psychology Today*, they did a study of fifty or a hundred people with sixteen jokes and they were unable to get a consensus on whether any joke was unanimously good or bad. It's such a personal thing. I can't say to people, 'Listen I'm a professional comedian, and this guy is good.' They'll go, 'No, he doesn't make me laugh; he's not funny,' and they're right."

In stand-up, as opposed to other art forms, people are far less willing to stand back and let the "experts" tell them what is and isn't high art. Unlike a Jackson Pollock painting or a John Cage quartet, with comedy, almost everyone "gets it" to some degree, so everybody becomes an expert critic. It is hard to impose gradations of quality on an art form that, when innovative and brilliant, often elicits the same response from people as when it is derivative and vulgar. After all, a laugh is a laugh is a laugh. The only solution would be to draw a distinction between "high laughs" and "low laughs" which, while instinctively done by comedians among themselves (any comic knows the difference between killing by doing dick jokes, which is easy, and killing by employing innovative material, which can be like pulling teeth from a wild boar), seems both elitist and unnecessary outside of their world.

It would not only be absurd for comics to define "comic art" for an audience; it would also be unfair, because it is so subjective. Jerry Seinfeld says, upon being told that his show the previous night was extraordinary, "I'm telling you, there was someone in that room who saw the worst show they'll ever see in their life. They walked out, saying, 'I can't believe that guy even has a career. I didn't like one thing he did.' That's just a personal theory of mine. I can't say it's a fact, but I'm convinced that every show you do, someone thinks it's the best thing they've ever seen and someone thinks it's the worst thing they've ever seen." But he feels that to be both hated and loved is a positive attribute because "anything that appeals to everybody can't be good, by definition; it is only average." For instance, he says, "What is the most simple, basic type of comedy? Probably a pie in the face." But, while this may make the maximum amount of people laugh at any given time, it certainly isn't what one would consider a classic, like Beethoven's Fifth Symphony.

Years ago, Steven Wright found it annoying when audiences couldn't separate hardworking, unique comics from dick joke acts but then he concluded, "Why should they care? They just want to laugh —so let them laugh at whatever they want... I know they'll laugh at disgusting jokes and maybe they'll also laugh at what I say, but I don't care. I don't want to say my stuff is better than theirs, because I don't think it is; it's just another version."

Another difficulty in defining stand-up as art lies in many audiences' inability to distinguish stand-up comics' work from the work of comic actors. After a set, Gary Lazer is often approached by people asking who writes his material, "and they'll give me a joke and say, 'Hey, you can use this if you want.' They didn't understand that I wasn't telling 'jokes' up there—that I was telling funny stories I'd written myself... that's the whole point." Tom Dreesen has observed: "One interesting thing about people is that when you ask about stand-up comics they'll say something like, 'Isn't that Paul Lynde funny?' Paul Lynde never did what we do—that's the important difference between 'us' and 'them.'"

The difference is particularly great today, as opposed to the pre–Lenny Bruce era, because most stand-ups write their own material. In mistaking stand-ups for comic actors, audiences not only deny them the credit for having written their own material, but they also overlook the unique nature of the performance. Stand-up is not simply an actor reciting funny lines that somebody else has written and directed, according to Tom Dreesen: "It is being out there alone, totally vulnerable, suspended in mid-air, which is probably why there are so few of us. Dick Shawn once said, 'People live from day to day, singers live from song to song, and the comedian lives from laugh to laugh.'" He feels, like Seinfeld, that it's unfair to critique comedy because of the audience's subjectivity, but adds that it's also unfair to the comics because of the nature of the business: "It's so personal—my favorite line about that is, 'A critic is someone who comes in after the battle is over and shoots the wounded.' You write, you develop, you work, and if the stuff doesn't work that one night, somebody wants to nail you right away."

Budd Friedman has found that misunderstanding about stand-up is not restricted to audiences. About the reviewer at the *Los Angeles Times*, Larry Christon, he says, "We had to educate him... I once called him an asshole onstage, but we've since become very good friends." He explains that, years ago, Christon reviewed a benefit performance Robin Williams did at the Improv and, not understanding that even the best comics use certain bits in their act over and over, he criticized Williams for performing some of the same material he'd used three months earlier at the Amphitheater. Friedman remembers,

"I said, 'What the hell is going on here?' and it turned out his background was theater . . . but he has since become a very astute comedy critic."

Instead of trying to measure the artistic merit of an act immediately, Paul Provenza says it must be viewed in the context of cultural history: "One of the things that separates pop art from high culture is durability—high culture lasts, pop culture is more ephemeral." For example, the Marx Brothers became wildly popular again about five years ago: "What happened in between those fifty years? Nothing—history repeats itself and quality is a constant. In that way some comedy does have the durability of high art—it holds up in the long run, over successive periods."

But still, even if comedy maintains its popular and critical integrity after many years, it stands apart from most other art forms (most notably, music) in *how* it is experienced by people. According to David Brenner, "Comedians appeal to the brain, as opposed to the emotions." He gives as an example rock music, which connects directly to a person's emotions, "and that makes people emote—which means they scream, rip clothes, faint, go into a frenzy—whereas when you're intellectually stimulated, the most you'll get is a headache. You're not going to rip your clothes off and run onstage when you're intellectually stimulated, otherwise Einstein would've had groupies camping outside of his house, cause he was the greatest brain that ever lived." And while he concedes that there are cases of comic groupies today, he believes that what differentiates them from rock groupies is "that element of hysteria."

The rational, cerebral manner in which comedy is experienced is the very thing that makes it a pure art; it is always viewed and appreciated in its most naked form, as opposed to rock music, which is draped in the most elaborate wardrobe modern technology has to offer. By not setting up an outrageous atmosphere of supernatural entertainment, stand-ups don't have the power to metamorphose otherwise normal people into whirling dervishes, but neither are they vulnerable to the dependence inherent in this power. Paul Reiser says, "Imagine some big act up at the Madison Square Garden, doing all the MTV moves, and suddenly some janitor accidentally hits the power button.

Suddenly it's like the *Wizard of Oz*, like, 'Okay, I was bullshitting you, I don't have anything—I'm about five foot seven, I've got bad skin, a little roll here, it was all made up . . . thanks, and good-bye.'

"With comedy, you're safe in that you're embracing your shortcomings, not hiding them. There's something magical about the lack of magic with which it all happens—no lights, nothing." He says that it is not only rock, but music in general that works this way: "If someone drops a glass while Horowitz is playing, it's over, but a comedian will deal with it. You're aware of your own limitations; you're not staking any great claims, so no one can pull the rug out from under you."

For Kip Adotta, stand-up comedy is the "purest art form—it's the only one where you must communicate a specific thought. With painting or music, it's what do *you* see, or hear. In comedy you must communicate a specific thought and receive a specific reaction—laughter." It also has more freedom in its conception than any other art form, according to George Carlin: "The thing a comic gets to do that no other artist can is to change the work of art during its creation—poet, painter, composer, symphony musician, even rock musicians—they've got that song to finish. And they don't know if it's going over well because of all the noise. With a comedian, the appreciator of art gets to vote all the way through, about every five seconds, on whether the work of art is going the way they'd like. And if it isn't, the comic gets the message immediately and can change it. The only person who comes close to that is a jazz soloist who has the ability to change what he's doing . . . but he's still stuck with a tempo, a key, and the chord changes for that song. So the comic, when he's extemporizing, is the freest artist there is." Jerry Seinfeld describes it as "pared down entertainment," and says that "just because it's so elemental doesn't make it any less art. The fact that it is pared down is an artistic statement in itself. Someone said, the only concept that runs through all art, which is positive, is economy—something that's just good and everything else is gone. Stand-up is really one of the ultimate examples of that, because it's the most economical art—in a given space and time, you're getting more entertainment and impressions of life than with just about anything else."

Another difference in the ways comedy and music are experienced is that comedy must always be listened to fully, while music may be appreciated (or ignored) on many levels. Jay Leno says, "You can have music, and you can have Muzak, but you don't get that choice with comedy. You'll never get into an elevator and hear, softly, 'These two guys go into a bar...' You don't hear jokes being whispered in doctor's waiting rooms. It's a thing that takes all your concentration; you can't listen to jokes subliminally. It's like in casinos, singers don't disturb anyone, they just keep playing—but if there was a comedian, everyone would stop and listen, and you'd get fired for distracting them from gambling."

This need for complete concentration is both advantageous and unfortunate for stand-ups because, while they're more often given a crowd's undivided attention than is a musician, they are also more vulnerable to a crowd's criticism—people are listening to, and judging, every word. Another problem (or, depending on one's point of view, advantage) is that the audience's response can not be faked. Brenner says, "It's not like with a singer—he sings off-key, you applaud anyway: 'I did it my way-y-y...' and you think, 'That was nice' [applauding] or you think, 'He stinks, doesn't he?' [applauding] People applaud no matter what they say, but with a comedian you never hear, 'God, he's awful [laughing] he really stinks' [laughing]. You never see that—what you hear is the real thing." Robert Wuhl feels that comedy differs from music in its immediacy and intimacy: "Songs can last a long time, but a joke is right there and gone. It's also very personal because you're dealing with you, as opposed to a singer who can hide behind a song. An actor can be behind a play—but stand-up is you. Granted, it's a persona, but it's you. The audience is thinking, 'I hate *him*' or 'I like *him*.'" But in spite of all of the differences, Jerry Seinfeld believes: "Comedy is a lot like music in that it's a very small notion presented with a certain timing and rhythm. And for some reason it's very entertaining. So that's the analogy between comedy and music. It's very similar. Very small notions, almost meaningless notions, but rhythmically presented."

Although they feel that stand-up can be an art form, whether or not it meets the same criteria as music, painting or dance, comics stress that, like all art forms, it all depends on the performer. Carol Leifer says: "I kind of have lofty ideals for comedy—that it should be life-affirming, and make you feel good; in that respect, I'm a big fan of Jay Leno and Jerry Seinfeld." Racist or sexist acts depress her because these comics drag down the craft and give audiences a negative impression about comics' messages. While some comics meet the artistic criteria of timelessness, others' dependence upon topical material takes them out of the running. Paul Provenza points out that "a painting will mean the same thing twenty-five years from now, but comedy can be very immediate, very ephemeral. It's now, it's here, it's gone tomorrow. George Burns isn't like that; the stuff he did thirty years ago works as well now as then, but he's special. Bob Hope—you look at the material he did on his specials five years ago and it doesn't hold up. Five years ago it was Loni Anderson—today it's Mr. T."

The ephemeral nature of comedy operates on an immediate level as well as in the long run. Regardless of a joke's content, it must be executed in a delicate, precise manner, or else it will simply disappear; like paintings in a museum, jokes must be presented in the proper context. Paul Reiser says, "Requests are hard in comedy. It is so ephemeral and intangible, by nature, that if you put it in your hand to deliver it to someone, it will evaporate. Even around other comics, if one says to me, 'Hey, tell Larry the thing about . . .' I have to preface it by saying, 'It's nothing, I do a thing about . . .' and then do it. You have to put it in context, and you can't let anyone see the seams, the beginning or end of a bit, because it's absurd." Without proper bracketing, "you realize that, in fact, it's nothing but you talking and making observations. You have to put it in quotes. When you go onstage, there are quotes around the entire thing—'I'm walking onstage, how are you, I'm walking offstage.' It has a context. You have to disqualify it to make it important. The context has to be absurd, otherwise you look foolish."

Veteran comic Alan King feels that part of placing comedy in its proper context is the comic setting himself up as an absolute professional, in "maintaining that great sense of obligation to your audience —never miss a show, never walk on a stage with a creased crotch, always have your clothes pressed . . . because if you're up there for an hour, why shouldn't you look your best." He sees stand-up not only as an art, but as one of the oldest: "We're storytellers; before the printed word there was somebody who went from town to town, whether he lectured, preached or amused—and most of the time it was a combination of all three. We're the storytellers, purveyors of the news, bearers of bad and good tidings."

As in all art forms, stand-up advances and changes with the innovations of progressive individuals. Often, these individuals are misunderstood or ignored in the beginning, but eventually they give birth to a whole new movement within the craft. Steve Martin, in the mid 1970s, revolutionized the industry: his "Wild-and-Crazy Guy" steered American stand-up away from the 1960s/Watergate topical path and into a silly, apolitical direction where it was picked up by Robin Williams, in the latter part of the decade, who filtered this zaniness into scores of his own characters.

King says that comedy is like painting, in this respect: "You look at early Picasso, he was a traditional painter—then all of a sudden he must have seen the ugliest broad in the world, and did a portrait of her, and it changed the face of art." Of himself, he says, "I'm a traditionalist, although I did make some breakthroughs. I wasn't aware I was doing it. I don't think any innovator is aware of the fact that he is innovating. It's the public that tells you. You just express yourself at the time, the way you feel. Like in music, I don't think anybody started out saying, 'Today I'm going to use cowbells and I'm going to bang on pipes'—it's an evolution."

Just as they are often uncomfortable discussing the process of joke writing with civilians, so do many comics avoid describing what they do as art, both for the same basic reason: it can either tune people out, or turn them off. Others, like Bob Goldthwait, have an innate distrust of the word "art" and view the entire subject with unveiled cynicism: "I was at a performance place in Boston not long ago, and I was like, 'What's the big deal about a performance artist space? Next they're going to put a mechanical bull in here—what the fuck . . .' Last night there was a lull in my act, and I said, 'Jesus, one more lull and I'm going to be a performance artist.' I don't like the word 'art' in general, it usually implies that you're hip, and I don't want to be hip."

Whether or not a comic feels that stand-up is a valid art form, it can safely be assumed that most view what they're doing as a valid form of work, at the very least. This, however, is something that many find themselves having to prove to other people over and over—that what they are doing is not only the means to an end, but an end in itself. In recent years, because of the increasing number of comics who successfully "cross over" into acting, it has become an assumption on the part of many people, particularly within the entertainment industry, that a stand-up is only doing this until he gets his big break. Seinfeld says, "As I've gone on in the business, I've gotten a lot of respect for George Burns, because he takes a lot of joy in stand-up. I know so many successful people in show business who aren't enjoying it, and to me that's so sad. It's so hard to get there, then when you do, you're not having fun—you're thinking, 'That guy over there...' and 'They wouldn't give me the percentage...' It's a shame. I love what I'm doing, I'm grateful, it's a wonderful way to live. I want to keep doing stand-up... forever." He adds, "I'm in it for the jokes. That should be my by-line... 'I'm in it for the jokes.'"

Kip Adotta believes that this "just passing through" assumption on the part of club owners and producers is used as a rationale for underpaying comics: "I started out to be a comedian and that's what I want to be. I'm not 'passing' here—this isn't my 'ticket to a series'—so why shouldn't I make money?" But in spite of staunch "I'm-a-comic-first" purists like Seinfeld and Adotta, the "I'm-a-comic-soon-to-be-an-actor" era has begun and is flourishing. In the context of the times, it really isn't that surprising. The superman-oriented 1980s are severely afflicted with the slash (/) syndrome; one must be a writer/producer, a singer/songwriter, etc./etc. (According to Gilbert Gottfried, "If Helen Keller were alive today, she'd be billed as a deaf/mute.") Comic/actors have begun to dominate a field that was once open only to comics. Chris Albrecht says in many cases stand-up is used by young actors and their agents as a casting tool: "When I was an agent I signed a couple of these good-looking guys who were pretty funny, but you couldn't get real excited about them. You're using their five to ten minutes to bring a casting person down so you can separate them from the rest of the herd of actors, before they go into the audition room."

Budd Friedman agrees that many actors today use stand-up as a way to showcase their talent. At the New York Improv in the 1960s, before casting agents visited clubs comedy was strictly the medium of comics. There was no other reason for someone to do it. Today actors can support themselves on the road with mediocre acts, "but they're not going to go anywhere. They might make it as an actor, but they'll never make it as a stand-up. There are more good comics around today. You just have to separate the wheat from the chaff, but there's so much chaff around that it's hard to separate the wheat. . . ." One comic said about the situation, "It used to mean something to be a comic— now you're a schmuck if you're not one." Ultimately, this cross-pollination takes its toll on stand-up as an art form.

Michael Fuchs of HBO feels that the current generation of comics differs from the last in that "back then there was more of a stand-up tradition—they were really professional comics. They didn't do movies and TV. There was the borscht belt and Vegas and that was a whole lifestyle." Today comics are involved in all areas of the media and, after they've achieved some success, they really have to make an effort to continue doing stand-up, because at that point they don't need it to earn a living: "Eddie Murphy, who could be a great stand-up, does it infrequently and he doesn't work that hard at it, whereas Robin Williams goes onstage because he loves to, not to earn a living, and he works hard."

More comics are crossing over today because, Fuchs says, "there's such a thirst for talent in the entertainment business now that, as soon as a young stand-up appears that seems to have some talent, he gets re-routed to a sit-com or to movies. Those opportunities didn't exist a while ago, so they stayed together as a group. You go back to the guys before my time, Joe E. Lewis, Jackie Leonard—they were legendary characters—'the nightclub comedian.' Also, some of the risqué material of the early days was quite exotic back then, so they had a special role, like Lenny, and it kept them from going farther: there wasn't that type of cross-fertilization. Sinatra becoming an actor was a famous cross-over from one medium to another; it didn't happen much, especially with comics."

Mitzi Shore says, however, that simply because those comics of the older generation worked exclusively as stand-ups doesn't mean they worked any harder or were any more artistic than those today: "That is so wrong—they work much harder and longer than those that worked on the road. In the old days, they had to drive everywhere, so it was a lot of time not spent performing. Here, at the Store, they have more time on the stage than comics have had in the history of stand-up comedy. And when they worked the circuit, they did the same act for fifteen years. You can't get away with that here—every night you have to change, add and subtract lines. I know what it's about, I've been there honey. I know the Catskill Mountains and what those guys did up there—cocked around for an hour on the floor—totally nonproductive. Here, when you work out, if you get six hot minutes, you're on television with it. It was cushioned then, no competition and totally undisciplined. Today, it's a different story."

Still, though it's a change from the past, the situation doesn't seem to hurt anyone. Showcase clubs in New York and Los Angeles, located in the country's media centers, are easily accessible to producers and casting agents, and, since comedy is king in show business now, every actor wants to present himself as an actor with comic potential. The club owners benefit by having more talent, more drinking customers and more of a big-time, show-biz feel, which appeals to customers. The actor/comics get to earn a little extra money, and the agent/producers have a nightly pool from which to hold floating auditions. So everybody's happy, right?

Wrong. Many comics are annoyed by the ease with which their art is being turned into a giant casting call. Paul Provenza says, "There's a problem with a lot of comics today that drives me crazy; they don't want to be good comics. There are very few guys out there who are concerned with being good stand-up comics. Jay Leno loves being on the road, loves working clubs, and wants to be a good comic. He's not concerned with doing comedy to get a sit-com—although it would be very nice if he did—but his main concern in doing comedy is not as a vehicle for getting a movie. There are a lot of guys who are doing comedy for the sole purpose of getting seen and getting a movie. They don't write and they've done the same act for the last six or seven years and it's sad. It's detrimental to stand-up comedy in general."

Jay Leno, widely admired by most comics for his continuing commitment and dedication to stand-up, says, "People ask me now, 'Since you're successful, what are you going to be doing in three years?' As if suddenly I would turn to dance. I don't understand. I find comedy much more rewarding. I think of something today, I try it out tonight, and I know tomorrow whether it worked or not. Whenever I do a sit-com, not that I'm so wonderful, but they'll say, 'Here's a joke— we'll make it funny when we get into the sweetening...' Then my friends see it and say, 'Jay, what was that about?' Being a comic, they always want to cast me as the guy whose socks roll up and down when he kisses the girl; it's out of my control. At least with my act, if people don't like it, I can honestly say to them, 'Sir, here's your money back —this is the best I can do.'" Finally, he asserts, as if there were room to doubt his conviction, "Let me put it this way, I'm not doing this because I'm hoping somebody will offer me *King Lear*; this is what I like to do."

Regardless of how enlightened civilians—and comics—become about the artistic attributes of stand-up comedy, Alan Havey believes it will always have the residual stigma of being a second-rate art form because of its "unenlightened" subject matter. He says, "It's hard for me to explain to people that watching TV at night, going to see *Rambo* at three o'clock in the afternoon, and walking down the street are things that further my art—not just ways of passing time." This is a compelling question central to the "comedy as art" debate: in order to satirize trash, the satirist must, in a sense, wallow in it himself... does this then make the final product trash? It's anyone's guess. But perhaps, if the outcome is funny enough, the question is irrelevant.

CLUB OWNERS AND BOOKERS

MICHAEL CALLIE   owner, the Laff Stop
TONY DEPAUL   manager, San Francisco Holy City Zoo
RON DINUNZIO   owner, The Punch Line
CHRIS DIPETTA   former Punch Line booker, now associated with Catch A Rising Star
BIL DOWNES   owner, the Boston Comedy Connection
RICHARD FIELDS   Catch A Rising Star
BUDD FRIEDMAN   owner, The Improv
BILL GRUNDFEST   owner, the New York Comedy Cellar
BERT HAAS   General Manager, Zanies
PAUL HERZICH   owner, Comedy U, New York
CAROLINE HIRSCH   owner, Caroline's, New York
JERRY KUBACH   owner, the Funny Bone
RICK MESSINA   New York area club booker/producer
HARRY MONOCRUSOS   owner, Garvins, Washington, D.C.
MITZI SHORE   owner, the Comedy Store
JERRY STANLEY   formerly the largest comedy club booker in the country

TV EXECUTIVES

CHRIS ALBRECHT   Vice President, Comedy Development, HBO
BERNIE BRILLSTEIN   personal manager, Chief Operating Officer, Lorimar Film Entertainment
MICHAEL FUCHS   Chief Operating Officer, HBO
CLAUDIA MCMAHON   Talent Coordinator, Star Search
LORNE MICHAELS   Producer, "Saturday Night Live"
BOB MORTON   Segment Producer, "Latenight with David Letterman"
BARRY SAND   Producer, "Latenight with David Letterman"
LES SINCLAIR   Associate Producer, "The Merv Griffin Show"
STU SMILEY   Vice President, Comedy Programming, HBO
LAURIE ZAKS   Talent Executive, "Nightlife with David Brenner"

MOTHERS

BEA BASS   Paul Provenza's mom
BLANCHE LEWIS   Richard Lewis's mom

TABLE OF COMICS

KIP ADOTTA has been performing as a stand-up since 1972. After appearing on scores of television shows and watching his career make a steady upward climb, he was accused in 1980 of urinating onstage (a charge he vehemently denies) during a Las Vegas performance. Following this incident, he claims to have been black-balled completely from television. As a result, he has shifted his full attention to making numerous club appearances and producing his own comedy albums, which have proved to be far more lucrative for Kip than TV had ever been.

RICHARD BELZER should be given some sort of award for making the words "Yeah, babe!" synonymous with the institution of verbal humiliation. As emcee at Catch A Rising Star in the late 70s, Belzer ruled the stage with an iron mouth and a mind that sped through the crowd in a vitriolic frenzy, stopping only to vocally plunder (or as he says, to "Belzerize") some unfortunate victim, empty the contents of a woman's purse and present it to the crowd, or perhaps perform as Mick Jagger ("like a rooster on acid"). In the 80s he moved into film (*Fame* and *Scarface*) and television (in addition to stand-up spots on other programs, he hosted a talk show called "Hot Properties"). While continuing to perform in clubs—and continuing to do it well—the rage

293

that once spilled openly from Belzer seems to have fermented nicely, leaving a smoother, more enticing performer.

Having begun to perform only in 1986, **TOMMY BLAZE** is a relative newcomer to stand-up. But because his emergence coincided exactly with that of the road circuit explosion, he began earning a living—and headlining—almost immediately. But it wasn't only this perfect timing that led to Tommy's rapid rise; it was also his style—he's a self-proclaimed "rock and roll comic." Mixing jokes with rock-star movements, clothing and attitude, he elicits a combination of laughter and rock-concert fervor from audiences as he treks from town to town and club to club.

JOE BOLSTER, the oldest of fourteen children, says it comes as no surprise to him that many psychologists consider stand-up a cry for attention. To watch Joe perform—to watch the way he uses a combination of tiny body movements and subtle vocal inflections to get his jokes across, it's hard to remember he's speaking not to a couple of rapt listeners but to a room filled with two hundred rowdy people—all of whom sit mesmerized (and laughing). While he is based in New York, where he divides his days between writing and commercial auditions, Joe thrives on the road where he says the gratification is always immediate—always only one joke away.

DAVID BRENNER left a job as an award-winning documentary film producer to "goof around onstage" for a year. After a stunning debut on "The Tonight Show" in 1971, he went on to hundreds of successful TV spots and nightclub appearances around the country. Currently, he hosts his own talk show, "Nightlife with David Brenner."

LOIS BROMFIELD says of herself, in a Dietrich-esque tenor, "Think of me as Doris Day, if she were a biker." Canadian-born Lois (who insists that "Canadians just drink beer, get drunk and buy a couple pairs of jeans every few months since they've vomited on the rest") came to New York at age twenty-two to "make it at The Improv," stayed a year and a half, then moved to Los Angeles where she began working out at the Comedy Store. Among her credits since that time are the "Alan Thicke Show," on which she was a regular, and a popular cult video in which she stars called, "Sorority Women from Hell."

A. WHITNEY BROWN'S career began in the streets, at age eighteen, where he worked as a juggler/comic in partnership with another man and a performing dog. Though he eventually became a successful stand-up solo act, appearing on "Saturday Night Live," "Latenight with David Letterman" and "The Tonight Show," he has given up that medium for a time, in favor of his current job—writing and performing on "Saturday Night Live."

GEORGE CALFA is a New York-based comic who, in addition to working the road and the showcase clubs in Manhattan, is pursuing a song-writing career. Since he began in 1979, Calfa feels that comic audiences have changed dramatically: today, instead of wanting smart, sophisticated humor, many people flock to the clubs in order to heckle, drink, and listen to "dick jokes." Still, for him, stand-up remains an enjoyable profession—but perhaps less so than in the "early days."

In addition to booking and managing several New York-area comedy clubs and running an 800 phone number through which club bookers may check the availability of and then book comics who subscribe to the service—a particularly useful tool in last-minute bookings— **FRAN CAPO** is also a stand-up comic. Still, in keeping with her frenetic pace, Fran cannot simply commit herself to straight stand-up. Her comic credentials have recently been augmented by two new honors: a place in the Guinness Book of Records as the world's fastest talker, and the release of her first rap single (as sung by her May Westian alter-ego, June East).

GEORGE CARLIN'S career has included a decade as a "straight comic," including several years as a comic team with Jack Burns, a decade as a "counter-culture comic," during which time he was fired in Las Vegas for using the word "shit" onstage, arrested in concert for using "obscene" language and embroiled with the FCC for demanding the right to use his "Seven Little Words" on the radio. Throughout these altercations, and a host of others, Carlin toured the country, playing clubs and colleges, and recording comedy albums that were then, as now, stunningly brilliant and consistently innovative. In recent years, in addition to his still-active travel schedule, he has appeared on a series of HBO comedy specials and a smash film, *Outrageous Fortune*.

PHYLLIS DILLER, in addition to her well-known work in stand-up, has appeared as piano soloist with numerous symphony orchestras around the country, starred on Broadway in *Hello Dolly*, written four best-selling books, and raised five children. Today, at age seventy, she stops performing only to have another in a long series of facelifts.

As president of the Professional Comedians Association, **JERRY DINER** wakes up daily prepared to grapple with two daunting objectives—personal success in the world of stand-up and the betterment of life for all working stand-ups. Despite long hours spent working for the PCA (which, among other things, puts out a monthly newsletter, settles comic/club disputes, conducts inquiries into club and television booking practices) Jerry continues to perform the regular duties of a stand-up: writing, working-out onstage, auditioning, and taking his show on the road.

TOM DREESEN began life as a poverty-stricken shoeshine boy in a small Illinois town. After getting in trouble with the law, he was given the option by a judge to either enter the navy or go to jail. Following his discharge, he worked variously as a sewer cleaner, construction worker, private detective, and at countless other jobs. After he met Tim Reid (later a star of "WKRP in Cincinnati") at a Jaycees meeting in 1969, the two formed a comedy team and toured the country, playing nightclubs in the North and the "chitlin circuit" in the South. When the act broke up, Dreesen moved to Los Angeles, where he lived in an abandoned car and tried to get onstage at the Comedy Store. Finally, he got a break in a Carl Reiner TV series, which led to other bookings, which eventually led to extremely lucrative Las Vegas-type bookings. Today, in addition to his nightclub and TV work, Dreesen opens across the country for Frank Sinatra.

BOB "THE BOBCAT" GOLDTHWAIT is, like Paul Reiser, a movie star/comic who appears to have no desire to break away from his stand-up roots. As a former member of two tightly knit comic communities, first in Boston, then San Francisco, Bob had a chance to develop his act with minimal pressure to get laughs at any cost (as is often the case with stand-ups today who develop on the road circuit) and so he became "The Bobcat," a character who seems to roam the stage saying what he considers funny, working almost in spite of the audience. And it just so happens that the audience's sense of humor meshes with his, as is evidenced by his recent TV and film successes, including several cable specials, three *Police Academy* films, and a starring role in *Burglar* with Whoopi Goldberg.

GILBERT GOTTFRIED'S illustrious, slightly ambiguous past includes his being a "Saturday Night Live" cast member in 1979, a regular on the "Alan Thicke Show," in 1983 and, between those two, having a starring role in a sitcom ("Toast of Manhattan") opposite an orangutan. In addition to performing these feats, he has managed to earn a reputation as one of the most talented, unique stand-ups in the country—at first among his peers and people in "the business"—and lately, as his stand-up work has been exposed more steadily on TV, among audiences as well. His recent burst of popularity has been aided by both a cable special and role in *Beverly Hills Cop II*.

ALAN HAVEY is a New York-based stand-up who has been performing since the late 70s, originally as half of a comic team in Florida and eventually as a single act. Several years ago Havey worked onstage with a flashlight, which he shone into unsuspecting peoples' face, and while he's grown away from using this prop over time, his act continues to involve a high degree of interaction with the audience. A former altar boy, he feels that religious repression contributed a great deal to his career choice and, in a roundabout way, is thankful for that.

ALAN KING began performing at age fifteen, working his way up through the burlesque and Catskills circuits to a position at the top of the stand-up totem pole. In addition to maintaining a full performing schedule, King is a successful entrepreneur: Chairman of the Board of Odyssey Films, Ltd., a major investor in the Astoria Film Studio, and vice-chairman of the board of Grand Champions Resorts Hotels.

CATHY LADMAN began performing full-time in 1981 after a series of unsuccessful stand-up attempts and assorted dead-end "straight" jobs. After several years of late-night spots in Manhattan and middle-act work on the road, she broke into the headliner league and moved to California. Currently, in Los Angeles, she is writing, racking up TV credits, and putting in regular stage time.

GARY LAZER decided on a stand-up career while working as a shoe salesman and figuring that, if he didn't try comedy at that point, he really would have no excuses left. In the few years since that time, he has worked out steadily in the New York showcase clubs, developing a loose, witty style that has, of late, earned him several TV spots and an increasing amount of road work.

CAROL LEIFER began performing stand-up while still in college in the late 70s and, supporting herself by working as a receptionist for a private eye, continued to do it after graduation. As the road circuit grew, Carol became a popular club comic, working her way up to headliner status relatively quickly. In 1985/86 she worked as a writer for "Saturday Night Live," while continuing to work out in the clubs at night. Currently, she has resumed her full travel schedule and lists among her television credits nearly fifteen appearances on "Latenight with David Letterman."

JAY LENO estimates that he plays roughly 300 dates a year and says, amazingly, "I don't care for traveling," but adds, "I like the work when I get there." Leno is, according to virtually all knowledgeable comic sources, the ultimate "road warrior." In the mid 70s, before the road circuit began, Jay played strip clubs, in Boston's "Combat Zone," nursing homes, college dorms, brothels—literally anywhere he would be paid. When clubs began opening around the country, he played them all, in addition to performing at colleges, club gatherings, conventions, and eventually television shows. Like Richard Lewis, his final boost to the top came from his frequent appearances on "Latenight with David Letterman." Leno today is enjoying the trappings of his rapidly growing fame, including TV specials, movie deals, and guest-hosting shots on "The Tonight Show."

RICHARD LEWIS'S neurosis-oriented, frenzied style of stand-up gives one an idea of how it would sound to hear Franz Kafka overdosing on Benzedrine. And though it seems that his manic pace would be impossible to sustain, Lewis has been writing and performing in this "unique" state of mind since the early 70s. Though he has appeared in several TV series and pilots through the years, it was not until his friend David Letterman got his own show in 1982 and began inviting

Richard to appear regularly that Lewis found and "clicked with" his rightful audience.

For **LARRY MILLER,** spiritual, mental, and emotional growth are just as crucial to his art as jokes. He feels that in balancing his life offstage and maintaining a positive outlook he becomes a more honest writer and performer, which is what an audience responds to most enthusiastically. Like Jay Leno and Jerry Seinfeld, Miller is often cited by his comic peers as one of the most adaptable, prolific, and professional stand-ups in the business.

In his early stand-up days, **STEVE MITTLEMAN'S** humor was based almost exclusively on self-denigration—most notably his lack of a chin ("I once grew a beard... it looked like a fur tongue...") But today, his material stems not so much from his own physical flaws as from human flaws in general; this, he feels, is a reflection of both self-awareness and a more positive outlook on life. Ironically, his unique looks continue to work for him outside of stand-up—he has appeared in dozens of commercials, a medium for which his face seems to be ideally suited.

Since beginning in 1974, **TOM PARKS** has played roughly 700 colleges. By choosing to work universities instead of clubs (his only choice in the beginning), he became a specialist in a comic genre that most other stand-ups work only to supplement club dates. While he has enjoyed great financial success because of this, particularly in recent years, he is currently trying to make the transition into the club circuit because, among other things, he feels that today's college students have changed tremendously in the past few years: "They've become little Nazis." So far, his transition has been a smooth one, particularly since his recent debut spot on "The Tonight Show."

EMO PHILIPS began performing stand-up in 1976 for $2.50 a show and, while his price has gone up considerably since that time, he does not seem to have altered his lifestyle accordingly. Dressed in what seem to be hand-me-downs (and that's putting it euphemistically), he traverses the country non-stop, accompanied only by an aging trombone (with a big "EMO" taped to its side) and a stand-up act that's the comic equivalent of a Martian landing—like nothing you've seen before or will ever see again. He speaks in a sing-song voice and sings in a speaking manner, almost always about something very-very strange. Something, in fact, exactly like this: "I was walking down the street one day and something caught my eye . . . and dragged it fifteen feet . . ."

PAUL PROVENZA is an Ivy League graduate who first performed stand-up at age sixteen. He currently divides his time between comedy club appearances, writing and acting, having most recently starred in a CBS-TV movie of the week, "Under the Influence," and made his second appearance on "The Tonight Show."

PAUL REISER is one of a dwindling number of "movie star" comics who continues to perform stand-up regularly. After two years of working as a stand-up, in 1981 Paul was cast in the film *Diner*, which instantly transformed him from a fledgling, nameless comic into a respected actor. He followed up with roles in *Beverly Hills Cop* and *Aliens*, and found that even after several films, his love for stand-up had not diminished—so he kept on doing it. Currently, many club dates, Letterman, and Carson spots later, he continues pursuing film (most recently *Beverly Hills Cop II*) and comedy with seemingly equal passion.

PAUL RODRIGUEZ is best known for his starring role in the 198 Norman Lear series which centered around a young Hispanic man called "a.k.a. Pablo." While the sudden fame from the program transformed him overnight from a complete unknown into a desperately hot property, it did not also give him the experience to live up to his reputation because, although he had become famous because of stand-up, he had not performed much at all. After several difficult years, in which he struggled to work at his craft instead of cashing in on his name, he developed his stand-up enough to star in an in-concert HBO special and perform the club dates he had formerly turned down.

RITA RUDNER is a former singer/dancer whose list of credits includes the role of Lily St. Regis in the Broadway production of *Annie*. Fed up with the outrageous odds against success and lifelong dependence inherent in her trade, she decided to try her luck at stand-up . . . and failed miserably, at first. After three years of solid work, however, she appeared on "Latenight" and from there her career has climbed steadily.

JERRY SEINFELD is frequently referred to by his colleagues as (among other things): the best writer in the business, a consummate onstage professional, and one of the most adaptable talk show comics working. His comic persona and observational style of humor are not based on shock value; instead, their success is rooted in Seinfeld's exploration of normalcy unto its innermost parts. Jerry's style can best be described as: a nice, thoroughly likable guy who, in spite of himself (or so it seems), notices one hell of a lot of stuff . . . that just happens (or so it seems) to be funny.

In spite of the fact that she began working as a stand-up in such glamour gigs as "mafia bars" and Central Park (outside, next to an open guitar case) **CAROL SISKIND'S** comic style strikes one immediately as warm. Unlike "violent" and "maniacal," "warm" is an adjective not frequently used in describing comics' acts today—and for good reason; clinking glasses, whispering patrons, and defiant hecklers are only a few of the many elements that discourage warm behavior by comics. But Carol has no intention of giving in. Armed with a steady, penetrating gaze and heartfelt material, she takes control of a room, subtly gathering strength like a quiet storm and leaving the crowd, often in spite of itself, in fits of laughter.

YAKOV SMIRNOFF emigrated to this country from the Soviet Union in 1977. After working as a busboy at Grossinger's (during which time he began translating his Russian jokes into English), he tried unsuccessfully to get stage time at clubs in Manhattan. Two years later he moved to Los Angeles and began working out as both a carpenter and a comic at the Comedy Store, also performing "everywhere . . . including pizza parlors" and selling light bulbs over the phone—and eventually he was "discovered." Currently, having enjoyed several years of successful TV spots and club dates, he is starring in a television show whose title is derived from his tag line, "What a Country."

CARRIE SNOW, who hands out elegant pink matchbooks inscribed with her name followed by the line, "Seven thousand sailors can't be wrong," takes a straightforward approach to her position in stand-up: "I don't want to be known as a 'female comic.' I just want to be known as a comic... with really big tits." Since her earliest days onstage in 1978, at the San Francisco Holy City Zoo, she has maintained her image as a brash, funny, tasteless, and shocking comic who, if she had only nice things to say probably would say nothing at all.

BARRY SOBEL has been a professional comic since age seventeen—and it shows. To watch him work onstage is to understand immediately the true meaning of "comic timing." Just when a pause seems pregnant or a lull too quiet, Barry doubles back on the audience, pounding them hard with a striking burst of wit, wrapping them tightly in a wall of laughter. Having recently completed a starring role on the ill-fated Ellen Burstyn show, he has now begun work as a consultant to Tom Hanks on *Punchline*, an upcoming film about stand-up comics—and, of course, he is still working the stage regularly.

JONATHAN SOLOMON was enrolled in Boston University's Theater Program when he first tried stand-up; shortly afterward he left school to pursue comedy full-time. Today, he is based in New York where, like most stand-ups in the city, he works out nightly in the showcase clubs and spends days writing, auditioning for commercials, films and TV shows... and squeezing his random daily observations through the mental sieve that turns life into comic material.

ABBY STEIN was, inadvertently, the reason behind the founding of the Professional Comedians Association. In 1982, when she suffered a near fatal bout of spinal meningitis and had no money to cover her medical bills, a large group of comics and several club owners banded together and threw a series of benefits to raise the money for her. After recovering, she began talking to Jerry Diner about the problems of being a stand-up and having no medical coverage or income if they became ill. They called a meeting of all interested comics and found that there was a need for more than a group medical plan: "At the meeting people said, 'Fuck hospitalization, what about this bastard who won't book a black comic?' and things like that. So we got into other areas real quickly..." Currently, Abby is still involved in the PCA, though no longer as president, and while she is trying to cut down drastically on her traveling, continues to perform regularly.

JUDY TENUTA   is an enigmatic figure—that rare human being who walks the delicate line between Siren of Love and Perpetrator of Unearthly Horrors. She calls herself "The Petite Flower" but then, mere seconds later, exhorts the audience to "Shut up, Pigs!" or, to an unsuspecting victim/audience member, she'll say coyly, "You remind me of my brother Bosco... only he had a human head!" Having worked her way up from emceeing male strip shows in Chicago, Judy is today a cult comic queen of no small stature, dispensing both wanton lust and verbal assault to sell-out club crowds across the country.

ADRIANNE TOLSCH'S   comic style has been very obviously influenced by her years onstage as an emcee at Catch A Rising Star. To state it frankly, the woman takes no shit from anyone. Though she looks diminutive behind the stage mike, her voice covers and encloses a crowded room like a garish party tent. Traveling constantly, she views both the freedom and constraints of the road as she views her various audiences, with a carefully measured mixture of relief, fear, and endless anticipation.

ROBIN TYLER,   a former TV comedy writer (who once occupied Donny Osmond's dressing room), rarely performs stand-up today, choosing instead to divide her time between lecturing on the history of women and comedy and producing women's Comedy and Music Festivals around the country. When she does perform (as on her comedy albums or at social and political benefits) her humor is delivered from a feminist perspective, which she explains does not mean it is about politics, but rather that it is simply political by nature: "If you're a feminist, your humor comes from that perspective, that's the only difference. I can do humor on my plants or dogs or cats, and it's still from a feminist consciousness."

In the late 70s and early 80s **MARC WEINER** and his puppets, The Weinerettes, were one of the most popular club/college comedy acts working the circuit. Whether dressed in a rain slicker, spraying unsuspecting audiences with water, or captivating hundreds of people with puppets no larger than his fingers, Marc was a rapidly growing stand-up sensation. His upward climb was halted in 1984, however, when he began observing the Jewish Sabbath, which prevented him from working on Friday nights or Saturdays, thus shutting him out of most club gigs and many television opportunities. Currently, his career has begun moving again; presumably after seeing that his religious convictions did not actually alter his intrinsic wit or comic ability, television executives and club owners are calling Marc again with increasing frequency, offering to work around his schedule.

TIM WILSON is a road comic who has worked his way through each successive club stage—opener, middle act and, most recently, headliner—but unlike many of his road peers who look with desperate longing toward their headlining days, he seems to have thoroughly enjoyed every level. In fact, though he has spent many nights in strange towns waiting for gigs to turn up, with not a cent in his pocket, Tim has always considered himself lucky to be doing stand-up—for any price. Fortunately, as a headliner, he has risen far above the "any price" level—a fact that he still seems infinitely surprised to hear.

ROBERT WUHL began his stand-up career as a joke writer for Rodney Dangerfield in 1977 and shortly afterward began to perform his own material. Since that time his career has moved in several different directions—as a film actor (starring in *The Hollywood Knights*), a writer (story editor of *Police Squad*) and a comic, starring in his own cable special, playing the club, and hitting the talk-show circuit.